AURAL THINKING IN NORWAY

Hardingfele made by Eilef Jonson Steintjønndalen in 1869.

AURAL THINKING
IN NORWAY

Performance and Communication
with the *hardingfele*

by
Pandora Hopkins

With Foreword by JAN-PETTER BLOM

and Appendix by MAGNE MYHREN

HUMAN SCIENCES PRESS, INC.
72 FIFTH AVENUE
NEW YORK, N.Y. 10011

Published by Human Sciences Press, Inc.
72 Fifth Avenue, New York, New York, 10011-8004

Printed in the United States of America
123456789 987654321

Library of Congress Cataloging in Publication Data

Hopkins, Pandora.
    Aural thinking in Norway.

    Bibliography: p. 291
    Includes index.

    1. Folk music—Norway—History and criticism.
2. Hardanger fiddle.   I. Title.
ML3704.H66   1985   781.7481   85-2519
ISBN 0–89885–253–6

Designed by Barbara Perrin.

Typeset by Eastern Graphics, Inc.
Printed and Bound by Bookcrafters, Inc.

Production supervised by Brice Hammack.

It is by the fruits that the tree shall be known. . . .
Let the hundred blossoms grow. Then indeed will
forms solidify that provide, for each particular
instance, the best tool for the thoughts and the
character of every individual.

—Olav Lid

The decorations that appear throughout this book are patterns taken from Sverre Sandvik's method for *hardingfele* contruction, *Vi Byggji Hardingfele.*

I would like to dedicate this volume to three people who, at different periods of time, have shared my multi-cultural life: to the memory of my mother, Eleanor Knutesen Edwards, whose conviction in the importance of artistic communication molded her life; to my father, Hugh Francis Hopkins, whose visual thinking continues to be manifested in his paintings and whose personal encouragement has spurred this project to conclusion; and to my son, Terrence Hopkins Grame, who played an integral and significant role in my research during five of my trips to Norway.

*T*able of Contents

Part I

Part II

Foreword

The present book by Pandora Hopkins is most welcome. It enters upon the scene just at the time when the esoteric musical idiom of the Hardanger fiddle (*hardingfele*) has begun to attain a growing international reputation, particularly in the United States. Still only superficially understood by most Norwegians, this instrument has been virtually unknown to the rest of the world.

Historically, and to a certain extent even today, the instrument and its music are controlled, transmitted, and modified by a small group of semi-professional fiddlers in their capacity as members of agro-pastoral communities of the innerfjordal and mountain valleys of south-central Norway. Certain of its basic organological and musical features, however, are no doubt historically related to an ancient and probably widespread European tradition so convincingly identified by Dr. Hopkins as the "lyra-way" style of playing. However, the general features thereby referred to have certainly been adapated, remodeled, and refined to make up a particular but diversified regional idiom that integrates particular features of form, harmony, rhythm, and ornamentation. Aural imagination, creativity, and borrowing—however supported by incentives related to fiddlers' competition for reputation, rank, and customers—are nonetheless inspired by the sound properties of the sympathetic strings and the rhythms of local dance forms.

One popular notion does not hold true for Norway: that exotic peculiarities of folk culture represent cultural lags that survive in marginal areas due to communicational isolation. Geographical mobility exploits the culture of niches, redistributing it over wide areas; this has been part of the adaptational strategy of Norwegians throughout history, and is particularly true for the populations of marginal agricultural areas like the native regions of the *hardingfele*. Seasonal transhumance, labor migration, and trading created regular contacts with people of the more densely populated areas of the lowlands and coastal districts. Generally speaking, geographical mobility in Norway is related to the somewhat surprising fact that nature has provided Norwegians with the most excellent communicational facilities: a coastline sheltered by thousands of islands, fjords extending into the middle of the country, and mountain plateaus —which facilitate rather than hamper contacts across valleys and fjords. Cultural diversification in Norway is, therefore, not a question of geographical isolation. Rather, it results from differences in adaptational strategies, the distribution of social networks, and the conscious emphasis on cultural discontinuities and boundaries between local and regional groups with references to minor differences in behavior and expressive styles.

Although the traditional middle class of professionals and artists used to think unidimentionally and hierarchically when evaluating aesthetic expressions, class mobility and the cultural-political reality of Norway —based as it is on regionalism and egalitarian values—have reinforced pluralism, as well as pride and self-reliance among "the folk artists."

Dr. Hopkins's self-reflective discussion of her own background and field experiences provides the reader with a most valuable context with which to interpret her book. She convincingly attributes to her encounter with the *hardingfele* tradition an effective cure of any notions concerning unilinear evolution and value hierarchy in musical expression; thus, she describes her conversion to the idea of pluralism in respect to cultures separated by time or space. The idea of cultural pluralism concerns the very essence of Dr. Hopkins's presentation, as it conveys to the reader her emotional attachment to the *hardingfele* music and her admiration for the intelligence and the creativity of its performers. But notions of pluralism certainly concern more than a question of attitude. In a cultural situation characterized by a widespread knowledge of a variety of musical idioms, as well as the simultaneous existence of a great variety of local and individual styles within the traditional idiom, Hopkins rightly, as one of her important themes, explores the ability of individual players to control matters of boundary—thus demonstrating their control over continuity and change in the music with which they personally identify. It is her thesis that this ability can only be explained, if one accepts the view that performances are acts of communication reflecting particular intentionalities on the part of the individual player. Theories, therefore, must be based on fieldwork-derived insights drawn from the "aural thinking" implicit in a particular idiom of expression. The author's familiarity with the Norwegian scene, its musical and extra-musical characteristics, fruitfully guides her in her ethnomusicological thinking about native "aural thinking."

The present study is deliberately eclectic and explorative. The author's intention was never to write a definitive monograph on the subject. Each chapter of the book presents a different perspective, kinds of impressions, associations, data, and analysis. It contains valuable information about the instrument and its history, about outstanding fiddlers, their viewpoints and attitudes, and about aspects of musical organization; as well as different kinds of sociocultural associations constituting the complex context of music making and creativity. Still, the book emerges as a single composite picture, due to the way questions are theoretically and methodologically framed.

In my view, Dr. Hopkins's work serves three aims of equal value. It informs the international community of folk music devotees—scholars and laymen alike—about an unique tradition; it serves the interests of specialists by providing organological and musicological information and analyses; finally, it presents, both explicitly and implicitly, an important argument about how to do ethnomusicology.

Jan-Petter Blom, Ph.D.
Department of Socio-Anthropology
University of Bergen
Norway

List of Illustrations

List of Tables and Graphs

Musical Examples

Acknowledgments

First of all, I would like to acknowledge my debt to Finn Vabø and Johannes Dahle, whose ideas have provided the springboard for the theories developed in this book. Sadly, Johannes Dahle is no longer alive, and I can only attempt to thank him by making full use of the art he has left living beyond him. In the same way, I can only recall with deep gratitude Eivind Groven, whose analytical demonstrations for my benefit have proven valuable indeed; Gjermund Haugen, whose introductory lesson opened my mind to a new understanding of aural tradition; Øystein Odden, whose quiet dedication to the Tinn tradition took many forms, one being the building up of an invaluable collection of tape recordings dating from the days of Knut Dahle; Eivind Øygarden, from whose vast knowledge of the whole scope of the tradition I profited, both informally and through attending formal lectures; Jon Helland, who introduced me to the intricate art of constructing the instruments; and Knut Jorde, who invited me to attend the meetings of the Rauland *Spelemannslag* and graciously answered all questions that came to my mind.

I would like to thank all the members of the Rauland and the Tinn *spelemannslagar* for their continuous help over the years. Ola Kai Ledang, Kjetil Løndal, Knut Jorde, Johannes Rui, and Øystein Odden have gone to the trouble of sending me tapes especially recorded for my research. For other important interviews and recordings made in Norway, I wish to thank Gunnar Dahle, Ola Øyaland, Trygve Vågen, Odd Bakkerud, Bjarne Herrefoss, Magne Myhren, and Olga Homme.

I have benefited from conversations with Dagne Groven Myhren, Ellen Vabø, Johan Vaa, Einar Steen-Nøkleberg, Agnes Buen Garnås, Karin Brennesvik, and Egil Bakka, who have kindly been willing to share their specialized knowledge with me; as well as from the statistical information provided me by Hallgrim Berg and Ingar Ranheim. To Sigrid, Ragnhild, and Olav Lid, to Elna Odden, to Eva and Halvor Kostveit, to Kirsti

Øygarden, to Sonnev Dahle, Randi Settalid, and Anna Dahle, I owe a very special debt of gratitude for their warm hospitality, their help in planning field trips and in setting up recording sessions; also to Terrence Grame for his participation in most of my field trips, and to Theodore Grame, who shared the first trip to Bergen. Rolf Myklebust, many years head of the Norwegian Broadcasting Station, continually supported my research by generously supplying information and copies of tape recordings from the station's archives—as has, more recently, Sven Nyhus. I wish to thank Sigrid Lid, Elna Odden, and Eva Kostveit for help in checking English translations. To the musicians who gave their time and professional knowledge to the perceptual experiment, I am extremely grateful; they are Blanche Blitstein, L. Shankar, and Michael Kaloyanides. I also wish to thank June Trexler for her help with the trial run.

Ola Kai Ledang has helped keep me up to date with *hardingfele* research in between field trips and has given me valuable feedback on sections of the manuscript in progress. To Tellef Kvifte, I owe a detailed reading of the first draft of this manuscript; he has kept me from making too many major blunders, and I have profited from his thoughtful suggestions, both as to content and as to organization of the text.

I wish to thank Barbara Perrin for her invaluable artistic contribution to this volume: especially, the inspired rendering of Tåkatind from a mosaic of runic inscriptions and the book jacket design with its evocative transformation of my aural thinking photograph; she has, in addition, executed most of the charts and graphs and provided professional advice on design and format. To the artist's skill of Hugh Hopkins, I am indebted for the map of the *hardingfele* regions. I would like to gratefully acknowledge Sverre Sandvik's permission to use throughout my book *felarosa* designs drawn from his method on Hardanger violin construction (*Vi byggjer hardingfele*); and also thanks to his publisher, *Tiden Norsk Forlag*. Another exceptional artistic contribution is Chris Lagaard's impression of a *spelemann* at work, which he sketched and presented to me at the end of my stay at the *Morgedal Turisthotell* in 1967.

I am grateful to Andres Blomhaug for permission to publish his photograph of Knut Buen teaching a class in Sauland. The picture was originally reproduced in *Spelemannsbladet,* whose permission I also acknowledge. Thanks to Magnar Sundt, who has permitted me to include other illustrations from the pages of *Spelemannsbladet* as well: Ill. 19b from the 1980, Nr 5 issue; Ill. 19c and 19e from issue 1981, Nr 4; and 19d from 1977, Nr 5. Tore Heskestad took the photograph illustrated in 20c and Halvor Kostveit the photographs in 14c and 14d. To them, I am grateful as well as to the following persons who provided me with photographs for inclusion in this volume and/or gave me permission to use their images: Eva Kostveit, Olga Homme, Trygve Vågen, Knut Buen, Finn Vabø, Øivind Vabø, Anund Roheim, Tore Heskestad, Loretta Kelly, Andrea Een, Johannes Rui, and Ola Haugen. The photographer, Betty Dunn, is responsible for the superb close-up shots of the *hardingfele*: the *Frontispiece* and Illustrations 6, 7, 10, 11, and 12. The production of this book has been under the expert supervision of Brice Hammack.

For permission to publish an updated version of an article that first appeared in *Cross-Cultural Perspectives on Music* in 1982, I extend my appreciation to the editors, Tim Rice and Robert Falck, as well as to the University of Toronto Press. I am grateful indeed to Øyvind Anker who originally recognized the significance of the Knut Dahle—Johan Halvorsen—Edvard Grieg correspondence and printed it in the 1943 edition of *Årbok for Norsk Musikkgransking*; with his permission, I have been able to include an English translation of a major portion of this correspondence in the present volume. Knut Buen, who has recently published the original text in his book, *Som gofa spølå*, has given me permission to publish, as an appendix to the present volume, the list of *slåttar* in the repertoire of Johannes Dahle. To Magne Myhren, I owe a revised version of this list made for the purposes of the present publication, in which it appears in English translation. Dagne Groven Myhren has permitted me to reprint a chart from Eivind Groven's monograph, *Equal Temperament and Pure Tuning*, originally published in 1943; in my book, it appears as Chart 2.

I have benefited from three grants during the course of my research: two field trips were supported by Rutgers University (1979 and 1982). The last trip to Norway was at the invitation of the Norwegian government; an intricate itinerary was worked out by Ingvard Havnen and Jon Aase, Director of the Norwegian Information Service.

Part I

INTRODUCTION

ETHNOGRAPHY: AN AURAL BIBLIOGRAPHY

TRANSCRIPTIONS

Introduction

Outside the cultural mainstream; a rich musical tradition is flourishing in Norway today. The *harding-fele* (Harding or Hardanger fiddle), an intricately embellished violin with sympathetic strings, plays an idiosyncratic, thick-textured music that should be well known to the outside world. It is this conviction that initially prompted me to attempt a book on the subject: a presentation of an aurally-transmitted tradition that is meaningful in contemporary Norway to many who have never had anything to do with the pastoral societal complex from which it developed. This undertaking, which seemed straightforward enough, brought me unexpectedly into the midst of a conceptual quagmire. It appears that few scholars or musicians are prepared to accept a culturally pluralistic view of Europe. Conveniently imprecise words, such as "folk" and "classical," continue to perpetuate undigested attitudes toward the comparative evaluation of different cultures—and even affect the definition of history itself.

A recent book on Scandinavian music, for example, devotes little space to Norway. The author, who had travelled through Scandinavia in search of documentary evidence for what he called "the Nordic sound," explained:

> From the fifteenth through eighteenth centuries, a creditable, if not crushingly original, musical tradition grew up alongside the royal courts in Copenhagen and Stockholm. What was going on in Norway during these years? "Not much" makes a fair reply. Norwegians are by no means deprived of creative genius, but political and economic reverses conspired to punch a hole in their country's history. During the baroque and classical eras the cultivation of music depended on a leisured aristocracy; but no Esterházys lived in Norway.

(Yoell 1974: 12)

The above-quoted writer included for consideration the nationalist school of composers, who have utilized elements from "folk" music in their works; it was the "folk" musicians themselves who were invisible. It is interesting to observe in his words the same approach to research as was displayed by a South African college professor some years ago, when he remarked to students at a Connecticut university: "Africans have no history—except imperialist history, you know; they have no written records." The Native-American activist, Vine Deloria, has complained:

> The anthropological message to young Indians has not varied a jot or tittle in ten years. It is the same message these authors learned as fuzzy-cheeked graduate students in the post-war years—Indians are a folk people, whites are an urban people, and never the twain shall meet.
>
> (1969: 87)

But it seems that, in Deloria's sense, Norwegians were also a folk people, at least until the late 19th century. The historic hole perceived by Mr. Yoell referred specifically to the lack of an urban prestigious musical tradition.

I CONCEPTS

a) *Cultural Pluralism*

It is of particular significance for the study of folk tradition in general that Norway has occupied, economically and politically, a very special relationship to the rest of Europe.

> Unlike Sweden and Denmark, Norway is a "new nation," one that did not enter the ranks of independent countries until 1905. Norway was never a centralized bureaucratic state to the extent that its neighbors were, and regional cleavages have always been greater; no matter what history might have wrought, the geography of Norway would have insured this. Norway developed along democratic lines earlier and more easily than her neighbors, partly because of the absence of a strong native upper class, and there was no nobility and no army. Religion continues to play a larger role in

> *Norway than in Sweden and Denmark, and traditional attitudes are stronger.*
>
> (Tomasson 1975: 539)

Rendered powerless on the international scene by five centuries of foreign domination, Norway was never in a position to maintain a court (or develop a court culture) of her own. Living in highly inaccessible mountain regions, the great majority of Norwegian citizens were very little affected by Denmark and other European powers, and Norway followed a line of development that was quite different from that of the rest of Europe in several important respects. Norway never experienced a feudal division of property, for example, and she early attracted the attention of economists who were interested in a country where ". . . land is held, not in tenancy merely, as in Ireland, but in full ownership." (Laing 1854: 22; also see Malthus 1966: 154f) Thus, a consideration of folk culture is of more than peripheral importance to an understanding of Norwegian society; the fallacy of considering only the centralized institutions of this nation may be illustrated by a sociologist who has described Norway as: "an extremely antipluralistic country," because she is "dominated by one school system, one set of institutions for higher learning, one church denomination, one national broadcasting company for radio and television; and all four of these are in addition state controlled." (Ramsøy 1974: 395) This is not a satisfactory analysis. The members of such a homogeneous society would never have voted against the Common Market contrary to the advice of their mass media and their government in 1972; such a society would not insist on maintaining the legal status of two written languages, a situation that has led one observer to call Norway "two nations within one" (Smith 1962: 23). All school children must learn both *bokmål* (book language; also called *riksmål*, state language) and *nynorsk* (new Norwegian; originally called *landsmål*). The former reflects the speech of the officials in urban Norway under Danish rule; while the latter was fabricated from rural dialects by nationalistic literary and rural leaders during the nineteenth century. The local dialects themselves have been deliberately perpetuated (both informally and by local legislation); and they enjoy unusual prestige in Norway. An important point has been made for the Norwegian dialects: "The fact that . . . two varieties are perceived as distinct, however, does not necessarily mean that their separateness is marked by significant linguistic differences." (Blom 1974: 411)

The language dialects coincide with other distinctive regional traditions, including musical ones. In respect to music, the above point has been made more forcefully:

It is the quality, not the amount of variation that matters, a fact that accounts for the observation that fiddlers and dancers, objectively speaking as well as according to native theory, have difficulty in achieving competence in more than one local tradition.

(Blom 1981: 310)

It is interesting to note that the Norwegian political structure, from a sociological point of view, has been termed, "a denominational system":

. . . the distinctive feature of a denominational system is its recognition of validity in pluralism . . . since only with diversity do individuals freely choose.

(Parks 1979: 10)

This is an important statement—which should help us approach an understanding of the Norwegian traditions of the inner mountain valleys; for indeed they are major ingredients in an essentially and successfully pluralistic society.

b) *Folk*

Those European traditions usually termed "folk" are in a scholarly no-man's land at the present time—falling between the cracks of changing convictions. There has been much self-criticism within the social science fields lately. Dell Hymes has coined the term, "distinctive other traditions" in pointing to the anthropological fascination with the seemingly exotic (1969: 31)—a phenomenon David McAllester has identified for ethnomusicology as the "romance of distance in time and geography" (1979: 193) while the folk music scholars have reacted against what Ola Kai Ledang has called a "nature mystique" and "national romanticism." (Ledang 1974: 5) Folk music is no longer considered of peculiar importance for cultural research (as an index to survivals of the past or evidence for dissemination theories or reflections of national character), as the realization has come about that all traditions—"folk" or otherwise—are social manifestations. Even the term itself has come under new scrutiny: Klaus Wachsmann put the problem squarely up front, when he opened his article on the subject in the new edition of Groves Dictionary with the following words:

The notion that there is such a thing as "folk music" as distinct from other kinds of music is widespread in Europe and America.

Elsewhere the need for such a concept is felt less strongly, and in some parts of the world, especially in Africa, people do not make such distinctions. It is an ambiguous term that has different meanings and shades of meaning.

(1980: 693)

John Blacking observed that he began to understand the Venda musical system after two years of field work in their part of Africa, but:

I no longer understand the history and structures of European "art" music as clearly as I did; and I can see no useful distinction between the terms "folk" and "art" music, except as commercial labels.

(Blacking 1974: x)

Similarly, Marcia Herndon, in her study of Native American music, concluded that there was "no rational system" for separating one kind of music from the other (Herndon 1980: 10). The last distinguishing feature to stubbornly adhere to the folk concept is that of orality (aurality), and even that has been seriously questioned "by ethnomusicologists . . . though they have not stated this in print." (Seeger 1980: 436) The latest (1979) edition of *Encyclopedia Britannica* still includes a description of folk music as:

. . . music that lives in oral tradition, learned through hearing rather than reading, and disseminated within families and restricted social networks.

(See Dundes 1975 for a folklorist's criticism
of the oral criterion.)

c) *Aurality*

What of the one distinctive quality still to adhere to the folk concept: that of aural transmission? We live at a time when understanding the nature of aural transmission is of prime importance; it seems necessary to decide whether those critics are right who lament that we are entering a "post-literate" state of society, always with the assumption that such a state necessarily implies a less intellectual nature; or whether, on the other hand, the act of thinking is primordial to various manifestations, of which verbal communication is only one (a viewpoint strongly advocated by Lévi-Strauss). These considerations loom important in a world in which the domination of one segment over another is justified largely on the grounds of assumed cultural superiority; thus, the term "developing nation," implies both the inevitability and the desirability of becoming like the more prestigious nations (i.e., those more industrially focused). It is indeed a sobering thought that, when we became too sophisticated to use the term, "primitive," (even with inverted commas), we began to use the word, "non-literate," then "pre-literate"; now, as noted above, "post-literate" has become a catch-word.

To gain perspective on this question, it is useful to realize that the ancient Greek philosophers also believed that the state of being literate necessarily altered the intrinsic make-up of a person or society—but, most instructively, the concern was from the opposite point of view. Thus, Plato has the Egyptian, Thamus, predict that the discovery of letters: " . . . will create forgetfulness in the learners' souls, because they will not use their memories; they will trust to the external written characters and not remember of themselves . . . they will be tiresome company, having the show of wisdom without the reality." (Plato 1885: 274f) Nowadays, of course, forgetfulness is commonly associated with oral transmission. We are told that, when written language became "fixed" in the print of grammars and dictionaries, it became " . . . more intellectual than sensual through the predominance of the sense of sight over the sense of hearing." —a matter described as central " . . . to science, to all ordering and classifying and rationalizing." (Hughes 1964: 36f, 39)

In view of the significance attached to what is seen as an essential difference between oral and literate transmission, and the connection with culture change, it is interesting that the most important (and widely accepted) theory concerning the nature of oral transmission has recently been challenged. When Milman Parry and Albert Lord analyzed the living epic song tradition in Yugoslavia, their intention was to uncover distinctive (and universal) features of oral epic performance that would enable them to make a decision on the genesis of the Homeric epics. In reference to the epic of *Pābūjī*, John D. Smith has written: " . . . at least one epic tradition exists in western India which, while it shares the basic features of Yugoslav composition, is non-improvisatory. Lord's theory cannot account for such phenomena; indeed, it was specifically designed *not* to account for them. Fundamental rethinking will now be necessary." (1977: 141)

This call for a fundamental rethinking of the accepted view of oral epic recitation (as necessarily involving change) comes at a time when there is an expressed dissatisfaction with existing methods for explaining, or predicting, the course of musical change in general. Indeed, it is part of a

call for a new research orientation. Alan Merriam has complained that
the applicability of present methods to specific examples of culture
change often remains difficult to see. (1977: 806) Anne and Norm Cohen
similarly found that their expectations, based on seemingly solid scholarly theory, were not fulfilled. (1973: 44)

More recently, Bruno Nettl has taken up Seeger's challenge and point-
edly questioned the perceived oral/literate duality in print:

> When we began to know something about world musics, we es-
> tablished a dichotomy between classical and folk traditions. . . . . .
> . . .
>   It is widely believed that there is a difference in essence be-
> tween composing art music, with notation or at least a background
> of theory, and folk or tribal music. . . . Yet to me there seems no
> reason to regard composition in cultures with oral and written tra-
> ditions as different species. The precomposition—composition
> —revision model, while most readily applied to western compos-
> ers who depend heavily on notation, also works for those who
> have none.
>
> (Nettl 1983: 360 & 29f)

d) *History and Time*

The implications of changing scholarly views towards the nature of aural transmission are indeed far-reaching; and, just for this reason, difficult
to pin down. Anyone who sets out to research a European aurally-transmitted "folk" tradition faces obstacles in the very conceptual tools developed by the scholarly tradition itself; for, as we have seen, an unfortunate
dichotomy has been set up between those cultures that have "historical
records" (the traditional apparatus of scholarship) and those cultures that
do not. It must be recognized that this circumstance stems from a valid
scholarly interest in the objective portrayal of coexistent cultural systems,
each on its own terms. Much as certain European philosophers "brack-
eted" the question of existence, social scientists, reacting against unpro-
ductive searches for authenticity or ultimate origins, have set aside the
historical perspective in their areas of research. "Historical musicology"
is now a term commonly applied to the study of "high art" cultures (even
contemporary styles); while the history of the so-called "traditional"
forms is often ignored. The notion has been prevalent that "European music was somehow the exclusive domain of historical musicology." (Porter

1977: 443); and the terms, "West," "westernization," and "European" are still used as if they referred to a single culture.

Until recent years, Norwegians—no less than the Akan or the Venda —had no need for the folk music concept, dependent as it is on different "levels" of culture; only during the second half of the nineteenth century was "music as a conscious form of art . . . born in Norway . . ." (Lange 1958: 22) From the beginning of what we have referred to as a mainstream tradition, there was a strong nationalist component in this music. At that time, the distinctive functions of folk and art seemed obvious:

> They talk of carrying rocks to Norway but we have enough rock. Let us use simply what we have. Nationalism, in music for example, does not mean composing more Hallings and Springars such as our forefathers composed. That is nonsense. No, it means building a house out of all the bits of rock and living in it.
>
> (Rikard Nordrack quoted in Lange 1958: 31)

Against general expectations, the traditions of Nordrack's forefathers —the hallings and springars themselves—have continued to develop and thrive through the more than a century since his death. We no longer conceive of folk music as a reservoir of raw material for composers, but just how it is to be regarded—in comparison with the art traditions of urban centers—has, as stated above, not been resolved. The question becomes even more difficult to answer in the case of a tradition that has just transplanted itself to the urban areas.

It is not surprising that a re-evaluation of ideas about folk music has occurred at the same time as a new assessment of the nature of aural transmission and the process of musical change, since it is clear that these are interrelated concepts; but these changing views will be impossible to resolve satisfactorily, until the historicity of aural tradition is faced.

> The problem now is to explode the concept of history by the anthropological experience of culture. The heretofore obscure histories of remote islands deserve a place alongside the self-contemplation of the European past—or the history of "civilizations" —for their own remarkable contributions to an historical understanding. We thus multiply our conceptions of history by the diversity of structures. Suddenly, there are all kinds of new things to consider.
>
> (Sahlins 1983: 534)

While this is true, and timely put, one of the new things to consider is that it does not go nearly far enough. For most of the traditions of Europe —both rural and urban—remain unrepresented by the textbook interpretation of history, and it is a dangerous mistake to identify the traditions of European scholarship with European culture as a block.

It is not only the aural historian who has a problem in regard to documentation: the conventional historian who works with written records has difficulties of his own:

> *History is a dialogue with the dead. And the difficulty of the historian's task, as well as the heavy moral responsibility that this task imposes on him, lies in the truism stated by Professor Woodbridge, that "the questions we ask of the dead, only we can answer."*
>
> (Chase 1948: 1)

However, in a different sense, the past is "present-at-hand" (see Heidegger 1962: 430f) as acknowledged by today's aural historians who have chosen to supplement written records with field techniques; and this present-at-handness of the past is important to our argument, because it leads us naturally to a dynamic, not static, view of musical structuring —and therefore of meaning.

e) *Structure in Context*

The alliance of music with mathematics, on the one hand, and verbal communication, on the other, is time-honored (See Reese 1940: 118; Chase 1973; and Powers 1980); and both relationships, in different ways, have made it possible at times to use similar conceptual tools. Perhaps those who have been irritated by the recent fashion for applying linguistic techniques to music may draw some comfort from the knowledge that this borrowing has not been a one-sided affair. For example, the structural nature of music has been so apparent that scholars interested in illustrating techniques of structural analysis have frequently turned to musical analogies (e.g., see Sapir 1949: 3r; Leach 1973: 40). Lévi-Strauss, inquiring into the reason why the field of music, more than other manifestations of culture, should have developed complex theoretical systems, has hypothesized:

Perhaps because the combination of musical expression with in-
tellect is less obvious, musicians do not seem to have experienced
the same constraints in explaining the logical scope of their art.
(Lévi-Strauss 1971: 582)

Lévi-Strauss had in mind analytical models drawn from European music theory. (Hopkins 1977: also see Chase 1972 and 1973) Musical structuring has been described in verbal terms at least since the Indian epic, the *Ramayana* (which included an account of the raga system). "Folk" traditions, by definition, do not come equipped with formal systems of analysis: but there is no reason to conclude on that account that complex structuring does not exist or that musicians are unaware of it.

The recent emergence of a communications oriented school of folklorists has been of special significance to our study. The "shift from text to context" (Dundes 1964: 28) "releases folklore from the literary bonds imposed on it in archives and libraries." (Ben-Amos 1974: 13) This research has been highly influenced by sociolinguistics and the concept of an "ethnography of communication." (Gumperz 1972) Just as applicable to music as to verbal communication is the following observation;

One might even hope that folklore would take the lead in showing
how the appreciation and interpretation of performances as
unique events can be united in an analysis of the underlying rules
and regularities which make performances possible and intelligi-
ble; in showing how to overcome the divorce between the emer-
gent and the repeatable, between the actual, the realizable, and
the systematically possible that has plagued the study of speech.
(Hymes 1974: 13)

Thus:

The concern is with performance, not as something mechanical or
inferior, . . . but . . . as something creative, realized, achieved,
even transcendent of the ordinary course of events.
(Ben-Amos 1975: 13)

David Burrows has drawn attention to music as being characterized by the dual nature of process and thing. Yet: "To particularize music, we must begin by admitting that . . . the primary occasion is a performance." (Burrows 1972: 241; also see Feld 1974: 212)

It is important to realize that this perspective on performance unexpectedly brings the temporal element right into the synchronic picture; it entails ". . . a thorough going break with any standpoint which divorces the study of tradition from the incursions of time and the consequences of modern history." (Hymes 1975: 71; also see Herndon 1974: 222) For, as has been pointed out:

> . . . we must consider tradition as a symbolic process that both presupposes past symbolism and creatively reinterprets them. In other words, tradition is not a bounded entity made up of bounded constituent parts, but a process of interpretation, attributing meaning in the present through making references to the past.
>
> (Handler 1984: 286)

The broadened conception of folklore has brought it closer to the field of folklife (Scandinavian *folkliv*) which has recently gathered importance in this country; in its very definition, it encompasses all kinds of cultural elements from all ranks of society without drawing lines of demarcation. In so doing, "Folklife studies insists on historical as well as ethnographical methodology." (Yoder 1976: 5) The Harding fiddle tradition, as noted above, flourishes over an area that has substantially increased in size since the turn of the century. "This fact bears witness to its close adaptation to the Norwegian environment, associations of usage and ritual without which it would be meaningless," to paraphrase a scholar who was applying these words to Ireland. (Evans 1957: 13)

But if we are to seek the most basic information about what is specifically musical, we must consider the mental processes that are primordial to any outward manifestation: "the perception of sonic order that must be in the mind before it emerges as music." (Blacking 1973: 11) From the perspective of cognitive psychology, Dane Harwood has stressed the "perceptual basis of musical structure and meaning within a given style":

> I wish to assert that all people "construct" their worlds; we impose categories on our perceived environment, and this "categorical perception" is as indicative of musical behavior as of vision, language—indeed, all human thinking.
>
> (Harwood 1976: 521)

In psychology, as in other fields, the need has been felt to bring elements together that have been carefully kept apart (and often seen as different in kind) for analytical purposes. Rudolf Arnheim criticized the assumed distinction between receiving information and processing it, between the percept and the concept. Psychologists have developed a broadened conception of gestalt principles to describe holistic thought patterns—an interpretation that includes, indeed stresses, learned patterns; for:

> Like a spatial context, on which Gestaltists have concentrated their attention during the early development of the theory, the temporal context influences the way a phenomenon is perceived.
>
> (Arnheim 1969: 166)

Since the above words were written, there has been considerable attention to the relationship of psychology to human communication. Computer scientists have discovered a problem for them: that "Perception, in short, is a two-way street, a notion that has long fascinated poets and psychologists." Dr. John Kender, a computer expert at Columbia University, is quoted in *The New York Times* (September 25, 1984): "People familiar with the psychology of the brain should have had suspicions." (Broad 1984: c1) Curiously, most of the research that has recently been done on musical perception and cognition ignores cross-cultural communication (for an exception, in addition to the scholars quoted above, see Davies 1978); those who have commented on the relationship have usually attributed the drawing together of science and music to the increased availability and use of electronic equipment by composers. In a recently published book on the psychology of music, the author of one of the included articles comments:

> There has always been a problem of communication between disciplines. The languages often seem incommensurable and the goals different. When music is involved there is a double barrier, a large one between musical practice and music theory and another between music theory and those disciplines that touch music at some point or other—acoustics, psychoacoustics, cognitive psychology, and others. Nevertheless, developments in these fields over the past 20 years have led scientific investigators increasingly toward musical problems. Theoretically minded musicians are turning to experimental psychology for useful concepts and better underpinnings for their theoretical constructs.
>
> The first wave of musical interest came with the electronic technology that followed World War II.
>
> (Erikson 1982: 517)

The same author later quotes Milton Babbitt concerning the path upon which: ". . . the composer finds himself when he becomes aware that the responsible use of the electronic medium involves him, formally and informally, in acoustical and psycho-acoustical research." Erickson concludes: ". . . the need for musical context is there, in the suggestion of co-operation between composers and psychologists." (Erikson 1982: 518f) As Harwood knew: "All people 'construct' their worlds."

f) Meaning

We must now confront the problem of musical meaning, the very existence of which has been denied by some. But the meaningful nature of musical communication is proven every time a musician fits into (or does not fit into) a performance group through demonstrating (or failing to demonstrate) knowledge of the particular tradition through his/her playing. Thus, when Louis Armstrong found himself outside the be-bop circle, which was intentionally exclusive, he complained:

> Bop musicians want to carve everyone else because they're full of malice, and all they want to do is show you up, and any old way will do as long as it's different from the way you played it before. So you get all them weird chords which don't mean nothing. . . .
> (Tirro 1967: 316)

Misunderstandings on this fundamental matter may be explained by confusion on the meaning of meaning itself. It is often assumed that the term implies a verbal reference, (see Seeger 1977: 183) but some musicologists have tended to oversimplify the nature of verbal meaning. In a very real sense, the more meaningful is a word, the more diffuse its associations; and only a few words, mostly technical terms which have been consciously restricted, have each a single referent. These considerations led at least one linguist to question the very possibility of analyzing verbal meaning (Bloomfield 1933: 140). That meaning in linguistic communication is dependent upon contextual, as well as verbal, association was a major discovery of sociolinguistics. Most scholars recognize meaning in music as other than what has been called "dictionary meaning" (Springar 1956: 508) or "ektosemantic" (Seeger 1960: 229); (Also see Nketia 1962). Usually, musical meaning has been identified with the idiosyncratic structure of a musical system and the transformations of its elements; and some have pointed out that shared knowledge sets the stage for a manipulation of expectations for affective purposes. (Meyer 1956: 770f; also see McAllester 1971: 399). Other musicologists have found meaning in the result of these manipulations, the "creation of time of a special kind" (Wachsmann 1971; 383) or "the obliteration of time" (Lévi-Strauss 1971: 582), while a psychologist has stressed the relationship that is implied by meaning, suggesting that "music functions symbolically in several ways, each involving the *processing* of a relationship." (Harwood 1976: 529)

g) *Intentionality*

All of these points are insights into the composite musical reality, and all have special validity for the present study. But it is especially important to realize that meaning implies a relationship of a particular, an intentional, kind. Even chance music, to give an extreme example, is dependent for its effect upon the manipulation of shared associations of musician and listener.

In reference to the unpredictability of change in music, two of the authors referred to above issued a challenge:

> *Perhaps tunes are transformed almost immediately, according to principles yet to be discovered. These are the questions that still want answering, and we hope a more thorough study of materials near at hand will answer them.*
>
> (Cohen 1973: 44)

In a short, exploratory article in which much use was made of folklore-sociolinguistic theory, I attempted a first step in taking up this challenge; there, I sought to "demonstrate the importance of intentionality as a determining factor in the occurrence (or non-occurrence) of change in music." (Hopkins 1976: 450) the present essay is essentially a second step in the same direction: it is a more detailed study of "aural thinking" — to adapt Rudolf Arnheim's concept — the cognitive nature of musical communication. An exhaustive treatment of the proposed subject would be of vast proportions and would far exceed the scope and the exploratory purpose of the present work. I can only attempt to outline — to bring together — associations, often different in kind, so that the composite picture may be suggested.

II PERSPECTIVES

a) *The Fieldworker*

> *Landstad and Bugge were both here, and got all my stories and songs.*
>
> (Metcalfe 1858: 57)

With these discouraging words, a resident of Telemark, Norway, responded to eager questioning by a British traveller. Fortunately, in the century and a quarter since the incident took place, there has been no sign that these fears were justified, that the pioneer Norwegian folklorists mentioned above weakened the rural tradition in any way. However, there must be few thoughtful field researchers who have not attempted to define their relationship to the people whose cultures they were studying. "Cultural relativism is a 'tough-minded' philosophy," wrote Melville Herskovits. "It is especially difficult in the disciplines where man studies man." (1972: 35)

Alan Merriam's very definition of the ethnomusicologist contains the idea of separation from the culture under observation:

> ... *his position is always that of the outsider who seeks to understand what he hears through analysis of structure and behavior, and to reduce this understanding to terms which will allow him to compare and generalize his results for music as a universal phenomenon of man's existence.*
>
> (Merriam 1964: 2)

An even more separatist version of the outsider concept is found in a Ph.D. dissertation:

> *When I "chose" an art which belongs to someone else, I took on a responsibility not to assimilate; ... I took on the additional responsibility not to distort through dissemination.*
>
> (Whitney 1974: 148)

This view—objective in the extreme—denies not only the possibility of an individual interpretation but even the function of dissemination to the scholar who is not a member of the culture being studied. It is in direct opposition to Alan Lomax's concept of "cultural feedback," the idea that exposure of "genuine, uncensored native art" through mass channels of communication "acts upon a culture like water, sunlight, and fertilizer on a barren garden; it begins to bloom and grow again." (1968: 9) Mantle Hood sees the ethnomusicologist as both a recipient and disseminator of information, for "communication among people is a two-way street . . ." (1961: n.p.) To Melville Herskovits, the fieldworker's recipience of information (i.e., education) is of major importance:

> . . . ethnologists who in nonliterate societies had come to know artists as individuals realized that they were not too different from persons of artistic bent in any other social group including our own.
>
> (Herskovits 1972: 190)

Recent ethnomusicological opinion agrees with the view held by Herskovits and Hood. In a valuable article summarizing this latest trend in thought, K.A. Gourlay calls for the acceptance of the researcher as what he has termed a "non-eliminable" factor in the field work situation. (Gourlay 1978: 1; see also Blom 1975: 207; Herndon 1976: 20 and 1980: 1; Seeger 1971: 385; Wachsmann 1971: 381) In criticizing Merriam's research model for "sciencing about music," (1964: 25) Gourlay points out:

> The difficulty is that the method he proposes to achieve this end involves a concept of the ethnomusicologist as both omniscient and non-existent, as subject to zero constraint and at the same time to absolute constraint.
>
> (Gourlay 1978: 4)

He further complains that:

> The end result of this conceptualization is an ethnomusicological "discipline" which includes everything from synesthesia to symbolism and from composition to culture history but omits both the ethnomusicologist and the performer.
>
> (Gourlay 1978: 9)

If we accept the non-eliminability of the researcher (and, logically, we can hardly do otherwise), we must either conclude with Whitney (quoted above) that the non-native student has no valid role to play at all—or else we must see his/her role as possessing a special validity of its own. Charles Seeger has pointed out that, even in making initial judgements on what is or is not music within a particular culture, the scholar must refer to a "band of ideation" derived from personal experience. (1971: 388) Some years ago, in an article on the purposes of musical transcription, I referred to this process as a comparative one:

> *Many persons have rightfully stressed the importance of comprehensive (i.e., contextual) knowledge in transcribing the music of a culture that is foreign to us. But, curiously enough, this knowledge is generally thought to be involved solely with the foreign culture. It seems to be tacitly assumed that once we have steeped ourselves in another tradition and its music, we may then freeze our findings in notation much as one would freeze orange juice or chocolate cake. It is true, adjustments must be made for pitch or rhythmic deviation—but note the word, "deviation." The concept of "deviation" was surely not in the original piece but exists only in the pictorial description of the music, and, perhaps, so it should; because what is transcription, after all, but a comparison of that which is unfamiliar to that which is familiar? . . . it seems that the old name, comparative musicology, may not have been prematurely applied. Every time we transcribe a piece of ethnic music into our notational terms, we compare it with our music. This ability to compare is important if we believe in trying to do what we are trying to do here—to talk about music.*
>
> (1966: 311f)

The preceding words are relevant to the situation at hand in two senses: first of all, they quite literally apply to the viewpoint from which the transcriptions in this volume were constructed. After all, staff notation was chosen (certainly not the most suitable notational system one can imagine for *hardingfele* music); and, further, the conventional method of transposition was used, so that violinists could easily read the notes. Thus, both sides of the communication have been taken into consideration: not only what is coming out of it, but also where it is coming from.

But in a broader sense, the concept under discussion must apply to cultural interpretation in general by someone outside the culture. The Norwegian Hardanger violin tradition has been recorded, transcribed, and analyzed by Norwegian scholars who, almost without exception, have been outstanding players of the instrument themselves. Yet, outside of

Norway, this rich body of music is virtually unknown. It is in this area of cultural interpretation and translation, if you will, that the non-native scholar (who must compare) has a peculiarly valid role to play.

If I am to proceed logically according to the assumption that an ethnologist cannot remain an outsider, but must affect the situation of which he/she is a part, I must include information about the concrete, personal situation that impelled me to write this book, I should introduce myself as I was when I first came into contact with *hardingfele* tradition: a conservatory-trained violinist enrolled in a doctoral program for musicology/ethnomusicology at New York University. Mine was an unusually intercultural childhood: born in France of English and Norwegian-American parents, my first spoken language was Spanish and, by the time I was 14 years old, I had lived at 30 different addresses spread throughout five countries. Despite these early influences, I had absorbed the prevalent hierarchical view of culture and it had served as an easy method for conceptualizing the seeming illogic of diversity. Graduate study had made chinks in this smug intellectual armor. First, I had been placed in the interesting position of viewing the same kind of communication network (music) from three different perspectives: that of the performing musician, that of the European music historian, and that of the ethnomusicologist involved in music outside the western hemisphere; and it was astonishing to see how different these views could sometimes be. Furthermore, studying the violin with Rafael Bronstein, the principal transmitter of the Russian school of violin playing in this country, opened my eyes to the existence of different ethnic styles of violin technique. Gustave Reese, through his monumental works on medieval and Renaissance music, definitively proved the case for multiculturalism in time. Finally, I studied with Curt Sachs at the end of his life, when he was fighting against time to get his last book finished—the one in which he flatly contradicted his own evolutionary doctrine (Sachs 1961).

But it was the Hardanger violinists who completely destroyed the hierarchical perspective for me; no longer would I be able to mentally pidgeon-hole traditions according to their institutions, their international reputations and modes of transmission. In time, I could have paraphrased John Blacking's remark: while beginning to understand the *bygde* traditions, I, too, no longer understood the history and structures of European "art" music in the same way as formerly. (Blacking 1974: x) However, in my case, it was a European, not an African, tradition that has brought this realization.

It was a rich slice of the *hardingfele* tradition that I initially came into contact with; and I had no intention of attempting to broaden my knowledge to a necessarily superficial survey of the entire picture. Thus, on my successive trips to Norway, I travelled principally to the same places and visited the same musicians, seeking knowledge in greater depth. It was some years, however, before I found a means for attempting to communicate what I had found so significant about this tradition. I derived much from the intellectual tools and terminology I discovered in the Folklore Department of the University of Pennsylvania, where I taught ethnomusicology while completing my doctorate. There I was introduced to the folklore-communications school, the folklife perspective, and the insights of sociolinguistics. It was Kenneth Goldstein's article, "The Ballad Scholar and the Long-Playing Record," (Goldstein 1966) that kindled my interest in the importance of attitudes toward the media of transmission. I came across it in the early years of my research, and it had served to head me in the direction of the folklore department. My theory of musical code-switching (see Part II, Chapter 4) was directly inspired by an analysis of linguistic code-switching published in an article by Jan-Petter Blom and John Gumperz (Blom 1972). There was a third influential article: in it Ola Kai Ledang (Ledang 1974b) detailed the results of a remarkable oral history project that produced information about expansion of the *hardingfele* area shortly after the turn of the century. *Visual Thinking* (Arnheim 1969) gave me reason to believe it was necessary, and possible, to describe the fundamental interrelationship of perceptual and cognitive processes—a matter of obvious significance to cross-cultural understanding. Finally, I should mention a series of informal seminars held at Penn: a periodic gathering of members of the music, engineering and psychology departments. These, I believe, were the most important influences from different areas.

b) *The Performer*

As K.A. Gourlay pointed out, not only the ethnomusicologist, but also the performer was left out of the old "outsider" model of research. Behavior, according to this method, is discussed in the abstract, without reference to the individual musicians who do the behaving (i.e., performing). The individual *spelemann* is the focus of this study. While I have been generously aided in my research by a number of outstanding musicians and scholars, there are two *spelemenn* whose music and explanations over the years have formed the basis for this work. (See III. 1 and III. 3)

Finn Vabø (b. 1931) shares with Oddmund Dale the leadership of

Fjellbekken, the Bergen *Spelemannslag*; he is well known as an expert dance accompanist as well as a frequent participant in national and international competitions and festivals. Originally a student of the fine western *spelemann*, Jon Rosenlid (1891-1974), Vabø later—after having established himself as a *Klasse A* player in the national competitions—received a grant to study with Gjermund Haugen in Telemark, who (like Vabø himself) always had a special interest in the concert tradition. I recorded him extensively on my first trip to Norway in 1965, at which time he made both demonstration and performance tapes for me. He proved to be not only a skilled player of his instrument but also able to provide an exceptionally comprehensive and articulate analysis of his tradition. One of his demonstration tapes consisted of a detailed illustration of the construction of *hardingfele* music (see Part II, Chapter 2); he also gave examples of different regional styles of playing, of how this music is taught to students, of some of the various tunings used; and he included information about legends and other extra-musical associations. To a large extent, the structure of this book is founded on Vabø's exceptional analytical comprehension of the Harding fiddle tradition.

In December, 1981, Norway lost one of the finest musicians in the world. Johannes Dahle was a reserved farmer who lived quietly in Tinn, Telemark, throughout the almost ninety years of his life. During his lifetime, he exerted a predominant influence over his entire region (the culturally rich Telemark); and his own compositions are heard all over the country, interpreted according to the various regional styles. He has never chosen to participate widely in public performances; but his reputation has drawn disciples to him—as well as the Norwegian Broadcasting Company, which has recorded over 400 pieces in his isolated farm house. Dahle has been decorated with the King's golden medallion for his services to Norwegian culture, and he is a member of an important family of *spelemenn* who have made the Tinn tradition one of the most significant in the country. At the turn of the century, it was transcriptions from the playing of his grandfather, Knut Dahle, that introduced the composer, Edvard Grieg, to his own national music. Johannes Dahle was a quiet proselytizer for the Tinn tradition, always generous with his time for those who were sincerely interested in publicizing it. He recorded both *slått* performances and commentary on them for me; the latter consists of explanatory material on the music itself and the narration of associated legends. Of particular significance to our study are recordings I have made of Dahle playing the same *slått* at intervals over a period of twelve years, keeping distinct from one another versions deriving from separate traditions; this did not prevent Dahle from composing new material of his own.

III INFORMATION

My basic store of information has been collected from the *hardingfele spelemenn* during seven field trips to Norway (in 1965, 1967, 1969, 1972, 1979, 1982 and 1983); most of the time was spent in Telemark, especially in Rauland and Tinn. My data derives from a variety of sources: 1) personal interviews; 2) direct experience in learning to play the instrument myself; 3) participation in community life, including attendance at the weekly meetings of a local *spelemannslag* (players' organization) where I could observe the learning of the music; 4) attendance at formal and informal concerts and competitions (of both the national and local variety); 5) tape recordings, especially my own field recordings (but also tapes given to me by the Bergen University Library, the Norwegian Broadcasting Station, and by private individuals); and 6) publications.

Interviews for this project have been granted by musicologists: Egil Bakka, Jan-Petter Blom, Eivind Groven, Tellef Kvifte, Ola Kai Ledang, Morten Levy, Sven Nyhus, Reidar Sevåg, and Eivind Øgarden; the *hardingfele* maker: Jon Helland; traditional dancers: Karin Brennesvik, Tone Lid and Ellen Vabø; traditional singers: Agnes Buen, Olga Homme, and Dagne Groven Myhren; and the following *spelemenn*: Odd Bakkerud, Gunnar Dahle, Johannes Dahle, Gjermund Haugen, Ola Haugen, Bjarne Herrefoss, Knut Jorde, Svein Krontveit, Kjetil Løndal, Magne Myhren, Øystein Odden, Johannes Rui, Torbjørn Tveiti, Hans Ullern, Finn Vabø, Øivind Vabø, Trygve Vågen, and Ola Øyaland. The special role of Finn Vabø and Johannes Dahle has already been discussed (above p. 47ff).

Publications of the Harding violin tradition are notable for their authenticity, almost without exception by scholars with personal knowledge. Most impressive are the nearly 2,000 transcriptions of *slåttar* (as pieces for this instrument are called) now available in the recently completed, seven volume series, *Norsk Folkemusikk* (1958-1981). The editor-in-chief of the first five volumes of this monumental edition, Olav Gurvin, coordinated the work (transcriptions from the individual repertoires and field collections) of the other three editors; all outstanding players of the instrument themselves, they were Truls Ørpen (1880-1958), Arne Bjørndal (1882-1965), and Eivind Groven (1901-1977). The final two volumes have just recently been completed by the collaboration of three other scholar-musicians: Reider Sevåg, Director of the *Norsk Folkemusikksam-ling*; Sven Nyhus, Director of Folk Music for the Norwegian Broadcasting Corporation; and Jan-Petter Blom, Associate Professor of Anthropology at the University of Bergen. Arne Bjørndal and the folklorist, Brynjulf Alver, jointly published the only book specifically about the Harding fiddle (1966); it contains a wealth of information, especially relating to the western tradition and draws largely from the personal experience of Bjørndal. Sigbjørn Osa has put together a method for Hardanger fiddle, meant expressly for those who already know how to play the violin (Osa 1952). Sverre Sandvik recently published the first method for making the instrument. (Sandvik 1983)

There are numerous monographs supplying biographical information about well-known spelemenn; two of these (on the nineteenth-century virtuosi, Myllarguten and Gibøen) have been combined in book form (Berge 1972), a rich source for legendary lore, oral history, and some comparative musical analysis (a contribution by Eivind Groven). Local histories are a valuable source of information; for my work, I found Ein-ung's two-volume history of Tinn, Telemark (which includes a chapter on the *spelemenn* of Tinn by Berge) an important tool. The fine *spelemann*, Knut Buen, has recently made a significant contribution to documenta-tion of the Tinn tradition with the publication of his book, *Som gofa spølå: Tradisjonen rundt spelemannen Knut Dahle 1834-1921* (1983). Special mention should be made of the exceptionally literate and well-documented organ of *Landslaget for Spelemenn* (the national fiddlers' or-ganization), *Spelemannsbladet*.

In addition to their major roles on the editorial board of *Norsk Folke-musikk*, Eivind Groven and Olav Gurvin published some of the earliest analytical articles on the styles of Norwegian rural music (see especially Groven 1969, 1971, and 1972; and Gurvin 1940 and 1953). Groven de-voted his life to proving the individual worth of the Norwegian indige-nous tradition and in promoting its academic respectability. He accom-plished this through occupying a wide variety of musical posts: he was the first director of folk music for Norsk Rikskringkasting and the initiator of a weekly folk music radio program that has become something of a na-tional institution—in itself a major means of dissemination. Brought up in the rich tradition of Telemark, Groven refused a conservatory educa-tion in central European music, preferring to educate himself in composi-tional techniques that were more relevant to his culture; he composed and performed both *slåttar* and symphonic works, often using either the *hardingfele* itself or the idiom of its music. (For a detailed analysis of his technique, see Kydland 1983). Groven helped to invent an electronic organ capable of reproducing, for any key, intervals that are in agreement with the harmonic series (i.e., just intonation).

A new generation of scholars has been concentrating on the production of a scientific, systematic body of research. Ola Kai Ledang has used modern technology to measure tuning systems and folksong variants; he has, more recently, been analyzing new trends in the folk music movement that concern its recognition on a broader, more realistic basis (Ledang 1967, 1971, 1972, 1974a, 1974b, 1975, 1976). Jan-Petter Blom combining specialized knowledge of sociolinguistics, dance, and the *hardingfele*, has analyzed dance motions, especially the communication between *spelemann* and dancer; his contribution to the seventh volume of *Norsk Folkemusikk*, a detailed analysis of the rhythmic patterns of the different dance forms used in the Harding fiddle repertoire, is a major achievement. (Blom 1981; also see Blom 1961, 1979a and 1979) His analysis (in collaboration with John Gumperz) of the process of linguistic code switching in a northern Norwegian town directly inspired my theory of musical code-switching presented here in the fifth chapter (see Blom 1972). Egil Bakka has brought together a mass of new information on the different streams of Norwegian dance traditions, the result of exhaustive field work (Bakka 1982; also Bakka 1977, 1978 and 1983). Sven Nyhus has produced several collections of transcriptions and explanatory material, especially valuable for information about stylistic changes that have taken place in the Røros violin tradition (see especially Nyhus 1973). Morten Levy has published some of his analyses of the Hardanger fiddle tradition in Setesdal (Levy 1967) and a book setting forth a rather controversial theory concerning the similarity of the Setesdal music to medieval European polyphony (Levy 1974). The formal structure of *hardingfele* music has been the subject for analysis by Tellef Kvifte, who has drawn from communications theories (especially the field of cognitive psychology) to account for the complex patterns of thought evidenced by a spelemann's elaborate improvisational technique. His work is of obvious relevance to the present book, particularly to Chapter 2. (Kvifte 1978 and 1981) The organologist, Reidar Sevåg, has culled the confusing, inconsistent, and at times conflicting pieces of information concerning the history of the instrument under discussion (Sevåg 1972, 1973, 1975, 1979, and 1980). Arne Martin Klaussen, interested in aesthetics and sociological aspects of the art world, published *Kunstsosiologi* (1977), a major and pioneering work; his recent sociological research on conflicts between different perspectives on the function (and definition) of the arts in present-day Norway is of particular value for the study at hand. (Klaussen 1979) A significant contribution to an understanding of the Norwegian contribution to the multi-cultural perspective is a collection of essays on the continuing growth of importance of nynorsk (Rue 1981). Of more than routine interest is Rolf Myklebust's informative *Femti år med folkemusikk* (1982); for it focusses on experiences involved with years of directing one of the pivotal forces in shaping the course of national interest in traditional music, the radio program: *Folkemusikkhalvtimen* (Folk Music Half Hour).

IV ORGANIZATION

In this book, I have tried to present the *hardingfele* without a priori judgments. It is so easy to extend the application of generally accepted concepts beyond their original utility—even when the different purpose (or sometimes the original one) calls for fresh examination. We consider this problem in some detail in the discussion of the meaning of the instrument (Part I, Chapter 1); there we find that certain significant analogies with other European instruments have been obscured by the use of the most common system of musical instrument classification. Even more dangerous—because the implications are hidden—is the use of certain words that name classes of things or concepts. The term, "folk," for the reasons discussed above, will not be found in this book as a genre designation, to refer to a category of music set off by distinctive characteristics; we cannot avoid the term altogether, however, for we need a label for the concept itself. Sometimes, I have chosen "indigenous" or "traditional" to refer to the *bygde* idioms, but neither is without its own ambiguity. As used here, "indigenous" is meant to evoke the idea of independent legitimacy—simply the fact that it is a part of its own meaningful setting. The word, "tradition," is used in the fluid sense discussed above (the quotation from Handler 1984: 286). It is not meant to convey the notion of out-of-date culture, the interpretation one often finds in romantic accounts of "the folk" or, interestingly, as used by the composer, Paul Hindemith, in the title of *Traditional Harmony* (Hindemith 1943). The terms, "fiddle" and "violin" are interchangeable, the first having been used as an informal name for the instrument since at least the 17th century. The *spelemenn* refer both to the *flatfele* (flat violin) and *vanleg fele* (customary or ordinary violin), the first preferred here for its greater objectivity.

I have founded this study on three assumptions 1) that all traditions indeed have histories, 2) that all musical systems are meaningful (in a musical sense), and 3) that theories must be generated from the insights of the spelemenn themselves. The first assumption calls for a re-evaluation of the static conception of history, defined by chronological time and supported alone by tangible documents. The second assumption requires the consideration of thought patterns present in musical perception itself and the third assumption molds the organization of this study, since it involves the relationship of emic information to etic interpretation. While the importance of this problem has been recognized for some time (See Hallowell 1955 and Pike 1954) and has given rise to a number of terms ("folk taxonomy", "emic", "ethno-history", "ethno-science"), there has been a new wave of interest recently that has produced fruitful ideas. (See Stone 1982 for a description of her "feedback interview"; and Pekkilä 1983 for his distinction between "musical concepts" and "ethno-theory"; also see Feld 1982; Nketia 1981; and Rice 1980). An important aspect of this problem that has been given little attention, so far as I know, is devising a method for presenting the particular situation within which a particular piece of information was obtained—an intangible, involving interaction between two or more persons. In order to suggest the context in which ideas arose or became meaningful, I have chosen to use a narrative. Part I, including an ethnographic account of my field work in Norway, is presented in a phenomenological manner: events have been allowed to unfold as closely as possible to the way they actually occurred, and there are numerous quotations from field notes. Personal interpretation has been kept to a minimum; however, there has been a continual attempt to include the responses of the viewer from outside the culture—to depict the interplay between events and their reception to keep both ethnomusicologist and performer in full view. My intention was twofold: first to draw from the original data (and from the spelemenn's own words) the areas for analysis; and, secondly, to present the tradition in its complex setting. It is in the second sense that this section of the book may be considered analogous to a bibliography (and subtitled, paradoxically, an aural bibliography); for it is here that the reader may seek for the sources of aural information. The reader should not expect to find all incidents, all interviews, or even all places visited in field trips detailed there. There has been a selection made according to the significance (for this piece of research) of the aural information given, and matters not directly relevant were not included; this is not a travel account, diary, or even field notes in the usual informal sense. Most interviews with scholars are not included (perhaps a debatable point), on the theory that most of such discussions were directly involved with printed works that could be referred to in the usual bibliographical references. There are two more points to be made on this subject. Quotations are sometimes presented not in their original context, but in the situation that made them become meaningful to my work, although the time and place or the original context is always provided via footnote. Perhaps most important of all is the fact that all direct quotations have been submitted for approval to the original spokesmen—a process that has continued for the last 3 field trips. Adjustments, corrections, and deletions have been made accordingly. Sometimes, such review discussions have netted revisions or amplification of original quotations that have been important enough to include in the original text (e.g., see beginning of Part 1, Chapter 3); On at least one occasion, the problem of defining a single word took up most of an evening (See Ethnography, p. 100).

Each of the five chapters of Part II is an analytical essay that derives from one or more direct quotations presented in the ethnography. Chapter 1, *Meaning of the Instrument,* begins with a remark on sympathetic strings spoken by John Helland of the renowned family of Harding fiddle makers. It is used as a springboard for the development of a theory about the essential nature of musical instruments, a viewpoint that allows the *hardingfele* to be seen as a cluster of associations, a mental construct of which the physical instrument is only part. Chapter 2, *Aural Structuring,* derives its material from Finn Vabø's own description of the construction of the music—which leads to an analysis of the internal aspects of the music; idiosyncratic features (as tetrachordal scale patterns and scordatura tunings) are put forth as principal generators of the musical construction. Vabø's classification of the Harding fiddle pieces in different ways for different purposes (for listening and for dancing, easy or difficult to understand, Telemark vs. Hallingdal style, etc.) leads to a discussion of the distinctive features that serve to differentiate one traditional form from another, attributes that sometimes go beyond the merely functional. The third chapter, *Aural Thinking,* contains the description of an experiment concerning the perceptual nature of the spelemenn's mental constructs. The outcome of the experiment clearly demonstrates that musicians, highly skilled in other musical systems, can only understand those aspects of Harding fiddle music that, in some way, are analogous to patterns present in their own music; thus, it serves to display the cognitive component in musical perception itself. The rationale, as well as the name of the chapter (and title of this book) were inspired by Rudolf Arnheim's work, *Visual Thinking* (1969).

Chapter 4, *Musical Codes and the Control of Change,* consists of an analysis of the individual spelemann's manipulation of traditional resources: to what extent the rules may be changed, under what circumstances, and by whom. In other words, this is a discussion of how the tradition operates in its cultural setting; concepts and terminology are drawn from sociolinguistic and folklore theory as indicated by the title. The final, fifth chapter, *The Emergence of a Classical Tradition*, contains an examination of the status of the Hardanger violin. The appendix is a remarkable contribution by the scholar and spelemann, Magne Myhren; it represents one of the most detailed pieces of research ever done on the repertoire of a musician (Johannes Dahle) belonging to an aural tradition. Originally, published in Knut Buen's *"Som gofa spølå"* (Buen 1983), Magne Myhren has kindly sent me a newly revised version for inclusion in the present publication.

Within recent years, linguists have issued a clarion call; they have seriously questioned the significance of prestige values officially attributed to different varieties of speech. A biographer of Naom Chomsky explains that the:

> . . . distinction between "language" and "dialect" is commonly drawn on political grounds. . . . The important point is that the regional and social dialects of a language, say English, are not less systematic than the standard language and should not be described as imperfect approximations to it.
>
> (Lyons 1970: 16)

William Labov described the logic of nonstandard English in a chapter of his highly influential book on Black English Vernacular; it is, he writes, a:

> . . . polemic directed against the deficit theory of educational psychologists who see the language of black children as inadequate for learning and logical thinking. . . . The major problem in reading failures is the political and cultural conflict within the classroom.
>
> (Labov 1972: xvi)

The dangers encountered in bringing nonstandard linguistic systems into patterns established for mainstream traditions have been emphasized: e.g., a traditional grammar that was developed on the basis of Greek and Latin, and writing systems that made North American Indian languages look like English and those of Siberian peoples look like Russian. "The determining factors . . . are all social and political rather than merely linguistic and pedagogical." (Fishman 1972: 12)

Norway has provided the world with a model for an official incorporation of linguistic pluralism, as well as a model for the viable coexistence of different cultural streams. Establishment recognition of the indigenous music—which, as noted above, continues to grow in importance—has not yet arrived; and it remains invisible to the outside observer. The problems are more complex, because they involve attitudes toward music as well as toward nonstandard culture. Rudolf Arnheim was impelled to write *Visual Thinking* by a practical concern for what he considered to be prejudicial attitudes toward the arts in education: "Our entire educational system continues to be based on the study of words and numbers. . . . The arts are neglected because they are based on perception, and perception is disdained because it is not assumed to involve thought." (Arnheim 1969: 3)

The introduction has been exhaustively (if not exhaustingly) loaded with quotations that reveal a recent and wholesale questioning of well-entrenched principles—assumptions concerning folklore, aural tradition, culture change, the nature of perception and of artistic communication, of history, linguistic and societal status—even of established methods of analytical conceptualization. In a platonic sense, perhaps most of us already "know" (have a gut feeling) that these dog-eared assumptions are not valid. Yet we permit our institutions (our book and record stores, our university departments and school curricula, our library catalogues, museum exhibits, and our archives) to reflect untenable lines of societal demarcation; we even forget ourselves sometimes in our scholarly journals and describe certain traditions as being context free or use the term, "westernization" in an inexact way. The exceptionally pluralistic view of culture in Norway (and the question of its eventual resolution) is presented as of general significance for cultural relations. Is there any more important subject at issue today? The "cultural grey-out," so lugubriously envisioned by Alan Lomax (1968: 4), has never in fact taken place: there are at least as many styles of music co-existing today as in the past, and it begins to be apparent that we have been drawing distinctions in the field of music, as in language, on political grounds.

When Johannes Dahle articulated his desire for dissemination of the Tinn tradition—and when he sent the tape of one of his newly composed *hardingfele* slåtts to an international composers' competition—he was, perhaps, issuing a challenge, not so much to our definition of nationalism as to our concept of internationalism and the mystique that surrounds it.

Map of Southern Norway

Ethnography:
An Aural Bibliography

First Field Trip: 1965 Bergen

You must understand the geography of Norway to understand its music. . . . An undulating countryside inspires a similar type of music. In the West, hardingfele music is close to that of the ordinary violin and to the music of Scotland. . . . In Hardanger, they have the purest tradition. . . . Some of the most difficult to understand slåttar come from Telemark, where they take the melody up again and up again—very much like their mountains. Those who don't like this music—Well, they play no instruments at all—or else perhaps they play the musical comb.[1]

Finn Vabø thus emphasized the different regional styles of his tradition, their reflection of the local topography, and their esoteric nature. Vabø's playing and his analytical commentary were my introduction to the body of music that was to become the subject of life-long fascination for me. (See Ill. 1) Our meetings took place in one of the complex of new (indeed, still largely under construction) high-rise apartment buildings in Bergen, Norway. It was July, 1965, and Finn Vabø had recently ceased to be a seaman in the Norwegian merchant marine to become a superintendent of these buildings—in order to give him more time to practice than was available on shipboard, he told me.

Vabø had been born and brought up close to Bergen in one of the sheltered and fertile raised beaches that line the rocky outcroppings of what have been called "the Atlantic Ends of Europe." (Evans 1958) The term implies common geographical and cultural characteristics between the Scottish and Norwegian sides of the North Sea—those correspondences that were pointed out in the above quotation. Vabø knew what he was talking about: as a seaman, he had experienced the ease of water-way communication between the different parts of the "Atlantic fringes"; and, as a participant in folk festivals in the British Isles as well as closer to home, he could knowledgeably compare their traditions as well as their physical features. It is interesting that E. Estyn Evans, from the point of view of a cultural geographer, agrees with Vabø in respect to these inter-relationships:

> I . . . enlist the assistance of fieldwork in an attempt to trace the evolution of a cultural landscape . . . Cultural facets serve as a buffer between man and his environment, and we delude ourselves if we suppose that we need to take account of the physical environment only . . . the raised beaches lining the sea-inlets of Scotland and Norway are of special significance for man, and provided him with his first safe foothold. . . . Today it is at the level of folklife and in the rural landscape that cultural parallels along the Atlantic coasts can most readily be discovered.
>
> (Evans 1958: 5,12,4,3)

I myself had experienced the rare good fortune of traveling to Norway for the first time as it had so often been approached in Viking days: by the water route over the largely submerged ridge that divides the Arctic from the Atlantic oceans. Setting sail in Reykjavik, Iceland, we had stopped at the Faeroe Islands, then passed through the strait known as the Pentland Firth (between the Orkneys and the northern tip of Scotland), and crossed the North Sea to the inland water way (*Indreia*) that provides a dramatic means of access to the Norwegian interior through steep-walled fjords that are in fact water-filled valleys deeply cleft in the rock. Backed by the heights of Mount Floyen, the low-lying city of Bergen appeared all at once at a sudden widening of the expanse of water; and it was immediately apparent that the capital of the mountainous fjord provinces of *Vestlandet* faces out to the sea and away from the land.

The route from Iceland to Norway crosses through, or close to, the boundaries of four seas and can scarcely be a tranquil or easy passage, even today. To the Vikings, however, it seems to have become almost a routine matter of communication, for references to it in the Sagas are casual indeed:

> When they were ready to sail they put out to sea and had a good passage. They landed in Bergen, and Thorid wasted no time in asking whether the king was in residence. . . .
>
> (Pálsson 1971: 95)

Earlier that year, and in collaboration with Theodore Grame, I had been involved with researching the traditional music of Iceland. We were collecting material on the rich body of vocal forms that (like the Icelandic language) had remained substantially unchanged in character since medieval days. As an instrumentalist myself, I had been particularly curious about the old Icelandic zither (the *langspiel*); but my question was always answered in the same way, by another question: "If you are a violinist, why don't you go to Norway, where they have that most interesting of all stringed instruments: the hardingfele?"[2] When we had completed our work in Iceland (and accompanied by our two-year-old son), we boarded a small freighter-passenger ship, the *Hekla*, for Norway.

Six months before my arrival in Bergen, the performer and scholar, Arne Bjørndal, had died, completing nearly sixty years of work on the *hardingfele* tradition. Since 1906, Bjørndal had collected some two thousand *slåttar* (as pieces for this instrument are called), first in manuscript form and later with tape recorder. He had participated in over a thousand performances; written a book (Bjørndal 1966) and a number of scholarly monographs on the subject; served as chairman of *Landslaget for Spelemenn* (the National League of Fiddlers) from 1925-36; was one of the editors of the monumental collection of *hardingfele slåttar* published in Oslo as Series I of *Norsk Folkemusikk*; and, during his later years, filled the office of music director at the Bergen University Library.

The Director of the Music Division at the University Library, showed me Bjørndal's study containing his extraordinary collection of tapes, books, transcriptions, manuscripts, and instruments—including the famous *Jåstad-fele*, the earliest known *hardingfele* extant (made in Hardanger and signed, Ola Jonson Jåstad, 1651). I was able to study this fiddle—which is smaller than later models and has only two sympathetic strings. I was also able to listen to recordings from Bjørndal's collection. I had stumbled upon a wealth of material to begin my researches on a subject that had already begun to be of intense interest to me. But it was not until I heard the *hardingfele* played in live performance that I felt the full impact of the music.

It was through the help of the librarians of the University Library that I received an introduction to Finn Vabø, protégé of Jon Rosenlid, *spelemann* from Nordfjord. After I had introduced myself and explained the reason for my visit, Vabø told me that he had been working overtime in his new occupation; and, while offering to give me a demonstration of the instrument, he apologized for being out of practice and for not having had time to replace a faulty top string, one that had a tendency to whistle,

1. Finn Vabø

he said. Nonetheless, his illustrations were remarkable both for their analytical clarity and for his brilliant virtuosity and musicianship. The instrument's characteristic silvery tone quality was the result of wire understrings that vibrated sympathetically, when the top strings were bowed. The polyphonic, thick-textured music played on his reverberant eight-stringed violin filled the room with an intensity of sound that may possibly be compared with that experienced in a bell tower of a cathedral. I asked Finn Vabø if he would consent to have his playing recorded; and the next day we began to make a series of both performance and demonstration tapes.

I noticed that the *hardingfele* was smaller than the flat violin; that it had a shorter neck and a bridge that was nearly flat—to facilitate the simultaneous playing of several strings, I assumed; it had to be higher to service the resonance strings on a lower layer. A far lengthier peg box was topped by a colorfully resplendent dragon's head; and the belly was shaped so as to form large and deeply indented f-holes. The instrument itself was magnificently decorated with intricate designs reminiscent of rosemåling and with mother-of-pearl inlay. (Frontispiece)

As a violinist who had specialized in the performance of Baroque music, I felt at home with the highly embellished music. Vabø demonstrated the kind of improvisation that was played on the *hardingfele*: basically, stock melodic outlines that are interpreted and embroidered upon differently in the various geographical regions of Norway; and he was able to produce some examples of the regional styles for my benefit.

> *The way they hold the bow, with the little finger often raised above—not even touching—the wood. You'll see they can't develop right arm technique: never learned to hold the bow correctly.*

I recalled this chance remark made by a member of a foreign symphony orchestra then visiting Bergen: an inefficient right hand position prevented *hardingfele* players from "progressing" to modern violin technique, he had claimed. As I watched Finn Vabø's bowing hand closely, I realized that the position thus criticized was in fact almost identical with that of the Russian violin school (and used by such renowned violinists as Leopold Auer, Jascha Heifetz, Nathan Milstein, and the Oistrakhs). In reference to left hand technique, I knew what Rafael Bronstein (the celebrated violin teacher in the Auer tradition) would say if he had been present, for he had often made the observation in comparing Baroque violin music with 19th century style: "Horizontal across-the-string fiddle technique is just as difficult as vertical position technique." Finn Vabø locked his wrist under the neck of his instrument to achieve as much finger power as possible—and, as I was later to discover, in order to accurately execute certain idiosyncratic ornaments; his bow was meanwhile being deftly manipulated to provide the correct (usually syncopated) articulations for the highly embellished, contrapuntal music.

Vabø's repertoire from his own native *Vestland* seemed limitless as he unhesitatingly performed one piece after another. The almost constant drones reminded me of Highland bagpipe music, as did certain characteristic embellishments. Vabø played a *halling* (Ex. 1) and explained that this was a dance form that was possibly related to the *Highland fling*; he pointed out that certain technical features of the western music—such as spiccato and left-hand pizzicato—are not found in the Hardanger fiddle tradition of other parts of Norway and probably reflect close communication with other European countries. Certainly, many of the western slåtts had characteristics in common with the lands across the North Sea and even further away in Europe, yet in spite of these obvious points of resemblance, there was much that was entirely different. Indeed, in most respects, the music was vastly different from any I had heard before. There were incongruous (to me) modal peculiarities and an unusual pattern of foot-beating that sometimes seemed to bear little discernable relationship to the rhythmic complex as a whole. Vabø further indicated that in other regions of Norway the foot-beaten patterns—and the superimposed rhythmic structure upon them—was more difficult to understand. Ellen Vabø, a skilled traditional dancer, rose to demonstrate the contrast between the dance step of the tradition right there in *Vestlandet* and that of Telemark. I shook my head; I was totally unable to follow intelligently. When I asked: "Who is the leader, fiddler or dancer?" both spoke at once, then stopped short to laugh. I realized that there would never be complete agreement on this issue. Then Finn Vabø continued: "Well, I take a chance. I say: Yes; The fiddler is the leader. The dancers must dance after the fiddlers. We can't play after the dancers—. If the dancers are good, then the players will be inspired."

Vabø explained the extra-musical associations of the pieces he played, for interwoven with this music for Hardanger fiddle is an immense body of legendary material. There were many slåtts said to have been inspired by the beauties of nature—often coming to the fiddler in a burst of inspiration or in the form of a dream. There were associated legends about Old Nick, fairies, huldras, and trolls; indeed, even a special troll tuning (a-e'-a'-c ') which, according to the old tradition, might only be used after midnight and before dawn. There was a tuning called "Light Blue," that was appropriate to dawn. As might be expected, the old Nordic heroic legends were prevalent, with their typically tragic (and extra-human) tales of plunges into waterfalls or nuptial dances interrupted by disaster. One such legend was tempered by a touch of dry Norwegian humor, however. In this story, the bridegroom, Øystein, upon arriving just in time for what he fondly imagined to be his wedding, found his bride celebrating her marriage to another man. Øystein could not rest until he had arranged a dance with his bride, for he was determined to retrieve the valuable silver belt he had given her. Upon obtaining his belt, the jilted lover concluded the dance with a *rundkast*, a gigantic leap and somersault high in the air—and departed.

I was surprised to learn that—in this "folk" art—the virtuoso tradition is strong. Many slåtts are called after individual players whose names are held in awe today. The most famous *spelemann* of the last century was Torgeir Augundson, known as Myllarguten (the Miller Boy); and Vabø played *Myllarguten's Siste Slått* (Myllarguten's Last Slått)—a piece meant for listening, not dancing, even though considered to be based on the *gangar* dance form. Vabø described the music as having "something crying in it." (Ex. 2) The Harding fiddler plays slåtts for dancing and slåtts for marching to the wedding processional; but he also plays *lydarslåttar* (listening slåtts). Even the listener has become immortalized in Hardanger fiddle lore: The name of the *slått*, *Aksla-biten*, means "shoulder bite" and is said to derive from the habits of a man called Elling Sjur, whose ecstatic love for the Harding fiddle made him sit as close as possible to the performer with his head resting on the fiddler's left shoulder. Apparently, during a famous rendition of this piece by Per Nilson Bolko, he was unable to restrain himself at certain points and actually dug his teeth into the fiddler's shoulder.

Finn Vabø owned a finely made *hardingfele* of considerable value and an efficient Tandberg tape recorder that he used in his practicing. The great volumes of transcriptions, *Norsk Folkemusikk* (Gurvin 1958), occupied a central position in his bookcase; but, although he was able to read music and had tremendous respect for the editors of this edition (all of whom were skilled players, as well as scholars, themselves), he had not found notated examples to be of prescriptive value. He had tried to use them in learning a new *slått*, but; "The music," he said, "is not there." Vabø plays regularly in numerous local, national, and international competitions and had amassed a collection of prize-winning silver cups. Then (as now), he earned money through his fiddling by playing for dance halls in and around Bergen and teaching through the local *spelemannslag* (players' organization).

My first field trip to Norway concluded with a week's excursion up the Western coast, where I became acquainted with the rural countryside: the asymmetrically arranged pockets of settlement between sea-inlets and snow-capped mountains typical of the Norwegian highlands—and so much of the "northern fringes" in general. In the small resort town of Voss, I witnessed both traditional dancing to the music of the Hardanger fiddle and also a wedding in the old style, the *spelemann* leading the bridal party up to (but not through) the front entrance of the church. The brilliant Vestland costumes of the wedding party were highlighted by the glistening crown and jewelry of the bride; and, as I watched the fiddler, I was reminded of the words of a nineteenth-century British traveller who had also been struck by the significant position in the ritual held by ". . . that most important of persons—the fiddler—working his bow with astounding energy." (Mockler-Ferryman 1896: 96) The music was somewhat familiar, and I eventually recognized it as the wedding processional played by Finn Vabø as an example of music that was "easy to understand," because it had an even beat. (Ex. 3)

I left Norway with the conviction that I had only scratched the surface in trying to understand an unbelievably rich tradition. So much depended upon the knowledge of the regional differences—knowledge that could only be obtained through first-hand experience—that I immediately began to plan a trip to another part of the country.

Second Field Trip: 1967
Oslo

> It may be said that the Norsk character caught some parts of its colouring from the stern, rugged nurse in the embrace of whose mountains their lot has been cast; with the great backbone of primaeval rock (Kiolen) splitting Norway in two, and rendering intercourse difficult. So that now you will hear a Norskman talk of Nordenfjelds (north of the mountains) and Sondenfjelds (south of the mountains), as if they were two distinct countries.
>
> (Metcalfe 1858: 3f)

As the Englishman who wrote the above passage discovered in his travels to Telemark, *Langfjellene* (the Long Mountains) also appeared to form an impenetrable barrier between eastern and western Norway, from

Setesdal to the Dovre Mountain range. The shape of Norway has been described as that of a very long, thin fish, its head in the south and its tail portion reaching so far up into the arctic region that the total length of this small country extends well over a thousand miles. Up until 1909, when the railroad between Bergen and Oslo was finally completed, it had been far easier to sail out from the west coast to foreign seafaring countries than to cross the mountains that divide eastern from western Norway in the southern, fatter portion of the country. (See map on p. 58) The "head of the fish" contains the central area of Hardanger fiddle territory; now that I had come into contact with the western tradition, I was eager to learn something about the style of music that had developed in the more isolated regions of the highlands; where the mountain hamlets look inward toward themselves, rather than outward toward the sea. I remembered that Finn Vabø had spoken of the Telemark tradition with special respect:

> Some of the most difficult to understand slåttar come from Telemark, where they take the melody up again and up again—very much like their mountains. Those who don't like this music—Well, they play no instruments—or else perhaps they play the musical comb.[3]

Unlike my first trip, when a chain of fortuitous circumstances had thrown me into the midst of an experience I could never have anticipated, my second expedition was carefully planned in advance. I owe to Sigrid Lid (then temporarily in the United States) and to her father, Olav Lid (well known in Norway for his strong support to cultural activities in general and to the traditions of his native Telemark in particular), recommendations and introductions that made my work progress, for the most part, as smoothly as if it had been programmed.

In June, 1967, I arrived in Oslo, planning to attend the national competition in Porsgrunn before heading for the mountains of Telemark. I was accompanied by my son, Terry, now nearly four years old. While in Oslo, I benefited from the resources of the *Norsk Rikskringkasting* (the Norwegian national broadcasting station). There I met with the director of folk music, Rolf Myklebust, who introduced me to the efficient and exhaustive network of national folk music collecting that has its focus in the station's archives. I also talked with his assistant, Liv Greni, who was in the process of preparing a radio program from her own field recordings of songs remembered by women, who, in their youth, had taken charge of the summer mountain-top farms known as *sæters*. It was my first introduction to the women's vocal tradition—so distinctively different (in modal flavor and rhythmic construction) from the predominantly male *hardingfele* tradition.

Porsgrunn

The national competition (*Landskappleiken*) began on Friday, June 31. The train ride from Oslo to Porsgrunn was notable for the sounds of expert fiddling coming from many compartments: both the last minute finger-exercise practicing of the perfectionists and the casual exchange of musical ideas or instruments of the more relaxed. My son picked up a ruler to imitate the fiddler's actions, and I was reminded of Finn Vabø's response to my question: "When do young people normally begin to play the *hardingfele*? What is the ideal age?" There had been a short pause before Vabø replied:

> Well, that is not an easy question to answer. It all depends on— We use a French term; do you know it? The milieu. The musical milieu.[4]

From our train windows, we could see the evidence of another important Norwegian tradition, so time-honored that a traveler's account of a similar scene more than a century ago well describes our own impressions.

> In the stream lie thousands of logs that have been cut down in the mountains. . . . One of the most characteristic features of a Norwegian valley are gangs of burly broad-chested men, armed with huge poles, the ends of which are shod with a hook and pike. Directly there are symptoms of the water rising after rain, these fellows appear suddenly, and are seen pushing the stranded timbers from the shore, dashing through the water in their great jack-boots, to islands or shoals, for the like purpose, or boating across the river to set afloat some straggling laggard; and, forthwith, all these, like so many great cadises, just disengaged from their anchor, and soon to take wing, go swarming down the stream.
>
> (Metcalfe 1858: 252f)

Porsgrunn, a small industrial city known principally for the manufacture of a utilitarian brand of china, manifested the color and excitement of the occasion. Most of the visitors (especially the women) wore national costumes that could be read by the knowledgeable as indicative of regional background. Bright-colored flags hung from poles attached to the roof-tops of the community center and of the prosperous hotel in the center of town; and Rolf Myklebust, from the National Broadcasting Station, was feverishly directing his radio and television crew, who were already engaged in making the necessary connections from the station's truck, parked outside the community center. Fragments of fiddling were now coming from scattered houses on the narrow streets—and pouring into all corridors of the hotel.

Soon impassive judges were sitting in their places in the community center, where two halls were to provide for the simultaneously-running dance and music sessions. There were competitions for flat-fele, of which there is also a rich tradition in some sections of Norway; as well as performances of vocal music and demonstrations of traditional instruments no longer in common use (the *lur, munnharpe,* and *seljefløyte*).[5] But it was the *hardingfele* competition, without question, that drew the most attention and provided the central drama of the festival. Momentum gathered slowly, however. On the first afternoon, the elderly players, categorized as *Class D,* performed in a casual, non-competitive manner for the small knots of their friends and neighbors who had, in many cases, sponsored their trips to the festival (sometimes from remote parts of the countryside). Unlike their younger colleagues, most of these men wore national dress. The *Class B* (less experienced) and *Class C* (underage) *spelemenn* drew larger audiences, as those dedicated to the tradition were naturally interested in its future. There was especial interest in the brilliant playing of Knut Buen (nineteen-year-old member of a well-known family of players and singers). But the climax of the week-end came with the *Class A hardingfele* competition on Saturday afternoon. By this time, everyone had assembled; for the most celebrated instrumentalists tended to arrive late. And all the back-room loiterers who had until then spent their time wandering from session to session—or simply gathered into clusters in the back room, talking and buying *pannekaker,* sodas and beer—now all crowded into the main hall—forcing the back doors to remain open for an overflow audience. The session of over two hours in length was characterized by the silent, tense attention of the crowd, craning to see and to hear—but absolutely immobile except for the slight motion and thunderous sound of the traditional foot-tapping. This tapping (which was identical with that of the players) changed its form according to the *slått* being played. It was not simply pulse-reinforcement but provided a rhythmic framework against which the (often elaborate) cross-rhythms of the *hardingfele* improvisation were superimposed; it reminded me of the way the *tala* is kept by a knowledgeable Indian audience.[6]

As I listened, I sought to understand what elements of the music were free to be varied, what must remain the same. I watched the judges' still imperturbable countenances and recalled Finn Vabø's description of what the judges were looking for in performances:

> You must have the right bowing and note skeleton, and then you must add something from your own heart.[7]

There was still a group of persons who remained outside the main hall, even during the climactic afternoon: when they were not actually performing, the *Class A* players themselves often preferred to talk shop and exchange music with one another than to sit in the hall. I was reminded of scholarly meetings, where the most powerful participants spend most of their time in the corridors rather than in the conference hall listening to papers. I wondered if, in an analogous fashion, business was being transacted backstage; and I later discovered that, indeed, instruments were being bought and sold, contacts that would lead to professional playing jobs were being established. Shortly before their turns to play, the performers disappeared into a back room, where they checked the tuning of their instruments and warmed up. I was struck by their professional mien and dark, business-like dress. Most of the younger ones (like Finn Vabø) stood as they played and held their instruments high on the shoulder; others performed in a seated position, sometimes holding the instrument down below the shoulder in the old style. Their movements were kept at a minimum and their expressions those of serious concentration (so characteristic of fiddle players the world over).

The final decisions of the judges were made public Saturday evening, when an atmosphere of intense suspense was maintained through the lengthy reading of names and awards, beginning with *Class D* and gradually leading up to the final decision on the *Class A spelemenn*. Bjarne Herrefoss (construction worker from Telemark) and Odd Bakkerud (brought up in Hallingdal, now a salesman of high fidelity equipment in Oslo) received the first prize jointly. There was a standing ovation for the winners, and some grumbling, too, (especially from persons whose regions were not represented in the final decision) as the individuals in the packed hall prepared for general dancing and the fiddlers headed for the Ringness beer they had denied themselves during the competition itself.

General dancing on Friday and Saturday evenings—as well as the dance competition sessions—required the services of professional *har-dingfele* players. There, it was possible to observe the more routine, non-competitive work of the *spelemenn*. I began to understand that Norwegian dancing was characterized by an unusual freedom of choice amongst traditional figures—that indeed there was a combination of free and traditionally unchanged elements that seemed to closely parallel the individualistic nature of the fiddling tradition. I was surprised to find that the most esteemed dancing did not have the patterned regularity I had been accustomed to expect from knowledge of other (especially British and American) folk dance traditions. When I asked about this, I was told: "Ah, yes. In the resorts, and in city performances, there is usually a set plan decided upon in advance by the dancers. This is to please the tourists. Tourists do not understand our dancing; they think our dancers are making mistakes, when they are not performing the same figures at the same time or forming obvious patterns on the stage. In those places, you do not see real Norwegian dancing."

On Sunday morning, as the final event of the weekend festival, the *hardingfele* was performed in the ancient Porsgrunn church (whose intricately-embellished, cross-shaped interior featured a canoe-sized replica of a Viking ship suspended from the vaulted ceiling). There had previously been some controversy concerning the propriety of fiddle playing within the church itself; in the end, Gjermund Haugen, the renowned *spelemann* from Notadden, Telemark, performed several of his own *lydarslåttar* as a prelude to the service. After Haugen's playing and while the ruff-attired pastor climbed a short circular stairway to his canopied lectern—half of the audience filed out of the church. Most of the rest of the congregation left with the conclusion of the lengthy sermon, after the collection had been announced. The few that remained marched slowly to the altar, accompanied by organ music, to lay coins at the feet of the pastor. It was later explained to me that the collection was a redundancy, since: "Our taxes support the state religion." It is interesting to note that the collection ritual is a carry-over from the past when this practical method of remuneration was invariably mentioned by British travelers who tended to sneer at the undisguised combination of sacred and secular. (e.g., see Lowe 1857: 174)

A local newspaper had interviewed me during the festival days, describing my interest in the *hardingfele* tradition—a circumstance that produced two incidents. Several teen-agers approached me as I was walking down the streets of Porsgrunn the day after the festival. Offering me a cigarette, one of them remarked: "This folk music is all right for older people. But we young people, you know, we prefer rock." I was surprised, because it was almost my first confrontation with a negative attitude. The younger people I had met up to that time had been enthusiastic members of the closely knit group of enthusiasts for the traditional culture; and I had been impressed by the diversity of age and occupation of the adherents. That evening, as my son and I were sitting in the hotel dining room eating our evening meal, a Norwegian businessman crossed the breadth of the room to introduce himself. He said he was passing through Porsgrunn on a business trip and that he had read of our coming all the way from America to study the *hardingfele* tradition. With a formal bow, he proceeded to present Terry with what he explained was the most precious possession he had ever owned. Not having a child of his own, he said he would like my son to have the only property his father had been able to pass on to him: a leather wallet tooled with the design of a Viking ship. The empty wallet had brought him more prosperity than his father had ever known, he said; then he added several kroner for Terry to spend in Norway.

Telemark

Finn Vabø (who had himself begun to play at the age of two) had avoided a precise answer to my questions concerning the training of *hardingfele* players by pointing to the importance of the "musical milieu":

> When they have it in their heads, they take not such a long time to learn.[8]

I was looking forward to traveling through the rural countryside to experience for myself the musical environment of Telemark. These expectations were in fact realized as we headed inland from Porsgrunn to Skien, known as the "Gateway to Telemark," and up the mountain slopes to Morgedal, Seljord, Rjukan, and Tinn. Typical of the highlands in so much of the "Atlantic fringes":

> Settlements are dispersed, consisting of single farms or small vestigial clusters of farms instead of village communities, and the arable land is interrupted by extensive areas of bare rock and bog, of mountain grasses, heather, bracken and gorse. Urban centres are typically small and of no great antiquity. Economically and culturally the business of rearing livestock is of paramount importance. . . . Transhumance has been a means both of utilising hill grazing

2. We were constantly confronted with the forms of the great players in public statuary, the kind one is accustomed to associate with generals and politicians. Statue of Torkjell Haugerud at the Bø railroad station.

> *to provide a healthy variety for livestock, and of conserving fodder
> and safe-guarding crops on the small home farms.*
>
> (Evans 1958: 2)

Up until recently, the pastoral economy involved seasonal nomadism (transhumance), the *sæter* women (whose rich culture has been referred to above) typically being in charge of the summer farms. This system has left its mark on the cultural landscape in Norway (as it has in Ireland and Scotland), and ". . . survivals of these 'multiple tuns' have been studied by the Oslo Institute for Comparative Research in Human Culture. We note the irregular plan of the open-field plots and of the settlements—lacking the discipline of a roadway—which is contrasted with the regular lay-out of the Swedish or Danish village." (ibid.: 9)

It would have been difficult to forget the *spelemenn*, even if we had been entirely distracted by the scenery and the pleasures of an outdoor life; for we were constantly confronted with outdoor statuary (the kind that one is accustomed to associate with generals and politicians) in the forms of the great players; for example, the statues of Myllarguten in Nordagutu, Torkjell Haugerud in Bø. (See Ill. 2)

Seljord, Telemark

What I did not expect to find was the extent to which the competition atmosphere I thought we had left behind in Porsgrunn made up an intrinsic part of the fiber of this environment. Only a week after the national competition, the farming community of Seljord had its annual festival under the capable direction of its postmaster. Seljord is important to the history of Norwegian folklore as the birthplace of Magnus Brostrup Landstad (1802-1880), the itinerant preacher who was an early collector of rural ballads and legends; his statue rises up impressively behind the community's old stone church that dates from the twelfth century. On this special occasion, flags flew from the official buildings in which the various events had already begun to take place, while clusters of country people in Telemark costume moved along the mountain roads from one session to another. To my surprise, I found many names in the program familiar to me from Porsgrunn. Odd Bakkerud, one of the grand prize winners in the national competition, had not been satisfied to rest on his laurels but arrived from Oslo to compete with the same intensity of fervor he had displayed in Porsgrunn. He electrified the farmer-audience in Seljord just as he had the festival adherents in Porsgrunn by combining musical ability with the pyrotechnics of virtuosity. One of the few younger *spelemenn* to play in a seated position with the instrument held low under the shoulder, Bakkerud rose dramatically to his feet at the climax of his *slått* without effecting any interruption at all in his playing. Some members of the Telemark audience found themselves responding to this action by the Hallingdal player by rising themselves, and there was thunderous applause when he reached the conclusion of the music.

Not all the performers at Seljord were of the caliber to compete nationally; indeed, most of the local fiddlers were obviously taking the opportunity to try out their skills in public. One of these men found himself in grave difficulties with intonation; and the knowledgeability of the local audience may be gauged by the reaction of one couple who was seated in front of us. The man and woman turned to each other at the same instant and, speechlessly, exchanged wry expressions; then they turned back again to give token applause.

As in Porsgrunn, I was impressed by the ability of so large an audience to sit in concentrated silence while fiddler after fiddler presented his model performance. There was a dance competition, too; as well as performances of the old epics and the ancient round dances in connection with the traditional outdoor dramatization of the history of Seljord. But again, as had been the case in Porsgrunn, the heart of the festival was unquestionably the *hardingfele* competition. I came to realize that there was a competition in one locality or another nearly every summer weekend and that exceptional players could make names and contacts for themselves by going from one to the next (much in the manner of traveling virtuosi in any tradition).

> One must first learn many *slåttar* as they were made up by others
> and passed from person to person in the tradition. Only when one
> has mastered all this music, is one able to compose new composi-
> tions.[9]

Finn Vabø had thus described the precision with which the *hardingfele* tradition must be acquired before any individual player is considered qualified to compose new material. He had proceeded to demonstrate his own method of instruction: his careful attention to details in the student's playing. I myself had a first-hand experience when I received an introductory lesson from Gjermund Haugen. As I was painstakingly being taught to play, not only the notes, but also the correct bowings, nuances, and embellishments, I was reminded of the similarly exacting instruction I had once received in mainstream violin playing. After two hours of concentration, I had learned to play the first piece often given to students in the *hardingfele* tradition: the same wedding processional already known to me from Finn Vabø's demonstration in Bergen and the wedding I had witnessed in Voss. (Ex. 3) Vabø, we should remember, had called it "easy to understand," because it had neither the rhythmic nor the tonal intricacies of the difficult *slåtts*. The man—a lawyer—who had introduced me to Haugen was enthusiastic. An American, he said, had been taught to play the *hardingfele*. Haugen smiled and said that we shared an understanding of the beauties of nature; but I began to realize fully for the first time what a gulf there existed between my knowledge of the mainstream violin and the knowledge I would like to have of the Hardanger violin.

My first instruction in *hardingfele* playing had occurred in Porsgrunn. By the time we arrived in Seljord, I had become seriously interested in purchasing a Hardanger fiddle of my own; and when I tried out an instrument with a few notes of the processional, the response from bystanders was an incredulous: "Why that is our march! That's the Seljord wedding processional. Where did you learn that?" They did not realize that their *slått* is probably the most commonly played in all parts of Norway.

Tinn, Telemark

When the men come here from the national broadcasting station, they generally place the microphone over there.[10]

Johannes Dahle positioned a chair to hold my microphone in the living room of his two-roomed cottage in Tinn, near the western boundary of Telemark. It was difficult to understand how the *Norsk Rikskringkasting* had succeeded in driving its truck up the mountain road we had found to be impenetrable by car; but I knew they had recorded over 400 *slåttar* by Dahle (some of which they have issued commercially). Dahle's little farm house was sparsely furnished, but each individual article of furniture (a rose-painted chest, a handwrought table) had clearly been chosen for the perfection of its craftsmanship. The luxury of indoor plumbing was not available, but electrical wiring was; and Dahle owned a Tandberg tape recorder. (III. 3) This fact became of some practical importance to me; for when I blew a fuse in my Uher (due to the vagaries of the voltage strength in the mountains), I was able to proceed successfully with my recording through the use of Dahle's efficient machine.

3. *Johannes Dahle*

*Here in Tinn, we have our own scale. I have it from my grand-
father, Knut Dahle, who had it from Gibøen who had it from
Lurås.*[11]

Johannes Dahle, in the soft accents of the Tinn dialect, described the
pitch system of the valley that had produced a series of master *spelemenn*, from the legendary Brynjulv Olson in the early eighteenth century
to the present day. (See Einung, 1926) Seated quietly, Dahle introduced
me to his tradition with a variety of *slåttar*, some composed by himself,
some by Knut Dahle, others handed down from the tradition of Myllarguten or Gibøen, for both giant *spelemenn* had directly influenced Tinn
fiddlers, he explained. One of Johannes Dahle's original compositions
brought a smile to the face of Elna Odden, who had accompanied me up
to the mountain to the *spelemann's* farm. During World War II, she explained, Dahle (who had always been more interested in fiddle playing
than farming) realized that (like all Norwegians who possessed property)
he must make full use of his land. He sent an urgent request to his friends,
Elna and Øystein Odden, to help him harvest the hay—which they
began to do immediately, meeting at sunrise every morning. But Elna
Odden, who said she disliked this kind of work above all others, always
managed—unaccountably—to break the handle of her pitch fork during
the day's labor. She kept silent about this matter, however; and, when the
day's work had been accomplished, she would lean the broken tool
against the wall of the barn. Every morning, curiously enough, it was in
its place, waiting for her—and neatly mended. Dahle never mentioned
the incident either; but one day, long after the war was over, he called
Elna Odden to come and listen to a new piece he had composed especially for her. It was called *Rakstejenta (The Hay Maid)* and is based on
the uneven beat rhythm of the Telemark *springar* (Ex. 4). Later, I was to
hear *Rakstejenta* played by different *spelemenn* in various parts of Norway; I was even to hear this *slått* played as far away as Decorah, Iowa, at
a Norwegian-American festival.

Øystein Odden, for many years chairman of the Tinn *spelemannslag*,
told me the story of the composition of *Tåkatind* (Ex. 5). Dahle and the
Oddens were returning from a national festival some years ago, and
Dahle was feeling unhappy, disenchanted with the competitive atmosphere. Indeed, Dahle rarely appeared in public. Like Håvard Gibøen
before him, he remained close to home, highly sought after by others.
Dahle's heavy-hearted mood lifted gradually, as the friends stopped to
watch the antics of a muscular, young horse who was showing off for
wild mares on the wide-open stretches of one of the more isolated parts of

Rauland. The wild stallion, called *Tåkatind*, had been sent by the Norwegian government for breeding purposes; and there are still many stories being told in the mountains about the prowess of *Tåkatind*. Upon arriving home from the festival, Dahle composed the *slått*, *Tåkatind*, in the form of a halling (the acrobatic solo male dance); his good humor had entirely returned.

> *He must have had a remarkable ear—Halvorsen. He immediately recognized the special notes of our scale here in Tinn—and sang them back correctly to my grandfather.*[12]
>
> (my trans.)

Johannes Dahle was giving an account of the meeting of Knut Dahle with Johann Halvorsen, the composer who had been asked by Edvard Grieg in 1901 to transcribe some of the Tinn repertory from Dahle's playing. It was the first real experience with the *hardingfele* tradition for either of the urban-bred Norwegians; and later, Grieg made piano arrangements of some of these slåtts. Johannes Dahle and Øystein Odden together played *Jon Vestafe*, one of the pieces transcribed for the piano by Grieg; and I realized that I had recorded Finn Vabø playing his version of the *slått* in Bergen two years before. Three other members of the Tinn *Spelemannslag* appeared; and I had a chance to record an ensemble performance[13] of a Knut Dahle *slått*, *Rjukanfossen*, which, according to the composer, had come to him in a dream, while he rested by the side of the great waterfall at Rjukan, Telemark.

It was not necessary to know that Johannes Dahle had been decorated by the King's gold medallion (brought out by the Oddens for my benefit) or to examine a number of his other awards to be aware that he was a great musician by anyone's standards. However, it was several years, before I understood the depth of his present influence on the tradition not only of Tinn but also of other localities in Telemark. The high esteem for this gentle, quiet man by the members of his own community was reflected in the presence (even during his lifetime) of a marble bust prominently displayed in the entranceway to the secondary school in Tinn.

Seljord, Telemark

> *I am looking into the trade routes. Perhaps seamen brought the idea of sympathetic strings back from Asia. Many people think the*

*idea came to western Norway from Britain; but it is also possible
that it is indigenous to this country.*[14]

(Trans.)

Jon Helland, senior, (highly skilled member of one of the most famous
fiddle-making families in Norway) described one of the problems he was
facing in doing research for a book on the history of the *hardingfele*. We
were talking in Helland's summer *hytte*, high in the mountains above the
valley of Seljord. Helland then described a new instrument he was in the
process of designing (in conjunction with Sigbjørn Osa, *spelemann* from
Voss who had performed on the *hardingfele* in European concert halls). It
would be larger and have more carrying power than the traditional fiddle;
and it would also have a longer neck to accommodate high position
playing. It would, in fact, be a combination violin-*hardingfele* especially
suited to being played in large halls. Helland responded to my inquiries
concerning the purchase of a traditional Hardanger fiddle for myself by
inviting me to visit his workshop in Skien, which I later did.

Skien, Telemark

Jon Helland's workshop was part of a large and commercially successful enterprise; the music store, under the directorship of Jon Helland, Jun-
ior, sold all instruments (from electronic organs to plastic flutes)—as well
as records and sheet music. In the workshops, I examined the blueprints
for the intricate designs hand drawn with pen and India ink on the backs
of Harding fiddles. Helland showed me the process involved in the
mother-of-pearl inlay that characteristically ornaments the rim of the
belly. I eventually bought an instrument made in 1869 by Eilev Jonson
Steintjønndalen, son of Jon Erikson Helland (1790-1862) from Bø, Telemark, who is credited with establishing the Helland form of the instrument. I was later to discover that one of Johannes Dahle's instruments
had been made by Eilev Jonson.

Oslo

*There can be no doubt that sooner or later music for keyboard in-
struments will make use of untempered tuning. . . . What affords
the greatest possibilities for the future in an untempered system, is
the fact that tones that lie outside our customary tonal system be-*

> come available. I am thinking especially of the ancient scales
> which have been natural for European and other peoples, but
> which, until now, have been out of the reach of art music.[15]

Eivind Groven expressed the point of view that had led him to invent
an untempered organ, the latest model of which (completed in 1965) is
capable of playing 43 pitches to the octave. The necessity for an un-
wieldy number of keys to the octave is obviated by the existence of a
transistor-operated computer.

Back again in Oslo at the conclusion of my trip, I had the opportunity
to meet with this extraordinary man, who was distinguished as a musician, as an inventor, and as a scholar. A native of Telemark, Groven had
chosen to educate himself in harmony and counterpoint, fearful that a
conservatory education would interfere with his knowledge of the Norwegian rural idioms. He has played and composed both traditional slåttar
and (notated) works for symphony orchestra that utilized such integrally
nationalistic elements as the uneven beat structures and the pitch systems
of the rural styles.

Groven (who was one of the editors of Norsk Folkemusikk) had been
director of folk music for the radio station in Oslo for forty years; and his
daughter, Dagne Groven Myhren, described the hostile attitude towards
her father's first presentations of rural singers on the air some years
ago. The urban listeners violently reacted against what they called "out-
of-tune singing" and, in angry letters to the newspapers, demanded a
"proper piano accompaniment." The public animosity grew to such proportions that Dagne Myhren remembers the Groven house actually being
stoned by angry demonstrators.

At the Porsgrunn Festival, Dagen Groven herself had given a performance of an old Norwegian song learned from her grandmother. For my
benefit, she sang some of the short, chorale-like tunes, called stevs that
form the melodic basis for many slåtts; and she discussed the interrelationships between much of the vocal and fiddle music. I remembered that
Finn Vabø said, "Only the spelemann can play a hardingfele slått and
only the singer can imitate it." Unbelievable as it may seem, there exists a
strong tradition in Norway of singing fiddle slåtts, a practice that closely
parallels the Scottish tradition called "mouth music."

Eivind Groven chose examples from his collection of tapes to illustrate
the variations in individual style from one performance to another of a
single slått within a single region. Of special interest was a series of examples showing the permutations undergone by one of his own slåtts as it
had passed from fiddler to fiddler through the years.

Magne Myhren (Hallingdal *spelemann* and folklorist, then a graduate student at the University of Oslo) joined Eivind Groven to illustrate the difference between the two regional styles. Dagne Groven Myhren commented.

> *I shall never be able to dance to the playing of my husband; for he was born and brought up in Hallingdal, while I was brought up on Telemark music.*[16]

All agreed on the fundamental difference between the rhythmic structures of the *springar* in the two regions.

Third Field Trip: 1969
Geilo, Hallingdal

On a short trip to Norway in the summer of 1969, I was able to visit Hallingdal during the time of the *Landskappleik* (National Competition) which was being held in Geilo that year. Geilo looks out on precipitous outcroppings of jagged rock; near the timber line, there is little growth of grass or trees to soften the scenery; and snow, even in summer, is never very far away. I noticed a sharp contrast between Telemark, where (in most areas) grass-covered slopes lend warmth to the spectacular mountain scenery, and the Buskerud valley set high in *Langfjellene*, the famous mountain barrier between western and eastern Norway. It was through these rocks that the railroad had to penetrate to connect Oslo and Bergen.

While the crowds drawn to the resort town of Geilo were larger and the atmosphere somewhat more commercial than it had been at Porsgrunn, the general form of the national festival repeated itself. Similarly, I was reminded of the Seljord festival when I attended the annual competition at Vinje, Telemark, later that summer.

Rauland, Telemark

> *Here you have a scene from "Draumkvædet" which is a medieval visionary poem dating from the middle of the 13th century. There are four tunes traditionally sung to the 52 verses: each melody is associated with a specific portion of the poem.*[17]

We had just met the folklorist, Eivind Øygarden, at the Rauland town hall (*kommunehus*), the small building that housed the official affairs of the *bygd* was situated on the edge of sloping pastureland. He was showing us one of the fantastic and colorful murals that decorated the walls of a meeting room. The painter, he told us, was the local artist, Sveinung Svalastoga. Øygarden, also the school inspector for Rauland, was an authority on the cultural traditions of his native Telemark; I was later to record his singing of *Draumkvædet* melodies. On my fourth visit to Norway, it was Eivind Øygarden and his wife, Kirsti, (school teacher and church organist) who found us a cottage in one of the sloping pastures near the *Kommunehus*.

Fourth Field Trip: 1972
Rauland, Telemark

> This is a perfect situation for you. You have the beauty of Telemark; and you will experience the manner of life of the traditional spelemann.[18]

My intention on this fourth trip to Norway was to live in the community, to participate as much as possible in everyday activities. During the first part of our stay in Rauland, my son and I dwelt in the *hytte* mentioned above; it was situated in a sheep meadow belonging to the Odd Kostveit farm; following tradition, the son and daughter-in-law of Odd Kostveit had just finished building a house on the father's farm, its lines were modern but it bore a sod roof, still waiting to be seeded. Our manner of living was hardly typical of that community today; our cottage had been designed for summer vacationers who purposely wished to leave behind the modern conveniences that are taken for granted in the urban areas, as well as by the younger generation in such a prosperous rural community as Rauland. We did live in the style of the older generation of *spelemenn* who find electricity a necessity for their recording apparatuses but otherwise feel no need to change an effective mode of life. When the snow fell consistently and the spring froze, we moved to a similar *hytte* near *Krossen* (The Cross Road), the small cluster of buildings that takes the place of a village center. Here, we found the bank, the *Kafeteria* (a favorite teenage hang-out), and the secondary school—a modern building equipped with swimming pool and sauna, yet displaying the traditional sod roof. School children under ten, including nine-year-old Terry, met at *Krossen* to take the school bus to *Småskolen* (the small school), where they studied from text books marked *nynorsk*. All Norwegian school children must pass examinations in both official Norwegians (*nynorsk* and *riksmal* or Dano-Norwegian), and each community determines which is to be the fundamental language for their district. The rural and tradition-oriented region of Telemark naturally favors *nynorsk*.

> You have the pitch all wrong. I will not stay to hear my dialect insulted.[19]

The young school boy was reacting angrily against what he deemed an incorrect intonation of the voice in the speech of a new school teacher from outside the *bygd* of Rauland in Telemark. This man had gone to the not inconsiderable trouble of learning the Rauland speech system, and he had been hired by the school board; but the lilt of his voice (an important phonemic ingredient of the Norwegian language) did not satisfy at least one of his scholars. This incident, which had occurred shortly before my arrival in Rauland, was related to me as an example of the significance accorded the retention of local dialects by the people of Telemark.

I became acquainted at first hand with the skilled craftsmanship that was an every-day part of existence: the intricate wood-carving on *stabbur* panels wrought by Odd Kostveit (owner of our farm); the paintings of his neighbor, Olav Fosslid (also a house painter); wall hangings woven by Eva Kostveit (daugher-in-law of Odd); silver smithing by Halvor Nystog.

The *hardingfele* players of the community belonged to the local chapter of the national association of fiddlers, *Landslaget for Spelemenn*, and most of the members of the Rauland *Spelemannslag* were farmers. Their chairman, Knut Jorde, owned a farm bordering on the *Kommunehus*, where the group gathered once a week; and their meeting room was the very one in which we had first introduced ourselves to Eivind Øygarden three years before. The dramatic murals on the walls contrasted sharply with the sober furnishings—a massive wooden table and a number of brown-stained church pews. Their meetings were lengthy and serious work sessions, interrupted only occasionally by a cup of strong coffee. I watched their work-worn and muscular fingers deftly execute the elaborately embellished music as they played together in ensemble or concentrated upon learning new material. *Slåttar* were acquired either from one another or from tape recordings of well-known fiddlers.

Despite their abilities (which were considerable), all the players in the group referred to themselves as amateurs. Early in October, Bjarne Herrefoss (who had shared first place with Odd Bakkerud at Porsgrunn five years before) arrived in the community from Bø to take part in construction work on the new Rauland *folkehøgskole*. The first time Herrefoss appeared at a meeting of the group, all activity came to a complete halt; Knut Jorde, as chairman, delivered a lengthy and formal speech in which he welcomed Herrefoss and made it quite clear that we were in the presence of a fiddler of a different rank. After that evening, Herrefoss came regularly to the weekly meetings; he always arrived late, without his fiddle, was persuaded to try one or another of the members' instruments, complained about his lack of opportunity to practice, and made himself available to answer questions. One of the tapes being used by the group to learn new material had been given to them by Herrefoss.

One of the most promising of the younger players in Rauland was a farmer who lives in that bleak and remote area called Møsstrand, famous for reindeer herds and in legendary lore. Trygve Vågen began to study the *hardingfele* at the age of five on a small instrument especially made for him by one of his six older brothers. Their ancestral farm is situated on the other shore of Møssvatn, the vast lake whose waters can only be traversed when they are either completely iced or free of ice (i.e., in summer or winter). Thus the children of this area receive their education at federal expense at a boarding school; and they enjoy extended holidays in spring and fall, when they must remain at home. Vågen's first teacher was a grandson of Gibøen; more recently, however, he had been acquiring the tradition from tapes recorded and sent by mail to him by Johannes Dahle. Vågen had received more than 70 slåtts from Dahle, whom he had visited personally only once. A silent man of great dignity, Vågen had enjoyed uninterrupted time for practice—time that he has also used for fiddle construction, the instruments' bellies carved from maple trees on his property.

I met and recorded Trygve Vågen at an informal social gathering at the home of Eva and Halvor Kostveit, the young couple who had recently moved into a contemporary style, sod-roofed house on the ancestral farm. Guests listened to Vågen's playing attentively and silently during the first part of the evening; and it was only later, when coffee and smørrebrød were brought in, that there was participation in dancing, and those guests known for their ability to sing were persuaded to perform. It was not an everyday occurrence to have Trygve Vågen in the neighborhood, and some persons who were unable to stay for refreshments dropped by for a short time to hear him play.

Folkemusikk-konsert i Bø

I samband med folkemusikkopplæringa byr
Haugerudfondet inn til Folkemusikk-konsert på Sandvin
I Bø, fredag 13, oktober kl, 19,30.

Program ved: Spelemennene Jens Amundsen, Jon
Bondal, Knut Buen, Gjermund Haugen, Tor Homleid, Einar
Løndal, Kjetil Løndal, Torjei Romtveit, Johannes Sundsvalen
og Sigbjørn Bernhoft Osa.

Kveding: Brita Bratland, Hanne Kjerstl Buen og Torbjorn Aalid Paus
Nytt dette sjeidne hove til å hoyre landskjente folkemusikkutovarar.
Inngongspengar kr. 10.—Barn og ungdom kr. 5.—

Torkjell Haugeruds Minnefond

Formal concerts were also part of the musical environment (perhaps the winter time equivalent of summer festivals). While a series of recitals by touring art musicians took place in Rauland, there were no concerts of traditional music held there during my stay. However, it was often possible to drive to another community for this purpose, and notices like the above attracted people from all the surrounding communities. Bø (about 60 miles north-east of Rauland) is another important Telemark center for the *hardingfele* tradition; it is the home of several families of outstanding musicians (the Løndals, the Buens). In addition to the well-known players listed in the above announcement, a number of younger *spelemenn* performed; some wore the long hair and jeans of their generation, and one was a young woman dressed in Telemark costume. Several of these young people were the students of Gjermund Haugen, the fine *hardingfele spelemann* whose playing I had heard before at the Porsgrunn church and whose exacting instruction I had experienced as my first lesson on the instrument.

MINNEKVELD
Universitets-Aulaen
23, november 1972, kl. 19.30
for
MULLARGUTEN
OG
GIBØEN

H.M. Kongen vil vera til stades,
Møtelyden ma vera på plass kl. 19.15

An unusually formal concert, attended by the King of Norway, was held in Oslo in honor of Myllarguten and Gibøen (who had died a year apart from one another, a century before). Most of the players who participated were from Telemark, home of both the honored men. The atmosphere was highly tense—for the audience had to be seated before the king could make his formal entrance; and the performers played the lengthy program of nearly four hours in unaccustomed silence; no applause, no tapping of feet.

A third kind of staged performance took place in Tinn, Telemark, at the formal dinner held by the *Ungdomslag* (the national youth organization) in commemoration of its anniversary. Johannes Dahle, whose name came up continually in the lengthy, official speeches at the dinner and whose bust stood at the entranceway to the auditorium where the event was taking place, did not attend; he led too quiet a life, he explained, to be comfortable at such large social occasions. The guests (dressed in Telemark costume) sat in silence on folding chairs during the four hours of speech-making and music. The latter was performed by the Tinn *spelemannslag* who played a number of traditional *slåttar*. In several of these pieces, they were joimed by Sigbjørn Osa, who had been invited to make a guest appearance. In addition, Osa provided a contrast to the sober atmosphere by presenting an act of jokes and banter that focused on his *hardingfele*.

When the formal part of the evening was over, all but one of the members of the Tinn *Spelemannslag* left for home. The *spelemann* who remained attached a pick-up mike to his *hardingfele* and joined bass, accordion, and piano player in making music to accompany the polkas and rhinelanders that (as in Rauland) the general public preferred for informal dancing. It was my first experience with an *elektrisk hardingfele*.

> *One of the members of the Chirstiania, Fusel, and Blågress plays*
> *the electric hardingfele. You can hear them on television and com-*
> *mercial recordings.*[20]

Later, I was to hear Einar Mjølsncs play the electric Hardanger violin on television. In Rauland, the spelemenn told me that Mjølsnes (playing a traditional instrument) had taken part in their annual competition the preceding summer. They spoke highly of his abilities, and did not seem averse to the new departure.

On my way to Tinn, I had experienced the opportunity to visit what must be one of the most unusual cities in the world. Rjukan lies, perennially shaded by rock, in an immense cavern formed in *Vestfjordalen*. Situated in an isolated corner of Telemark, it presents a complete contrast to the open mountain reaches surrounding it. Once famous as the home of a magnificent waterfall that stalwart British hikers of the nineteenth century considered a goal of prime importance to attain, Rjukan was turned into an industrial island early in the century, when, in the interests of technological progress, it was conveyed into a means of obtaining cheap hydroelectric power. It was there in Rjukan that we met Elna Odden, who drove us to Tinn for our second visit to that tradition-rich center of *hardingfele* playing. We stayed with Elna and Øystein Odden for several days, during which time Øystein Odden took great pains to answer my questions regarding the Tinn tradition and gave me access to his tape recordings; some of his recordings of Tinn *spelemann* dated back to the early part of this century and included performances by Knut Dahle, grandfather of Johannes and the *spelemann* who introduced the *hardingfele* tradition to Grieg. I spent the afternoon with Johannes Dahle, recording his playing and asking specific questions about musical performance.

> *You have my tapes. All you need to do now is to practice with*
> *them. . . . But your bowing; it is not correct. You see, the bowing*
> *goes against the notes. . . . The boy, he needs a smaller instrument;*
> *I can see he plays vanleg fele.*[21]

> (my trans.)

Dahle, correcting my bowing of *Rakstejenta*, made me aware of the importance of bowing style to the rhythmic complex. I came to realize that absolute precision in this respect produced the syncopated nuances that had eluded me; and, once again, I was impressed with the meticulous attention to detail in *hardingfele* instruction. Dahle smiled as he turned to my son who, strongly affected by his surroundings, had asked

Øystein Odden to teach him a tune on my *hardingfele*—to surprise the great Tinn *spelemann*.

There was a new decorative object on Dahle's rose-painted chest: a wood carving of a brawny horse: Tåkatind, Dahle explained. It had been made and sent to him by Knut Buen, once the child prodigy of Porsgrunn and now a well-established *spelemann* of the first rank. This was the second image I had seen of the famous horse that had inspired Dahle's *halling*, the first being a snapshot shown to me in Rauland.

I re-recorded *Rjukanfossen* and found myself making associations that I could not have made five years before, in the early stages of my research. Not only was I now personally acquainted with the grim city, but I was also aware that the special impact of *Rjukanfossen* today has to do with events that occurred long after the *slått* was composted by Knut Dahle more than eighty years ago. Originally, of course, it was intended to celebrate the magnificent waterfall for which it was named: and the *slått* came to his grandfather, Johannes said, in a dream, as Knut rested by the side of the falls, homewardbound from far-away Møsstrand.

Years later, during World War II, the occupying Germans took over the now-existent Norwegian power plant with the purpose of developing heavy water. It was here that the Norwegian underground (of which Elna and Øystein Odden were Rjukan members) made plans to sabotage the out-going ferry boats that were to export this important component of the atomic bomb. The melodramatic Hollywood movie, *The Heroes of Telemark*, has since celebrated the sacrificial act in which many Norwegians friends and close relations of underground members perished in an effort that was a major turning point in the war.

Perhaps the most thoroughly tragic of all the *hardingfele* slåtts is the gangar, *Førnesbrunen*, which I recorded for the first time on this visit. As told to me by Johannes Dahle, the legend hearkens back to Medieval days and the Black Death. The title name is that of a courageous horse who is given the melancholy task of transporting the dead bodies of plague victims through the desolate stretches of Møsstrand to the Rauland church. This *slått* is a prime example of program music, and the listener is expected to hear musical imitations of the sound made by horse's hoofs struggling through deep snow, of the eventual stumble due to a broken snow shoe (*trug*), of the whinnying for help; and finally, of the death cry of the horse, who expires as human help arrives just too late. (Ex. 6)

> There are three Kivlemøyane slåttar, a gangar and two springars. They are very ancient and about the Christian religion. There were once three sisters who, they say, lived in the mountains and

played musical instruments—probably the lur—on Sundays. They played so beautifully that people in church were drawn outside to listen; whereupon the priest came out and turned them into stone. I have these slåtts from Knut Dahle who got them from Håvard Gibøen who had them from the old tradition.[22]

(trans.)

The *Kivlemøyane* cycle is a tour de force for virtuoso *hardingfele* players. Indeed, it is a test; those who can play this cycle of pieces are accomplished artists in their tradition. After recording them for me, Johannes Dahle played one of his own slåtts—a *springar*—which is based on another legend dealing with the same religious confrontation. *Urdbø-Ūrdi* is named after a great pile of rocks (ūrdi) that may still be seen on the Urdbø farm in Arabygd. According to legend, the god, Thor, paid a visit to the community many years ago, soon after Christianity had come to Norway. He demanded—and received—refreshment in the form of beer which, however, was proffered to him in bowls so inadequate in size that the mighty god of thunder became enraged; he picked up the boulders to hurl against, and demolish, the new church.

It is only that I think the world should know about our special tradition here in Tinn.[23]

(trans.)

Thus Johannes Dahle responded to my expression of gratitude.

Fifth Field Trip: 1979
Tinn, Telemark

It is not—as it should be. . . .[24]

Johannes Dahle

Two months before, Johannes Dahle had been rushed to the hospital emergency room, his arm paralyzed—the first sickness of his life, he maintained, at the age of 89. Now, able to play again in the stillness of his own home, he was upset over what he yet had not regained. He offered to record *Jon Vestafe*—for my research purposes only. Gently, he corrected my use of the word, *slått*, to *lått* (Tinn dialect). It was the last time I was ever to see the great musician.

Ola Øyaland, the present leader of the Tinn Spelemannslag, is now considered one of the principal inheritors of the Tinn tradition.

There was a course here in Tinn. Yes, I joined the classes. I found it immensely interesting to learn to read notes.—I enjoyed it.[25]

Ola Øyaland

However, Øyaland answered in the negative when asked if he had made use of his notational knowledge.

Gunnar Dahle, younger brother of Johannes, has, within recent years, come into his own as a national musical figure.

I have just finished recording the Knut Dahle slåttar with Knut Buen. Einar Steen-Nøkleberg is playing the Grieg piano pieces.[26]

Gunnar Dahle

Dahle was referring to the disc produced by Caprice (CAP 1153) that contains performances of the original Tinn *slåttar* as well as the Grieg-Halvorsen arrangements.

New tape recordings of *Jon Vestafe* by Øyaland and Dahle were remarkable in providing two different perspectives on the Tinn heritage —both different again from that of Johannes Dahle. Now I had the evidence that a particular slått, *Jon Vestafe* (as to actual pitches and indeed most of what gets written down in transcription) had remained remarkably stable with different players and through time (1965-1983); but the recordings also manifested the variety of avenues available within the most strictly coded scheme (of the ancient heritage) for freedom of expression—enigmatic to all but those who had the knowledge, the skill, and the creative ability.

Evident was a growth of *local* interest in the *hardingfele*, the reversal of a recent trend: for, except in the charmed circle of the dedicated family groups, rural young people had tended for some years to yearn to become "more modern," as they saw it—during the same period of time that the youth of the cities were interpreting the traditional culture as of special relevance to their desire for freedom of expression. Well known as a dedicated teacher, Gunnar Dahle spoke warmly of his students, many of them quite young. Of special interest was the exceptional promise of his own twelve-year-old grandson; this great-great-grand child of Knut Dahle lived near enough to be a regular student of Gunnar. He had recently won a prize in a local competition and might well be one of the principal carriers of the Brynjulv Olson-Knut Dahle tradition into the 21st century.

The male-female cultural dichotomy was sharply changing, judging from the information I received from Gunnar Dahle who informed me that many of his *hardingfele* students were girls. He also told me of a young female dancer of the *halling*, who had just won her battle for permission to compete—and win—in a local competition. I remembered the words of Tone Lid, who was able to perform the acrobatics of the *halling*, but had no desire to do so in public ("It is just as difficult to be graceful.") and wondered if she had changed her viewpoint over the last decade.

Rauland, Telemark

Olga Homme arrived at my cottage in Rauland dressed in a leather jacket and riding a motorcycle—hardly part of the national-romantic imagery associated with the sæter maiden; yet without doubt closer in spirit to the original role. Indeed, the fine traditional singer had, as a young girl, experienced life on a sæter; and, amongst the songs she had recorded for my machine, were some that portrayed life on the mountain top farms in more realistic terms. (III. 4)

Tuddal, Telemark

A center for the promotion and production of traditional arts and crafts has been created in Tuddal, the inner-Telemark valley, under the direction of Knut Buen and aided by other culture leaders, especially other prominent members of the Buen and Løndal families. Before my departure for Norway, I had been told of the 2-day Tuddal *hardingfele* festival, advised that it would be a meeting place for urban youth interested in traditional culture and Telemark spelemenn. In Telemark itself, before the opening of the event, the general local consensus of opinion was:

> No, you don't want to go to Tuddal the first day. Nothing's going on then. Anyone can get up and play. The second day, that's when we all go—to hear the invited players.

When the Telemark spelemenn and the inner circle of adherents arrived in Tuddal on the second—the *invited*—day, they found that all the ur-

4. Olga Homme

ban participants had left for home the night before, after a rousing party with much informal music-making at the Buen home. The 2-day festival had drawn two entirely different groups of participants. Only the Master of Ceremonies, Knut Buen, and other members of the group that had created the festival apparently felt at ease in both atmospheres.

Oslo

Back in Oslo, preparations were underway at the University to host the biennial meeting of the International Folk Music Council (now called the International Council of Traditional Musics). One of the opening events was a recital to take place in the hall of the Munch Museum; Knut Buen and Einar Steen-Nøkleberg were scheduled to play the Knut Dahle *slåttar* and Grieg's piano versions. There was a publicity photo of Knut Buen published in the museum's calendar (see Illustration 16), representative of the fact that the host of both halves of the Tudall festival was experienced and quite at home in the recital milieu as well.

Sixth Field Trip: 1982
Oslo

A Rutgers University grant supported a short three-weeks stay in Oslo during the mid-winter break; this time I planned to devote myself principally to the resources of the University Library and to the Norwegian Folk Music Archives (*Norsk Folkemusikksamling*) now housed at the university. No sooner had I arrived than I was invited to be interviewed on the radio about my interest in the *hardingfele*; I demurred, pointing out that I had not attempted to speak Norwegian in nearly three years, but was told: "Oh, that doesn't matter. It will mean so much to the *spelemenn*." But, for some reason, all my Norwegian words left me completely when my interviewer announced in a jocular vein:

> Here is someone who has written a dissertation on—of all things —the hardingfele.

> (my trans.)

I would like to draw a charitable curtain over the rest of this incident, only to add that, when the program was aired that evening, I was working my way through old field notes in my room on the top floor of a mid-town hospits. Suddenly, my next-door neighbor switched on his radio, and I heard: "Here is someone who has written a dissertation on—of all things —the *hardingfele!*" I reached to block the sound from my ears, when I heard an anguished "Whooop!" and the radio was summarily turned off. I felt grateful that some people in Oslo evidently were still of the anti-traditional music persuasion—but a little guilty about not having listened when Sven Nyhus later asked me how I liked the Dahle tape of *Rakste-jenta* he had searched out to play for my benefit at the end of the program —and even more so when I later received a note from Elna Odden thanking me for playing that tape.

Some of the urban youth who were involved in the new "folk" movement participated in a *hardingfele* party I attended shortly thereafter. The event was already in full swing when I arrived to find Magne Myhren, in a seated playing position, concentrating on his intense musical dialogue with effortlessly moving dancing bodies. Most of the people, arranged along lengthy tables, were quietly watching and listening; although some were standing and drinking, just as quietly, in an adjoining room. I recognized Kjetil Løndal, immobile as he viewed the scene from a centrally-located vantage point and started to walk over to thank him for a valuable tape he had made for my perceptual project, but something made me turn and find an empty seat at one of the tables instead. This party etched a deeper impression on my mind than had previous, similar ones due to insights in a paper I had recently come across; it had been written by Marybeth Neal, an American graduate student who had spent some time studying Norwegian music in Oslo, and it contained a comparison of *flatfele* and *hardingfele* parties:

> . . . the *hardingfele* parties were solemn affairs. The meal was eaten in almost complete silence, and then the dancing began. Only one fiddler played at a time, as is the tradition with the *hard-ingfele.* . . . The fiddler at such parties is always an expert, usually a visiting professional from the country. The dancers were also excellent, executing the dance steps with great skill. The dancers didn't talk much and tended to select their partners from a select group of friends. . . .
>
> (Neal 1978: 4f)

Nevertheless, I was warmly greeted at my table, as Karin Brennesvik, one of the prominent dance leaders in Norway and the power behind the active Kongsberg (Telemark) dance group, introduced herself to me. There was much comment on the expert dancing of her young daughter, then on the dance floor; and we exchanged ideas on the importance of the individual distinguishing characteristics of the bygde dances.

Seventh Field Trip: 1983

An unsolicited, and quite unexpected, invitation to visit Norway came from the Norwegian Ministry of Foreign Affairs in 1983. Within the space of ten days, I would be able to set my own itinerary; thus, I was in a happy position of being able to meet with many of the musicians who had given me information and receive their impressions (and corrections) of my interpretations of their material, a process that had already been initiated both by correspondence and during my last two trips to Norway.

Oslo

When I visited Dagne Groven Myhren, she astonished me by showing me her Hallingdal costume. "Hallingdal! Does that make me a liar?" I riffled through my manuscript to find the chapter we had indeed already discussed on several occasions before. Dagne Myhren shook her head:

> In fact, just recently, I danced the Hallingspringar in public. But my dancing the Telespringar and the Hallingspringar are two different things; it's not the same. The point made is correct; and it says something important about the essential nature of our tradition.[27]

Einar Steen-Nøkleberg was describing rehearsal sessions for the Caprice LP made jointly with Gunnar Dahle and Knut Buen. Steen-Nøkleberg had taken laborious pains to learn the Telespringar rhythmic pattern and then had, as much as possible, introduced it into the Grieg paino pieces ". . . whenever I could; sometimes a full bass line makes it impossible.":

> I nearly fell off the piano stool, when Knut showed me how the Telemark springar should really be played.[28]

Bra feleinteresse i Sauland

Aldri har det vel vore så stor interesse for hardingfelemusikk i Hjartdal kommune som det er nettopp nå. Gjennom Friundervisninga har spelemannen Knut Buen frå Tuddal, hatt 8 kurs med omkring 50 elevar. Elevane skriv seg frå folkeskulestadiet til folk om lag 70 år, og det er mest like mange kvinner som karar. Skal ein døma etter interessa nå i mars, er det grunn til å tru at hardingfelemusikken vil ta seg bra opp. — Det lovar i alle fall godt — seier populære Buen.

A.B.

5. *Knut Buen teaching in Sauland*

Bø

I met Agnes Buen Garnås in her house in Bø—built and intricately embellished with wood carving by members of her family. In answer to a question about creativity in the contemporary *hardingfele* tradition, she responded:

> *Yes, the* spelemenn *continue to invent new* slåttar *all the time. Sometimes, it seems as if the judges at competitions prefer the old. But Knut was awarded first prize for playing an original composition last year, a* lydarslått.[29]

Concerning the interest of Telemark youth in the *hardingfele*, I was told that "Knut was inundated with students at Tuddal; there were more than he could handle." (See Ill. 5 for a picture of Buen's class in Sauland.)

I also spoke with Karin Brennesvik who informed me that the same enthusiasm continued to be manifested among youthful dancers. She told me that her dance group had been invited to the United States and would perhaps be making the trip the following year.

Rauland

In Rauland, I met with Eva Kostveit and Johann Vaa. I asked Mr. Vaa for an English translation of the word, *kluss*, which he had used in a published article that had created some controversy among the readers of *Spelemannsbladet (The Spelemann's Newspaper)*. There, he had described Grieg's music as "successful *kluss.*" (Vaa 1981: 15) A discussion ensued that took up most of the evening. I pointed out that Einar Haugen's standard Norwegian-English dictionary lists the following English synonyms for this word: "blot," "splatter," "splotch," "mess;" but he asserted that none of these words conveyed the particular sense he had in mind, because "There is nothing wrong with the music on its own terms." Rejecting such words as "fake," "synthetic," or "ersatz," he eventually decided upon a description rather than a synonym: "to change a thing that ought not be changed. If you still do it, it is not so good as originally or it is quite another thing."

I asked Eva Kostveit about local activity so far as the Hardanger violin was concerned:

They are teaching hardingfele *in the school in Rauland now—in the evening class. The same man teaches* hardingfele *and guitar and both instruments are in demand.*[30]

Eva Kostveit also informed me that a summer course in *hardingfele* making had become a regular summer offering at the *Akademie* in Rauland, taught by Sverre Sandvik (whose method for building this instrument had recently been published). (Sandvik 1983)

Ola Øyaland, Hans Ulleren, and Elna Odden travelled down to Rauland from Tinn the following morning. It was the first time I had seen Elna Odden since the double tragedy of her husband's death and that of Johannes Dahle. I was eager to discuss the two versions of *Jon Vestafe* I had transcribed from the playing of Johannes Dahle, particularly interested in their feedback to my theory that the two examples represented the individual styles of Myllargutten and Gibøen. I had based this conclusion on 1) Dahle's identification of one version with Gibøen, and 2) musical analysis, which had uncovered two modally different styles of music. To my surprise, and somewhat to my discomforture, Ola Øyaland replied:

No, they are both from Gibø tradition. But one is from the Rauland, the other from the Tinn tradition of Gibø-playing.[31]

Of course, this correction did not cast doubt on my main point: the ability of the *spelemann* to maintain the performance of more than a single rendering of *slått* material. Indeed, Ola Øyaland proceeded to give me more solid evidence by demonstrating his own skill in this respect—by performing both versions of the *slått* himself. (See Ex. 33 and Ex. 35)

Bergen

Nearly twenty years after our original meeting, Finn Vabø, now employed as an engineer, described a sudden and new explosion of interest and enthusiasm for learning to play the Hardanger violin. In Bergen throughout the present century, there has consistently been support from the small, closely-knit group of traditional music enthusiasts; however, an unprecedented number of forty would-be students appeared upon the announcement of a new course offering. Finn Vabø and Jan-Petter Blom received the assistance of additional instructors, including Øivind Vabø

—who, at sixteen, is considered one of the most promising of the young spelemenn around today. (III. 21)

I asked Øivind and Finn Vabø to describe Øivind's *hardingfele* training in the home milieu, and it was the father who responded first:

> When he was a little boy, he would come in to me at bedtime and ask me to play so he could go to sleep. He takes things I play— things he's heard around, since he was this high—. . . . If he comes to me and says, "I want to play Myllarguten's Siste Slått," I play, slowly, and then we start together.[32]

It was a different *lydarslått*, however, that Øivind chose to play for my tape recorder (*Ungkoneslåtten*).

Once again, we discussed the direct quotations I had used in my manuscript, and Finn Vabø elaborated somewhat on his original remarks concerning the balance between accuracy and creativity:

> They must learn the music and then they must give a little bit from their own heart—If they listen to others when they play, take something from another and then give something special from their own heart. In folk music, you can learn a little bit from every hardingfele spelemann—not necessarily only the good players. If you give something from your heart, I have my ear. If two players play the same piece with a slightly different part. . . . I have one variant more.[33]

The revival movement among Bergen Youth—students who were unlikely to have instruments in the attic or *hardingfele* makers or players in the family—has created a need in Norway (as it has in the United States) —for cheap instruments and effected other, less obvious, changes. For example, a new emphasis on group performance that was apparent in some localities was thus explained:

> In the areas north of Bergen where there are many inexperienced players, they play very often in groups; it helps the new players who don't feel confident to play alone yet.[34]

The large crop of young students had caused the *spelemenn* to search out amusing and attractive pieces of little technical difficulty. Vabø played one such example, *Knapp Halling*, composed by Jon Rosenlid, who had been his principal teacher.

What about the new broadening of outlook on the definition of traditional culture. Yes, it was not generally accepted that there was more to Norwegian indigenous music than the *hardingfele*: The *flatfele*, the guitar, and the accordion had won the battle to be accepted. In fact, Finn Vabø announced that he was at that time exchanging lessons with a friend who played the accordion. However:

> *It seems as though he gets more time to practice* hardingfele *than I do to practice the accordion.*[35]

Transcriptions

The composer, Morton Feldman, once told an interviewer: "I always worked with whatever notation I felt the work called for." (Griffith 1972: 258) These words reflect a viewpoint, prevalent among contemporary composers that diverges sharply from the conventional perception of musical notation as an absolute system of abstract symbols; for example, the definition found in a standard dictionary of musical terminology runs: "the art of expressing music in writing" and advises that: "A fully developed system of notation must be so designed as to clearly indicate the two main properties of a musical sound: its pitch and its duration." The author points to staff notation as possessing the "most satisfactory" symbols and seems oblivious to the fact that, in the contemporary composition of his own culture, matters other than these have often assumed greater importance—especially, of course, *timbre* (tone quality). (Apel 1942: 495f) No mention at all is made of notational systems from other parts of the world although they reflect a variety of musical values. Most astonishing of all is the fact that the author of this article does not seem to be aware of the diversity of musical communication-systems represented in his monumental treatise on the history of western musical notation. (Apel 1949)

It is important to stop and consider the nature of the relationship that exists between visual symbols and the musical sounds they represent. Often loosely called "music," the symbols are in fact visual patterns of a traditional nature that serve as a mnemonic aid: to remind the musical memory of what it has already learned. "Indeed, what we have in notation is nothing other than a picture of music—more or less exact. The most precise notation one can imagine is not the music itself but a sketch of the aural structure. . . ." (Hopkins 1966: 311)

It can be shown that staff notation, even for the music most closely associated with it, provides only an approximate outline. Some years ago, the psychologist, Carl Seashore, conducted a series of experiments with well-known virtuosi (including such figures as Tibbett, Menuhin, and Kreisler) to determine the physical make-up of the sounds they produced in actual musical performance. In the "Analysis of Artistic Singing," the author concludes that:

> The conventional musical score—the composer's documentation of the tonal sequences which he feels will express beauty, emotion, and meaning—is for the singer only a schematic reference about which he weaves, through continuous variations in pitch, a nicely integrated melodic unity. In a very real sense, a singer never sings on pitch.

(Seashore 1936: 25ff)

In "The Analysis of Violin Performance," we find that: "The violinist deviates over 60% of the time from the tempered scale notes with deviations .05 tone or greater and over 31% of the time with deviations .1 tone or greater." (Seashore 1936: 202) Rhythmically, "The violinists deviated over 80% of the time from exact note values. Half the deviations were more than .15 sec." (Seashore 1936: 228) Similar results were found with piano virtuosi in respect to duration and synchronization of notes written to be played simultaneously (Seashore 1936: 282, 289, and 306ff)

When first confronting the problem of transcribing hardingfele slåttar into musical notation, one is tempted to invent a new system which (like those devised by Morton Feldman and other composers) is specifically designed for the idiosyncratic features of a particular style, or even piece. However, most spelemenn have shown a complete disinterest in musical notation; indeed, they would be neither the initiators nor the recipients of information communicated in this way. On the other hand, and for the sake of those outside the initiated group:

> . . . a century of transcription seems to have given rise to a "model" of how a slått should look on paper . . . includes a complicated system of transposition inspired apparently by the violin itself, a limited number of time signatures, a thorough system of ornamentation, consistent two-part structure.

(Levy 1970: 157)

Any musical instrument that uses scordatura tunings poses special notational problems; and the Hardanger fiddle uses over 20 different tunings. The customary method of notating Hardanger fiddle music favors the performer-violinist over the analyst and is in fact a kind of tablature, for finger position is more the determining factor than absolute pitch. It is a form of staff notation in which the notes as written only represent standard pitches when the instrument is tuned like an ordinary violin. When the most common *hardingfele* tuning is used (a-d¹-a¹-e²), the notes on the lowest string will sound one whole tone higher than written. If so-called "troll tuning" (*trollstilt*) is used (a-e¹-a¹-c#²), notes on the third string sound as written, while those on the top sound a minor third lower. The Hardanger violin is usually tuned higher (often as much as a minor third higher) than the *flatfele*; thus the notes placed on the staff (as well as the note names above) indicate relative, not absolute, pitches. It should be realized that this notational model (sanctioned by the fact that most analyzers interested in this body of music have been violinists) is a combination of prescriptive and descriptive types; descriptive because each example represents, to the extent possible, one particular performance — not a recipe for one's own individual performance.

In the present book, I have used the notational system described above for the lengthier musical examples in Part I. On the other hand, for the short examples of Part II, obviously meant only for analytical purposes, I have used ordinary notation. There can be no confusion about which system is being employed, since, in the first case only, examples include a designation of the tuning for both upper and lower strings.

There are other notational difficulties that have necessitated special consideration. For example, the ubiquitous ornament, *likring*, is meant to be performed on the accented part of the beat, thus taking time from the principal note. I have chosen to indicate this by positioning it in the appropriate part of the measure, using a slash to show that its value has not been subtracted from the note it decorates. A special technique, consisting of a rapid trembling of part of the hand, produces this embellishment. (See p. 173) The peculiar bowing style is a factor of major importance to both the rhythmic nature of the piece and the textural quality of the sound. A special right arm technique (with even rate of motion, and silent connection) promotes the continuous ringing of the sympathetic and drone strings. The syncopated effect of over-the-beat slurring is mainly, although not altogether, achieved in the melodic line. Again, it must be emphatically stated that these characteristics of performance practice can only be properly learned aurally — a factor that is perhaps even more evident in connection with the idiosyncratic rhythmic interpretations of regional dance forms. In reference to the *springar*, Jan-Petter Blom has written:

> The springar *tunes are invariable written in 3/4 time. This conven-*
> *tion makes reading easy, but unfortunately obscures both the gen-*
> *eral characteristics of the springar rhythm and its highly significant*
> *dialectical differentiation.*
>
> *By 3/4 meter one normally refers to measures of three homolo-*
> *gous, binary or evenly divided beats (2/8, 4/16, etc.), the first of*
> *which carries the dynamic stress. These features do not hold true*
> *for the* springar.
>
> (Blom 1981: 309)

The foot-beating of player and listener provides a percussive accompaniment, an integral feature of the music. The reader should be cautioned,
however, that the feet characteristically do not stamp simultaneously, but
produce a dotted rhythm of the short-long variety. The special composition of the Telemark *springar* rhythm is the focus of Chapter 3. While one
foot stamps an uneven three beats, the other accents only the first two. I
have attempted to suggest this rhythmic configuration with the time sig-
nature $\frac{1}{4}^2$ in the transcription of *Rakstejenta* (Example 4). To suggest the
character of the light and shorter third beat, I have used the symbol ∫
above the notes in the opening bars.

Horizontal lines over note-heads indicate an indeterminate length-
ening of the notes; the dotted figure is also expected to be interpreted
with flexibility. No attempt has been made to convey exact pitches or to
include the sounds of drone and sympathetic strings. These and other
matters of performance practice are discussed in the second chapter of
Part II. However, it cannot be too emphatically stated that notation by itself is of little use.

It is hoped that the transcriptions in this book will be used along with
direct musical experience.

bowed strings   sympathetic strings

Ex. 1: West Coast *Halling* after Finn Vabø (my recording; Bergen, 1965)

bowed strings   sympathetic strings

Ex. 2: *Myllarguten's Siste Slått* after Finn Vabø (my recording; Bergen, 1965)

Ex. 3: *Seljord Wedding Processional*, Finn Vabø (my recording; Bergen, 1965)

bowed strings   sympathetic strings

Ex. 4: *Rakstejenta* after Johannes Dahle (my recording; Tinn, Telemark, 1967)

Ex. 5: *Tåkatind* after Johannes Dahle (my recording; Tinn, Telemark, 1967)

Ex. 6: *Førnesbrunen* after Johannes Dahle (my recording; Tinn, Tele-
    mark, 1972)

Part II

THE MEANING OF
THE INSTRUMENT

AURAL STRUCTURING

AURAL THINKING

MUSICAL CODES

EMERGENCE OF
THE CLASSICAL

The Meaning of the Instrument

Perhaps seamen brought the idea of sympathetic strings from Asia.
Many people think the idea came to western Norway from Britain;
but it is also possible that it is indigenous to this country.[1]

Jon Helland

 Remarkable is the fact that the Hardanger fiddle has remained essentially unchanged throughout three centuries. Like the Irish harp, the Highland bagpipe, or the Chinese ch'in, the Hardanger violin has played an intimate role in an esoteric communicative network that, within its society, involved non-musical, as well as musical, features. Unlike the other above-named instruments, however, the *hardingfele* has not been associated with the prestigious segment of the social order; its aurally transmitted music developed in the pastoral-seafaring society of the southern mountain regions of the country.

Musical instruments sometimes emerge into view—as did Athena —full-grown and all-at-once; but the sudden appearance of an important tool or making music may be more difficult to account for than is the birth of the goddess of wisdom. "Hard evidence" for the history of a "folk" instrument is difficult to come by; for such information must be based on whatever instrument specimens happen to have survived, the authenticity of labels, and the availability of written or pictorial documentation. This is particularly true of the Hardanger fiddle tradition, which developed in a country that had little formal communication with the rest of the world for so many years. Thus, it is not surprising that opinions on the early history of the *hardingfele* vary. Some believe in the authenticity of the Jåstad-fele (made by Ole Jonson Jåstad and bearing a label dated 1651) (Bjørndal 1966: 18), but the reliability of all evidence relating to the *early hardingfele* has recently been questioned; and the present scholarly consensus is that the Harding fiddle may have developed little earlier than the year 1700 (Sevgåg 1980: 327).

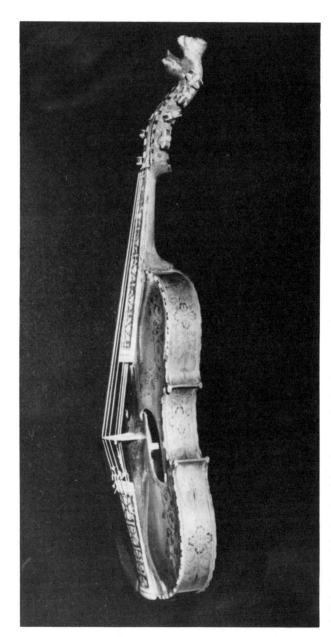

6. Side view of the hardingfele, showing flat bridge, sympathetic strings, deeply indented f-holes and decoration.

To our knowledge, resonance strings were used by Eastern peoples some centuries before their appearance in Europe. Today, they continue to be a feature of different versions of the Islamic spike fiddle, of certain Asian bowed lutes, and in both the plucked and bowed lutes of India (e.g., the *sitār* and the *sārangī*, probably the most widely known of these instruments). (See Sachs 1940; Bessaraboff 1941; and Slobin 1976.) According to established organological thought; the Baroque violin received its characteristic shape by Italian craftsmen (Straeten 1933: 45f; Boyden 1980: 826). Except for certain idiosyncratic details (flat bridge and finger-board, deeply-cut and elongated f-holes, decoration) (Ill. 6), most scholars have dismissed any idea of Scandinavian derivation. (Panum 1905: 112ff; Baines 1961: 173; Bjørndal 1966: 18; Sevåg 1980: 325). Even the flat bridge, generally considered to be the most important special feature of the Hardanger fiddle, actually existed, to varying degrees, in some of the fiddle-type instruments of seventeenth and eighteenth-century Europe. Yet, the Hardanger violin, which developed as part of a societal complex that has undergone great changes in recent years, is more important to Norway in general today than before the dissolution of this way of life. The special meaning it has always had for the mountain communities has increased to the point where it now functions as a national symbol. How and why did this seemingly foreign importation become enmeshed in Norwegian culture? This is the puzzle we must begin an attempt to solve in the present chapter.

The *hardingfele* maker, Sverre Sandvik, in his recently-published method, observes: "Always there is secrecy and mystery surrounding the hardingfele. We know that there have been made fiddles of the type we call *hardingfele* for at least 300 years here in this country. . . . Norway is poor on literature about fiddle building. There has never before been a method on the making of a *hardingfele*, the art of building having been passed down from father to son or taken care of in the family or circle of friends." (Sandvik 1983: 7ff; my trans.) The point being made here is relevant to the subject of documentation: the impossibility of expecting the same kind of documentation for instruments that operate through informal channels as for those that function as part of a formal communicative system.

Any attempt to fathom the meaning of the Hardanger fiddle must begin with the identification of the different symbols that form its composite significance; and questions of derivation will necessarily be raised along the way. This does not involve an investigation into its provenance as such, a matter that is veiled in obscurity and is irrelevant to our purpose. It does involve the history of component parts. A musical instrument—a tool for a time-manipulative art—is responsible for a complex form of communication that concerns the relations among a large variety of aural (as well as visual and tactile) symbols; and the tools of the historian for uncovering the past in the present are necessary for understanding this communicatory structure.

It is a truism (and basic to information theory) that a communication, to be completed, must involve shared knowledge between transmitter and receiver. As with speaking one's native language, the manipulation of symbols by artists, craftsmen, and musicians—as well as their comprehension by the knowledgeable—is not dependent upon translation into other terms; but any one who seeks to attempt a conscious analysis must interpret (within appropriate time and space context) references that may often be oblique (allegorical, satirical, etc.) in their meaning. The very concept, "meaning," implies a relationship between two entities; furthermore, it refers to a specific kind of relationship: one that involves *accuracy* of transmission and, therefore, assumes intentionality on the part of the transmitter. This relationship in symbolic communication (unlike that of signs or symptoms) is diffuse and complex—as is indicated by the original Greek meaning of the word, "symbol": "to cast together." A musical instrument is primarily a tool (an instrument in the literal sense) and as such it is, at one and the same time, a reflection of the system of sound patterns it was designed to produce and a method for carrying out the intentions of the performing musician; for the word, "tool" (or "instrument") can only be used to designate a meaningful relationship. The resultant, highly symbolic, communication is fraught with extra-musical associations of different kinds—attached to the musical sounds themselves, their structure, and to the shape of the musical instrument. In our search for the meaning of the Hardanger fiddle to its culture, we shall examine the different aspects of the instrument, one at a time; we shall begin by looking at the *hardingfele* in its primary role, as an instrument for producing music.

I *The Hardanger Fiddle as a Musician's Tool*

The most striking characteristic of the *hardingfele* is its set of sympathetic strings—especially when we take into consideration the fact that this instrument represents almost the only flourishing tradition in contemporary western Europe still to employ them. They also are an essential feature; without resonance strings, a violin cannot be a Hardanger violin, nor can it transmit *hardingfele* music. (III. 7)

7. *Close up of the sympathetic strings. Note double cruciform pattern of finger-board inlay.*

How can the acoustical contribution of sympathetic strings to *harding-fele* timbre be explained satisfactorily? Even the most obvious difference in tone quality between a Stradivarius and the rudest of machine-made violins is difficult to account for via physical measurements.[2] Similarly, the evident contrast that is in fact heard between the timbre of a regular violin and that of a Hardanger violin is not, with one important exception to be discussed later, immediately apparent. A researcher at the Institute of Physics at the University of Oslo conducted an experiment with the sympathetic strings of the Hardanger fiddle and concluded that their principal function was to promote the unbroken continuity of sound: ". . . since they are able to dominate in the last part of the decay, they will make the transition between two succeeding notes softer. . . . The actual meaning of the sympathetic strings may therefore be in the transients." (Michaelson n.d.: 7f) This emphasis is interesting, because it brings out a close connection between bowing technique and the contribution of the sympathetic strings to the textual complex of the music.

However, our own recent research has indicated that there may be another important acoustical phenomenon present as well. With a focus somewhat different from that of the Oslo project, we have been examining bowed tones that have not gone through a filtering process to eliminate extremes in frequency; and up to this point, in the initial stages of our research, there has been an indication of the consistent presence of tones well below the playing range of the instrument, whenever—and only whenever—the sympathetic strings are left free to vibrate. Indeed, however, it should be stressed that much further work is needed before any definitive conclusions can be drawn.

Sympathetic strings are found in the Balkan areas of Europe itself (notably, with the Bulgarian *gadulka*); and Norway's next-door neighbor, Sweden, employs them on its *nyckelharpa*, virtually the only other instrument in western Europe to utilize them today. But this was not always true of Europe: during the seventeenth and eighteenth centuries, there developed in Europe a proliferation of musical instruments that employed sympathetic strings. The first written evidence of their use documents the practice in England. The German organologist, Michael Praetorius, reported that the English had been using resonance strings on what he called the *viola bastarda*, a small bass viola da gamba especially suited to chordal playing. (Praetorius 1619: 47) At about the same time, Chancellor Francis Bacon (d. 1626) described this practice in some detail:

> It was devised, that a Viall should have a lay of Wire Strings below, as close to the Belly as a Lute: And then the strings of Guts

mounted upon a Bridge, as in Ordinary Vialls: To this end that, by this means, the upper strings strucken, should make the lower resound by Sympathy, and so make the Musick the better; Which, it be to purpose, then Sympathy worketh as well by Report of Sound, as by Motion.

(Quoted in Sachs 1940: 366)

From that time on we hear of the *application* of narrow gauge understrings to a number of the many and various forms of European chordophones.

The word, application, has been underscored intentionally; for it is clear that resonance strings only became an integral part of these European instruments for the purpose of contributing to a certain desired sound: namely, an increased density of timbre and a continuous tonal backdrop. We shall find evidence of the value of this perspective in attempting to understand the *viola d'amore*—the instrument often considered to be the most likely model for the *hardingfele*. It is important to realize that not all *viole d'amore* had resonance strings; some instruments being designated as such because of the presence of bowed strings made of metal. A typical seventeenth-century source stresses the "sweetness and novelty" of the "5 wyre strings played with a bow." (Evelyn's Diary quoted in Danks 1976: 14).

Contemporary descriptions of the viola d'amore have provided us with an important insight into the meaning of this musical instrument: the equivalence of metal bowed and sympathetic strings demonstrates the essential importance of the *kind* of sound engendered. The complete description of this instrument by John Evelyn (quoted in part above) provides further clues, for the well-known diarist noted that he had enjoyed:

. . . *for its sweetness and novelty, the viola d'amore of 5 wyre-strings plaid with a bow, being but an ordinary violin play'd on lyra-way by a German.*

(Danks 1976: 14)

Thus, Evelyn defined the *viola d'amore* not only as possessing metal strings but also as being played "lyra-way," a term used for the performance of a thick-textured fiddle music characterized by the simultaneous sounding of several strings in drones and, sometimes, true polyphony. It always implied a flat bridge, a short neck, and the use of scordatura tunings (i.e., the practice of tuning the strings variously for different pieces). Although it is obvious that scordatura tunings made a greater variety of note combinations available under the fingers of the hand, Sibil Marcuse has pointed out that they were not just a matter of expediency:

> The reason generally given for such numerous tunings is that it permits an increase in the variety of chords easily available; however, it is more likely that the object was to produce maximum sympathetic resonance of the open strings by having them tuned to the triad of the key in which a piece was to be played.
> (Marcuse 1975: 321)

Evelyn's *viola d'amore*, as we have seen, is not only identified by the metallic ring of its strings but also by the thick texture of the music it was designed to produce. It was one of a group of musical instruments having in common the characteristics of playing "lyra-way." Sometimes, the application of one or more of these features to an established instrument would effect a seeming metamorphosis—the instrument in question suddenly emerging with a totally new name; this circumstance has caused, understandably, much confusion among scholars in later years. Thus, a small bass gamba (as already mentioned above) became a *viola bastarda* when outfitted with sympathetic strings in Germany; its English version was actually named for this function, the lyra-viol being simply defined as "a viol played lyra-way."[3] (Playford 1982) Even the small size of the lyra-viol was explained in terms of convenience in playing many-voiced music. Toward the end of the seventeenth century, a larger number of strings (from 11 to as many as 40) added to a full-sized gamba created a "barytone" (which was also, and significantly, called *"viola di bordone"*).[4] A century later, Leopold Mozart described the "English Violet" as a viola d'amore with 14 (rather than 7) sympathetic strings.

Two instruments, both prominent in European literary and pictorial sources of the sixteenth century, were obvious predecessors of the Baroque lyra-way chordophones; both used scordatura tunings and possessed flat bridges and off-board drone strings—gut strings hanging freely to the side of the fingerboard, out of reach for finger stopping but available to the thumb for open string strumming. Both played a chordal style of music characterized by the continuous sounding of several bowed strings at once in addition to the abovementioned drones. In respect to their physical shapes and playing positions, however, they contradicted one another. The *lira da broccio* (flourished from 1475-1619) was related in size and shape to the violoncello, the bass member fo the violin family, but it was played in an upward position, like the treble members (the violin and viola) of that family.[5] The *lira da gamba*[6] (flourished from 1550-1680) was both shaped and played like the *viola da gamba*— despite the fact that it was usually of a size somewhat smaller than the *lira da braccio*.

The Hardanger fiddle may now be defined as a Norwegian violin with sympathetic strings, played lyra-way. The characteristics shared by the lyra-way instruments are of greater musical importance than simply the production of a common tone quality. The thick-textured, resonant sound produced is integrally involved with a specific musical style, one characterized by constant drones or polyphony; and this style reflects a kind of musical thinking that manifests itself in such constructional devices as echo effects, motivic imitation, and the use of contrasting timbres (of different strings or combinations of strings). It requires a horizontal (across the string) kind of violin technique which can even (as we shall see in the following chapter) cause the formation of a particular scale.

The lyra-way instruments functioned essentially as solo instruments, equipped to play melody and harmony parts together or an accompaniment to a vocal solo, but not well equipped to play a single thread in an harmonic fabric. Mersenne, after describing the flat bridge of the *lira da braccio*, explained that it had to accommodate the great ". . . multitude of strings, which must be played three or four at a time by one stroke of the bow, so as to produce chords. He continues by explaining that the resultant sound is ". . . very languishing and suitable for exciting devotion and . . . used to accompany the voice and recitatives." (Mersenne 1636: 263) Nearly a century later, Roger North, in describing eight different "intents" (functions) of music, gave the lyra viol tradition as the only example of his first category: solitary music; which he said, was to be recommended as ". . . a medicine without any nausea or bitter and is taken for pleasure or cure." (North 1959: 257) We are reminded that John Playford in his *Musick's Recreation on the Viol, Lyra-Way* directed his introductory remarks to: ". . . such as desire to Learn who live in remote Parts, far from any profest Teacher." (Playford 1682) A devoted amateur player, this time of the *viola d'amore*, detailed his concern about the lack of interest in his instrument, a circumstance he explained by the changing style of music in the eighteenth century:

> As by virtue of its nature the viola d'amore can never be a secondary instrument, but most always remain more or less a solo, he that wishes to concentrate solely on it would be a useless musician in any ensemble.
>
> (Danks 1976: 41; trans. by Danks)

The Hardanger violin of the isolated mountain valleys is, also, essentially a solo instrument, playing either dance accompaniments or *lydarslåttar* (listening pieces). It should perhaps be noted that all lyra-way instruments could be and, at times, were played in groups; this did not interfere in the slightest with the identification of them as fundamentally solo instruments. (III. 8)

Accepted organological theory actually obscures the existence of lyra-way instruments as a genre. According to the establishment classification system (the Sachs-Hornbostel system), chordophones (that is, string instruments) can be reduced to four fundamental types (according to the relationship of strings to sound board): zithers, lutes, lyres, and harps; while lutes and lyres are subdivided into bowed and plucked types. (Sachs 1940) European bowed-lutes from the sixteenth century on are considered to belong to "two distinct families": "leg viols" or *viole da gamba* and "arms viols" or *viole de braccio* (referring to the playing position of the higher-range members of the family). It has been shown that the two families have different derivations and that the principal physical characteristics of each, listed below, are separate and distinct from one another:

viola da gamba	*viola da braccio* (violin family)
flat back	rounded (bulging) back
sloping shoulders	rounded shoulders
6 strings	4 strings
frets	no frets
C holes	f holes

(Sachs 1940: 374; Bessaraboff 1940: 292; Hajdecki 1892: 27ff)

As we have seen, the lyra-way instruments occur in both viol and violin shape; and their harmonic function gives them a close relationship to some categories of plucked chordophones. To quote John Playford in reference to the lyra-viol:

> *This way of playing on the* Viol, *is but a late invention, in imitation of the* Old English Lute *or* Bandora . . .
>
> (Playford 1682)

But the same kind of close relationship with plucked instruments has also been noticed for the Italian lyras (Galpin 1910: 92)

There is no doubt that the viol and the violin represent different physical types and that this was evident from the time when the violin first

8. *Ensemble playing of a solo instrument. Johannes Dahle and Øystein Odden (a); Tinn Spelemannslaget (b).*

appeared on the historical scene (Leipp 1969: 23). It is also true that contemporary writers categorized and named instruments according to qualities that had nothing to do with (even contradicted) physical characteristics; these were the functional and stylistic features that made up the lyra-viol concept. At this point, it is necessary to look for analogous descriptions of the violin and viola da gamba traditions. Consistently and from the earliest accounts, we find that the European violin was conceived of primarily as an orchestral instrument. Quite typical is the explanation by Marin Mersenne:

> *Although one can sometimes play two strings on the violin at the same time to make a chord, nevertheless many violins must be used to make a whole concert, such as the Twenty-four Violins of the King;*
>
> (Mersenne 1636: 242)

Mersenne later remarked that it was possible to have as many as 500 violins playing together, ". . . although twenty-four are enough, in which are six trebles, six bass, four contratenors, four altos, and four of a fifth part." (Mersenne 1636: 244)

Viols were considered elegant, refined instruments designed in the different voice ranges to play consort music; indeed, every prestigious household of the time had to have its "chest of viols." Jamb-de-Fer wrote:

> *Why do they call the one viols and the other violins? We call those viols that gentle people, merchants and other people of virtue pass their time.* . . .
>
> (Quoted in Leipp 1969: 23; my trans.)

Of viol consorts Mersenne observed: "Now they are made of all sorts of sizes, in which one can enclose some young page-boy to sing the treble of many delightful airs while the bass player sings the alto. . ." "Your *Best Provision* (and *most Compleat*) will be, a *Good Chest of Viols*; six, in Number; vz. 2 *Basses*, 2 *Tenors*, and 2 *Trebeles*: All *Truly*, and *Proportionably Suited*." (Mace 1676: 245)

It is clear that there was a specific purpose behind the efflorescence of violins and gambas into families of all sizes from treble to bass: quite simply, the fact that both types of instrument were used in concerted music. This impressive circumstance may have been the cause for an undue emphasis on the shape of chordophones in classifying them; it has probably led some to expect all instrument shapes to manifest themselves in similar family groupings, and in fact there has been some effort to find a viola d'amore family—an attempt, one would think, rather similar to a search for a group of keyboard instruments in all ranges.[7]

In sum, violins were assocated with their orchestral (and professional) function; viols were thought of primarily as chamber music instruments for amateurs; while the lyra-way instruments (which could, and did, possess the physical characteristics of either of the other two groups) were designed to stand by themselves, for solos and accompaniments. The various attributes of the third kind of instrument appeared in a wide variety of combinations, from small modifications in the bridge and bow of a regular violin necessary to perform a Bach solo sonata to the elaborate assemblage of drones (both plucked and bowed) and sympathetic strings of the barytone. It is important to realize that a functional change is not always accompanied by a name change, as happened with the lyra-viol, the viola d'amore, and the barytone; thus, the violin and bass gamba can be used for solo sonatas, while the Hardanger fiddle and lyra viol can be played in ensembles. For it is inherent in the functional perspective that there be a focus on intangible qualities that are likely to be different in kind and fluid in nature. (See Chart 1)

The efficacy of this line of approach for understanding the *hardingfele* tradition has been indicated by Norwegian scholars. In highlighting the importance of the flat bridge, Bjørndal and Alver have called it the feature that performs the ". . . functional task of implementing a polyphonic style," (1966: 23) thus pinpointing the fact that it is not the invention of a certain kind of bridge but the impulse for a certain kind of music that is significant. Reidar Sevåg has more recently suggested that the "bourdon style . . . so typical of Harding Fiddle music" should be studied:

> *First, this style was familiar also to the ordinary violin in Norway and is still practiced in a few districts. Next, written sources state that the violin, possibly also older types of stringed instruments, were known in western Norway as far back as about 1600. Probably therefore a playing style of old bierfiddler character had already been established in these districts at the time when the Harding Fiddle came into existence, and just as this new fiddle grew out of instruments already at hand, it must have taken over, carried on and developed the existing styles of playing.*
>
> (Sevåg 1972: 22)

Sevåg thus draws attention to the historical importance of the lyra-way style to Norway. Indeed, this technique can be shown to have been

	"Bowed harp"	Crwth (Wales)	Hurdy-gurdy type	Lyra da braccio (Italy)	Lyra da gamba (Italy)	Viola d d'amore	lang-spil (Iceland)
Functional characteristics:							
Flat bridge or No bridge	●	●	●	●	●	●	●
Scordatura tunings	?	◐	●	●	●	●	?
Drone strings	●	●	●	●	●	●	●
Sympathetic strings	✗	✗	◐	✗	✗	◐	✗
Metal strings	✗	✗	◐	✗	✗	●	✗
Self-sufficient	●	●	●	●	●	●	●

Chart 1. Comparative chart of lyra-way characteristics

Barytone	Viol played lyra-way	Violin played lyra-way	Nyckel-harpen (Sweden)	Jouhi-kantele (Finland)	Eesti-kannel (Esthonia)	Gadulka (Bulgaria)	Lyra (Greece)	Harding-fele
●	●	●	●	●	●	●	◐	●
◐	●	●	●	◐	?	●	◐	●
●	●	●	●	●	◐	●	●	●
●	◐	◐	◐	X	X	◐	◐	●
●	◐	◐	◐	◐	●	◐	◐	●
●	●	●	●	●	●	●	●	●

linked to Scandinavian music consistently over a lengthy period of time. Besides the regular violin referred to in the above quotation, the Norwegian plucked zither, the *langleik,* is characterized by numerous (as many as 7) drone strings to accompany a single melody string; shaped somewhat like a flat-backed lute, it is known to have existed in Norway, like the violin, as early as 1600. (Ledang 1974: 107f) Earlier Norwegian examples remain obscure. However, in Iceland up to the turn of this century, there existed two distinct kinds of bowed zithers: the *langspil* and the *fiðla.* Related to the Norwegian *langleik,* the former possessed either one string or two pitched in unison, plus an additional string that functioned as a drone one octave below. Of the 3-stringed variety, only one of the identically-pitched strings was bowed; the other was permitted to vibrate freely as a resonance string. (Ledang 1974: 107f; Panum 1920: 10f). The *fiðla* has been mentioned in Icelandic literary sources since the Middle Ages; by 1900, however, it had ceased to be a living tradition, and for information about the instrument we are now dependent upon a very few extant specimens, including some careful reconstructions, and accounts obtained from the last performers of the *fiðla.* Reliable scholarship has shown that the *fiðla* possessed two strings that were bowed simultaneously either over a flat bridge, or more likely, no bridge at all; one of the two strings functioned as a drone and was thus left to vibrate freely, while the left hand fingers stopped the other, melody, string from beneath. The finger stopping technique involved holding the left hand between sound board and strings of the instrument with the back of the hand downward and the fingers unfolding upward so that either knuckles or fingernails would do the touching. (Jóhannsdóttir 1972: 27ff; Thorsteinsson 1906: 70f) From these descriptions of the Icelandic instruments, we can extrapolate the principal lyra-way characteristics: drone strings, resonance strings, the simultaneous sounding of more than one string due to either a bridgeless situation or to a flat bridge. Yet these instruments were not of the fiddle type.

More than fifty years ago, the Swedish scholar, Otto Andersson, assembled a vast amount of information concerning ancient Norse stringed instruments (Andersson 1939). The subject for Andersson's focus of attention is the instrument called by him a "bowed-harp"—an instrument that eludes all conventional methods of organological classification. According to the accoustical-typological criteria of the Sachs-Hornbostel system, most examples of this instrument would be classified as a lyre or zither. Indeed, we have met it in its zither shape, when we discussed the Icelandic *fiðla;* and can find it in its lyre shape by looking at the famous twelfth-century sculpture in the Nidaros Cathedral at Trondheim. Andersson has chosen to make use of a literal translation for his use of the word, "harp," not only to have a convenient, generic term, but—more importantly—to draw an analogy between the role of this instrument in Nordic culture and that of the harp in Celtic lands. It is for similar reasons that van Gulik renamed the Chinese zither, *ch'in,* for the elegant European instrument in *The Lore of the Chinese Lute.*

The bowed-harp is a further problem to classify according to the usual method, because it is a bowed instrument that:

   1) is not a lute type (i.e., possess a neck)
   2) does not have a fingerboard (its strings being stopped from below)
   3) does not have incurvations on the sides of the body (often assumed as necessary to bowing)
   4) often has no separate bridge (the string-holder serving two functions)

The absence of these features—considered critical—have caused scholars to reject much of the evidence (literary and representational) for the predominance of bowed instruments in Old Norse society. Terminological problems have further contributed to this confusion: the word, *harpa,* as indicated above, has been accepted as a generic term for stringed instruments. However, the indications are also strong that it was, at least sometimes, bowed, since it has appeared with the word, *draga* (draw, drag, or pull). It is more often associated with the verb, *sla* (literally, strike or beat), a fact that has caused scholars up to the present day to classify it as a plucked instrument (for this misunderstanding, see Sachs 1940: 274; Marcuse 1975: 181; and editor's note in Andersson 1930: 145). However, Andersson has shown that the Icelandic verb also could have the meaning: "to set in motion," in which sense, he points out, the word is still used today by musicians in Sweden. (ibid: 154) We can bring further evidence to bear on this matter from the Norwegian *hardingfele* tradition, where, it will be remembered, a form of this word specifies a piece for the *hardingfele.* It is interesting to note that Finn Vabø originally described the term, *slått,* as referring to the bowing action of the fiddler: "Do you know the German term, *schlagen?*" he asked me. "It is the same word —*beat* in English."

Besides, *harpa,* there are two terms that also refer to stringed instruments in Old Norse literature: *gigja* and *fiðla.* All three of these names may be found associated with the uncontested term for the bowing motion: *draga*—as well as with *spela* (to play) and *sla;* yet in Old Norse literature they are listed in such a way as to indicate that a distinction was made among them. It seems evident that there used to be several varieties of bowed instruments in Scandinavia, just as indeed there are today. The bowed-harp, known to us both through the Icelandic *fiðla* and through surviving examples and representations studied by Andersson in Norway, Sweden, Finland and Swedish Estonia:

> . . . has held a place in the instruments of the northern peoples since the early Middle Ages, at least; it has been associated with their poetry and ideas of music, and has maintained its primitive form until the present day.
>
> (Andersson 1930: 30f)

Closely associated with these instruments is a group of instruments in which the harmonic nature of the music is guaranteed by a mechanical bow in the shape of a wheel. Taken up by a variety of social orders from the Middle Ages to the present day, it has been known by different names, including *hurdy-gurdy, organistrum, drehleier, vielle,* and *symphonia* (Clemencic 1968: 110). Andersson has drawn attention to the last term listed here and to the use of the terms, *simfon* and *fon* in the sagas as probably referring to such an instrument (1930: 182). It is also of interest that the hurdy-gurdy was once known in Europe as a "harp" (see Comenius quotation in Sandys 1864: 157); at other times it was called, "lyra" (Virdung 1511: 22). Today, a related instrument exists in Sweden: The *nyckelharpa* has a similar (fiddle/zither) shape but without the wheel, and the strings are stopped by mechanical keys. The bow moves over several strings at once, and the *nyckelharpa* is usually outfitted with a number of sympathetic strings.

We now have a contextual frame for the study of the Norwegian national instrument. It is clear that, within the Scandinavian context, the *hardingfele* is part of a time-honored tradition of lyra-way instruments that appeared in a wide array of shapes and sizes. Within the European context, we can now see that the *hardingfele* was the only one of the lyra-viol instruments to outlast the Baroque; as noted above, it has displayed a remarkable consistency over a period of at least 300 years. This was in direct contrast to the other lyra-viol instruments (including the *barytone,* the *viola d'amore,* and various kinds of gambas with sympathetic strings) which were always exceptional instruments, appearing sporadically, likely to be greeted with flurries of excitement, but never becoming long-standing traditions of particular cultures; this is the reason that the data on their cultural ties is confusing and, often, conflicting. Even the regular vi-

olin underwent several important changes during the late eighteenth century, modifications that again demonstrate the primarily functional purpose of musical instruments. In order to accommodate the new style of
music: the neck and bridge of the violin were strengthened (to permit the
greater tension of higher-pitched strings); the neck and fingerboard were
made longer (to facilitate position playing); and the highly arched bridge
became a standard item. With the sole exception that its body contour
has become closer to the Italian model, the Hardanger fiddle has retained
its original lyra-way, Baroque structure to the present—including short
neck and finger-board, small body, high belly, flat bridge, sympathetic
strings, elaborate ornamentation, carved dragon's head, and idiosyncrat-
ically-shaped f-holes.

At this point, we should turn our attention to the violin body as a functional characteristic itself. It should be realized that the attachment of
sympathetic strings to a violin-shaped body was unusual; even the most
characteristic examples of the *viola d'amore* with sympathetic strings,
were basically treble viols. The significance of this can only be understood, if we remember that the violin has been of prime importance to
Norwegian traditional music since at least 1600 (Sevåg 1972: 22). While
the violin as we know it appeared on the European scene in the early
sixteenth century, it was not completely accepted as an elite instrument
until close to 1700. Mersenne criticized violins for having "too much
roughness," although he thought they could become, with appropriate
modification, nearly perfect instruments (Mersenne 1636: 254). The English lawyer, Roger North, wrote: "the use of the violin had been little in
England except by common fiddlers," referring to the early sixteenth century. It has been pointed out that:

> The result was that the viols (played da gamba, i.e., between the
> legs) were nearly always richly adorned, whereas the violins
> (played da braccio, on the arm) were generally very simple in out-
> ward appearance.

(Clemencic 1968: 64)

By the last quarter of the century in England, the violin family was
displacing the violin in the public's affection. Thomas Mace, writing in
1676 of what he called "the Scolding Violins," predicted that they "will
out-Top Them All":

> . . . I have begun to speak of the Sprightly, Generous, and Heroick
> Viol; which Instrument I Love, and Highly Value; . . . Whereas

> *now the* Fashion *has* Cry'd These Things Down, *and set up others in their* Room; *which I confess make a Greater Noise; but which of the* Two *is the Better Fashion, I leave to be* Judg'd *by the* Judicious.
>
> (Mace 1676: 233f)

Mace was right: violins did make a "greater noise"—and their acceptance seems a logical outgrowth of the utter fascination with pure volume of sound that led to experiments with metal and sympathetic strings. The body of the violin (both because of the increased thickness of the wood and its shape) is built to produce a louder, more powerful sound than the clear, bell-like timbre of the flat-backed viols—or the subdued tone of zithers and lyres. Just as important was the playing position of the violinist, who shouldered the instrument (thus separating it almost entirely from the damping properties of the body) and brought the bow down from above—rather than teasing the strings into vibration; with the viol player's under-handed bow grip.

Even in Italy, the violin was not fully accepted, until nearly a century after its first use in orchestral scores:

> Before Corelli, the art of violin playing was absolutely unknown: the employment of the instrument was left to the rule of thumb practice of some ignorant musicians who could not be qualified by the honourable title of artists.
>
> (quoted in Pincherle 1956: 178)

The Harding fiddle, within its highly circumscribed and non-elite society, seems always to have been treated with care and esteem. The fingerboards and tailpieces of the earliest examples that have come down to us were carefully inlaid with animal horn, bone, and mother-of-pearl; pegboxes surmounted by carefully carved animal heads. A mark of special favor, one might call the sympathetic strings with which these instruments were equipped. Similarly lavish attention was reserved, in the mainstream European culture of the day, for the prestigious plucked lutes and, as noted above, for members of the *viola da gamba* family.

II *Extra-Musical Associations*

> *It was Corelli who raised fiddling to the dignity of an art, by the side of the other reproductive arts; who first (in his own land at*

least) freed it from the medieval tavern and trampdown reminis-
cences, and the fiddler from the unsavory reputation of quackery
and trickery and smelling of strong drinks which hitherto had
clung around him like wet clothes round a swimmer. . . .
(Quoted in Pincherle 1956: 178)

In the preceding words, we seem to see the itinerant rural musician plying his trade in country fairs, weddings, and local taverns rather than hired by a court or church. The socially snobbish attitude is evident in this quotation; and the "ignorant" musician so ridiculed may actually have been as skilled and creative as the *hardingfele spelemann*; but, of course, there is no way of determining this today. There is also no way of discovering just what was meant by "quackery and trickery." Could the author have been referring to extra-musical meanings in southern European fiddle music? We do know that there associations have played an important role in harding fiddle communication, and it would be interesting to know whether such concepts were peculiar to Norwegian fiddlers in Europe.

The direct musical transmission of specific moods is commonly associated with the Far East or the Mediterranean. We usually use the Greek word, *ethos*, to describe this, although the concept is reflected in our word, mode (mood), and probably behind the German-Baroque notion of the *affektenlehre* (which referred to the portraying of a single emotion by an entire piece of music). With the *spelemenn*, it was not scale patterns or compositions that were primarily accorded this kind of musical power, but rather tunings (which, as we shall see in the following chapter, are basic to the structure of the music).

It has been pointed out (see Marcuse quotation, above) that the practice of using a variety of tunings (scordatura) had more practical significance than simple utility, that these tunings were also desired to augment the acoustical resonance of the instrument. But with the *hardingfele*, the significance extends much further: a certain tuning was considered evocative of a specific state of mind and there was a perceived difference in the affective transmission. Thus, particular tunings (as with East Indian music) are still considered appropriate to particular times of day and situations. Troll tuning (*trollstilt*), for example, is considered appropriate to the period between midnight and dawn, and it is used in *nøringslåttar* (special *slåtts* played to the bridal guests before they rise from bed in the morning).

More than any other figure, including the Pastor himself, the *spelemann* was the leader of the traditional wedding celebration, and he had to understand and put into motion customs and ceremonies that formed a several-day ritual of which the religious ceremony at the church was only a part. Special slåtts were appropriate for each step along the way, from greeting slåtts (velkomeslåttar) to be played as the spelemann met each group of guests on the day before the wedding to farewell slåtts (jageslåttar), played during the eating of the final meal on the third or fourth day after arrival. There were, in addition, listening slåtts (lydarslåttar) to be played at times when quiet was specified (for example, in the bride's house just before the wedding procession got on its way); and particular slåtts to accompany: the eating of the traditional wedding food (rømmegraut); the first dance with the bride; the bridal pair to their nuptual bed, and so on. The spelemann, of course, led the procession to and from the church for the wedding ceremony itself and was in charge of all-night dances that required, not only an abundance of energy, a fund of knowledge, and a large repertoire of pieces, but also leadership and diplomatic ability of the charismatic kind that allows one to control the actions of a crowd. (Bjørndal 1966: 71ff)

The affective connotations were an important part of Hardanger fiddle communication; and the ability of the spelemann to manipulate them gave him a power that was recognized in the community. Arne Bjørndal, drawing upon his own experience, described this responsibility of the spelemann as the traditional wedding feast drew to a close and the guests, who had been together with much to drink and very little sleep for several days, continued to coexist for a little while longer:

> All mingled together in the wedding party, good as well as bad, loving and hating. They could be as in a witch's cauldron. At such moments, the spelemann must be careful about what slåtts he played. It had better be music that talked to the senses. A well-chosen slått could quiet the storm. Were the slått "alken" or "skriput," as they say in Hallingdal, it was dangerous. The halling Skripalat'n must not be heard where there are idlers ready to brawl. They who were looking for a fight would fly at each other then.
> (Bjørndal 1966: 80; my trans.)

The importance of these ethical connotations today is de-emphasized by most spelemenn, who exist in a world of competitions, concerts, and dances. Like Finn Vabø, most will say: "We used to believe it was dangerous to use troll tuning after dawn and before midnight." Yet, this knowledge remains part of the communicative picture for the initiated; and the spelemann maintains a position of authority that derives from more than simple admiration for his abilities. In a deeper sense, these attitudes toward the spelemenn's extra-musical powers are very much alive today in the form of the genius concept, important in a tradition where top virtuosi may receive status as legendary figures.

Verbal associations are as important at the present time as they ever were; these exist in the form of songs or legends, and they are replete with symbolic imagery. *Slåttar* are sometimes built on pre-existent songs; or, in other cases, words are added to the basic tunes of the fiddle pieces afterward. The usual song-form associated with *hardingfele* construction is the *stev*, a simple, choral-like melody to which words (unpretentious and light-hearted, often ribald) have been set. (For example, see following chapter, footnote 3)

Of all the kinds of extra-musical associations, the narratives attached to *hardingfele slåttar* are the most recognized as being of integral importance: The spelemann does not think his transmission of a *slått* complete without associated legend. Indeed, in many cases, even the pure sound of the music itself cannot be properly understood without this information, for musical word-painting is sometimes present: the imitation of moans, bells, or other sounds. This legendary material can be very roughly grouped into four categories (not mutually exclusive): 1) Those concerned with the monumental crises of the past (e.g., the conflict between the Norse and Christian religions, the Black Death, etc.); 2) Those perpetuating knowledge of national or local events (as the routing of Scottish mercenaries at Kringa); 3) The narration of seemingly more homely events (ostensibly, at least, concerned with ordinary people, animals, or natural objects); and 4) The history of tradition itself (transmitting the names and feats of extraordinary players, dancers, and *slått* singers, or describing the genesis of a particular piece).

It is important to realize that, in all of these legends, the kind of history being transmitted has to do with matters more diffuse (and more significant) than names and dates. The waterfall nymth (*fossegrimen*), who is credited with giving slåtts to *hardingfele spelemenn* (usually in dreams), communicates by extension a certain point of view about the connection of magic and music (and perhaps about cultural creation in general). A certain kind of wry sense of humor is transmitted from one generation to another along with such yarns as the one about Øystein who took pains to retrieve his silver belt from the bride who had jilted him. The prominence of certain cultural symbols is naturally reflected in the legendary material. For example, there is probably no more ancient symbol of Nordic culture than the horse, and legends and stories about horses are as abundant today as they were in the last century (Metcalfe 1858: 168ff).

Two of the most evocative slåtts I received from Johannes Dahle concern horses, and they express the two sides of their symbolic significance. The first, composed by Dahle himself within recent years, is a musical commenoration of Tåkatind, the proud young stallion sent by the Norwegian government to service the wild mares of Rauland. Tåkatind's fame has increased over the years, and his likeness has been reproduced many times by people in the surrounding area. Appropriately, Dahle's Slått is in the form of a virile halling. (Ex. 5) (III. 9)

In Førnesbrunen, the listening gangar that is known as the "tearful slått," we have a portrayal in musical tone-painting of the other role traditionally accorded the horse: man's loyal helper who patiently suffers martyrdom. Førnesbrunen is one of the most ancient slåtts: both the legend and the music were written down in the middle of the last century, and by now there is quite an extensive bibliography on the subject. (See Bjørndal 1966: 109) As we have seen, these circumstances have not prevented the slått from thriving in aural tradition. There have been many versions of both the legend and the music: the form of the legend I received from Johannes Dahle—the one that appears in Part I (Ex. 6)—is considered by Bjørndal to be the original (Bjørndal 1966: 138). This is the version that connects it with the Black Death and the remote section of the bygd of Rauland called Møsstrand—the home of two quiet, introspective spelemenn: the young Trygve Vågen and, a century ago, the highly revered Håvard Gibøen. Musically, the Førnesbrunen slåttar are lydarslåttar (listening slåtts), the symphonic poems of Hardanger fiddle music. (For other transcriptions of the slått, see Gurvin III: 195-20)

III The Artifact

We have been examining the hardingfele in its primary aspect, as an instrument for producing music: both (I) sound patterns and (II) the associated extra-musical connotations generated along with them. We have seen that even the body shape of the instrument should be considered as one of a number of functional qualities that make up this musician's tool. However, a musical instrument is also a three-dimensional object: an artifact with a tactile and visual presence; and, as such, it communicates on a completely different plane. This is the aspect of musical instruments that has led one organologist to call them "sounding statues." Pointing to the horse hair of the fiddle bow, he asserts:

> No creature in Eurasian belief is of greater or more fundamental importance than the horse, and thus we might expect that it would

9. *Sketch of Tåkatind by Barbara Perrin.*

> find its way into the lore of instruments as well as furnishing so
> prominent a constructional material. This indeed is so, and from
> Japan to Norway there is clear evidence that many stringed instru-
> ments have a symbolic relationship to the horse.
>
> (Grame 1973: 38)

One of the signs of this symbolic connection may be found in nomencla-
ture for parts of the instrument; for example, throughout this geographical
area the term for the bridge of a violin is often connected with horse culture. In Norway, the name for bridge in several regions is *hest* (horse); in
other regions, *stall* (stable).

The Harding violin, considered as an artifact rather than an instrument
for musical production, is embedded in a new complex of associations.
We have been struck first of all with the great care and skilled craftsmanship lavished upon most specimens—a matter of significance because of
its existence alone. Now, our attention has been drawn to specific symbols: a horse hair bow brought down to strings held by a "hest."

The horse played a prominent role in the ancient Norse religion, where
it was featured in all the major festivals and sacrificial rites—always as a
symbol of virility.

> The Vikings felt just as much affinity for their horses as for their
> ships. The horse was not only a fast, reliable animal and personal
> friend—it was more than that—it embodied the power of the
> gods. Wodan's eight-footed warhorse could tear like the wind
> across the earth and through the air and is always mentioned
> when any noteworthy ride is to be undertaken.
>
> (Oxenstierna 1965: 216ff)

Horse symbolism was strong enough to survive the advent of Christianity.
St. Stephen was transformed into a stableboy by medieval painters who
liked to picture him in his new role as consecrator of an ancient Yuletide
custom, celebrating fertility and light, that involved an early morning gal-
lop by stableboys on their horses.

In light of this evidence for the historic importance of the horse in Norwegian culture, it is interesting that Svale Solheim drawns an analogy
between the celebration of the old horse-fights and the highly popular
race/dance festivals held within recent years on certain farms:

> These sæter gatherings were, from olden times, clearly connected
> with the gathering of the summer's produce at the sæter and with

the hay-making which took place about the same time. A closer examination of the prevailing customs points to a harvest festival which originally had a much wider scope, and which can be traced into the past.

(Solheim 1956: 8)

Solheim quotes an eye-witness account of a gathering at Helleset (c. 1800):

There were crowds of people on the open plain, and they were dancing and drinking, fighting and racing. And it had been like this every year from the remotest antiquity.

(Solheim 1956: 9)

But what is particularly significant from our point of view is the description of the *spelemann's* role:

Before long, the fiddler would take his seat on Steinmannsseinen (the Fiddler's Rock) and, soon after, his instrument would ring out. Then dancing started, and the brandy would pass from mouth to mouth.

(Solheim 1956: 9)

Sometimes fighting would break out—often with knives, sometimes on horseback; but it is stressed that the proceedings always began with dignity. The best *spelemenn* and dancers in the entire area would assemble and enter seriously into formal competitions that would run concurrently with the horse-racing, selling and bartering. Sometimes, there would be two groups of dancers, both taking advantage of the *spelemann* situated between them. It seems apparent that the *spelemann* was entrusted with a responsibility here similar in scope to the one he habitually assumed at wedding celebrations.

Evidence of the fiddle as a horse symbol has been found in the cultures of northern peoples from the Mongols to the British. The horse has consistently been a male symbol—the prime symbol of virility—over the area whose people have drawn an important distinction between male and female culture:

It is interesting to notice that it is the Mongol usage to allot the right side of the yurt to men and the left to women. We are surely dealing with a very ancient tradition related perhaps to the or-

dered routine of a pastoral nomadic life. For the Mongols the right and left sides were symbolized respectively by horse and cow. In the humblest Irish farms, which lack sanitary conveniences of any kind, it is customary for the women to use the byre and the men to use the stable.

(Evans 1957: 66)

Up until recently, the summer nomadism (transhumance) that was typical of Norwegian rural life (as it was typical of mountain-sea cultures in most of the Atlantic Ends) provided a practical foundation for the growth of separate sexual traditions. Wherever men were involved seriously with the seaways during the summer months, women were responsible for the farm work up on the summer highland farms—the sæters—during the most productive part of the agricultural year. There they sang the *kulokk* (the melismatic cow call), *smørbøn* (butter-making song), *bånsull* (lullaby), and other forms that make up part of the remarkable sæter song tradition. In respect to artifacts, they concentrated on weaving, embroidery and lace work:

These delicate and beautiful things were usually made in their spare time by the same women who had spent the day in heavy work in the home, the stable or the open fields . . .

(Arneberg: 15)

Thus, a distinctive complex of symbols for each sex is firmly rooted in separate roles that were established far in the past.

The Hardanger violin tradition developed as a fundamentally male tradition. There have been a small number of fine women performers, as, for example, Signe Flaten Nesset of Seljord and Christiana Lund of Telemark; but—until recently—they have been as rare as male weavers. It is important to realize what is also obvious: that the *hardingfele* is a prime example of highly developed skill in woodworking—a craft intimately associated with two most time-honored male lines of work in Norway. These are, of course, seafaring and lumbering. The carved animal heads that characteristically surmount the peg boxes (illustrations 10, 11 and 12) are indeed reminiscent of Viking prow figureheads, those samples of naval architecture that have been called: "highly developed examples of construction, which are unique in the history of art and are of the highest artistic as well as utilitarian merit." (Kauli: 11) When the dragon and other imaginary serpents that were so much favored by Viking artists were

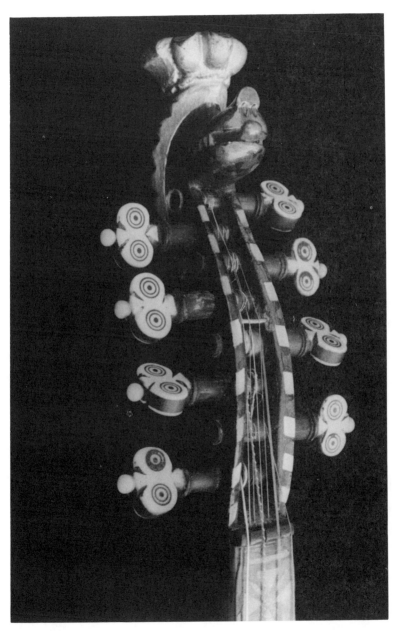

10. The carved animal head that characteristically surmounts the pegbox.

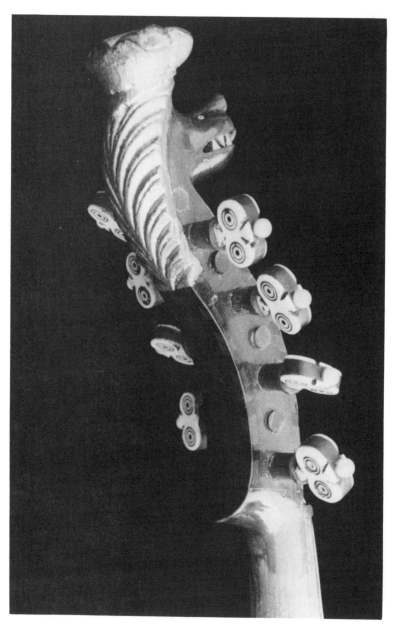

11. *The circled dot commonly found on* hardingfele *pegs.*

12. The five finger symbol.

carried over into Christian decoration, we find them perched on the roofs of pagoda-like churches:

In Norway the natural building material is wood, and we must therefore expect to find the distinctive architectural features of the country in this medium.

(Kauli: 12)

Animal carvings represent the most ancient and consistent Norwegian motifs for both abstract and naturalistic decoration—also found in relief work and jewelry.

The elaborate, and stylized, decorations drawn freehand with pen and India ink onto surfaces of the Harding fiddle are rather freely abstracted shapes derived from leaves, stems, and flowers of plants (Ill. 6). It is plant ornamentation that we think of today as being characteristically Norwegian, especially as it appears in *rosemåling* on wooden bowls, chests, and other articles of furniture. These designs reflect contact with the fashions and styles of other countries; but the Mediterranean herb species, the acanthus, or the Dutch tulip underwent various transformations in being adapted to the regional requirements of the Norwegian mountain communities. Coexisting with the regional styles, moreover, are certain characteristics that are common to *hardingfele* decoration in general. The painters call this style *felarosa*.[8]

The Hardanger fiddle used for the illustrative photographs in this chapter exhibits most of the features that are typical of Telemark, where it was made in 1869: graceful, elongated leaf forms, delicate flowers on long stems, symmetrical patterning, and the vine motif. (Stewart 1953: 88-105) At the same time, these features contain within them typical Harding fiddle motifs. In view of the ceremonial role played by the *spelemann* and the extra-musical connotations found in his tradition, we must take seriously the fact that certain protective symbols may be found in *felarosa*. Versions of similar patterns transcend the national boundaries of Mediterranean and European countries, according to Westermarck. (Westermarck 1926: 442ff and 476 for Scandinavian usage) The double cruciform figure imposed upon floral patterns is commonly found in the pen and ink designs and inlay work (See Ill. 6 and Ill. 7). Less obvious, but also in widespread use are protective motifs against the evil eye— reflecting the belief that a person, even unwittingly, can cause harm through the glance of an eye (Elsworthy 1895: 131f, 136, 142; Westermarck 1926: 442, 450, 454) Fiddle examples include the circled dot found on fiddle pegs and the five-finger (sometimes, six-finger) symbol. (See illustrations 11 and 12; also see Westermarck: 449) It is interesting to note that cruciform, eye, hand or cloven foot symbols have a long history of usage in Telemark agricultural life in general. (Berge 1942: 692f, 696)

As a material object, the Harding fiddle is a manifestation of highly-developed skills in wood-working and rose painting, reflecting the male traditions of lumbering and seafaring. But there is another tradition that is involved in the production of the Norwegian instrument. Indeed, there may have been a politico-economic reason for the choice of metal sympathetic strings at the time the *hardingfele* was being developed. Larsen tells us that, in the early part of the seventeenth century, the Danish king, Christian IV:

> . . . had a feverish eagerness to utilize Norway's supposedly fabulous mineral wealth, all of which, according to the theory of the age, was the property of the crown. He gave mining a great impetus, the effect of which was not lost throughout this period. The ironworks of the preceding century were continued and enlarged and new ones opened. . . . In spite of some crises the industry held its own through the years, and gradually the owners became residents and the capital Norwegian.
>
> (Larsen 1948: 299)

The Kongsberg silver mine was opened in 1624; copper mines followed, in 1633 and 1644. These facts are probably of more interest than simply supplying documentation for the availability of metal and metal-working knowledge for the manufacture of wire strings. It should be realized that fairs tended to be established at these important economic centers; and these fairs were of central importance to the fiddle tradition itself; instruments were bought and sold, music exchanged and the *spelemenn* made names for themselves at fairs. Most famous was the Kongsberg fair. (Bjørndal 1966: 235) The metal working skills had been highly developed in Norway at an early date, for intricate jewelry making as well as for more practical purposes; and "Nearly every farm had a smithy. . . . Iron was obtained in numerous bogs." (Stewert 1953: 116) Thus it would seem that the benefit of the formal development of these resources must have been partly, at least, of a sociological nature.

Just as a consideration of the Harding fiddle as a tool led to a focus on the magical powers of the *spelemenn*, the discussion of the instrument as a material object has taken us, once again, from the concrete to the intangible. The Danish scholar, Hortense Panum, has drawn attention to certain qualities of a medieval Scandinavian instrument she calls a "harp" that were also true of the ancient tradition in that area:

> In Nordic, especially the Danish folk-songs, the "harp" is frequently mentioned, often while emphasizing how magically impressive is the playing. It is still a private instrument, played by both men and women of the nobility. . . . The domestic harp of the folk-songs differed essentially from the harp of Nordic antiquity in being a domestic instrument, used especially by the nobles and in being used only for solos and not for accompanying song.
>
> (Panum 1940: 136f)

Information not available in Panum's day suggests, as we have seen, other correspondences between contemporary and ancient Nordic instruments—relating to musical style and type of instrument. It is, however, extremely interesting that she has noticed a similarity in reference to such qualities as solo function, elite usage, and magical powers. A combination of these suggests the ceremonial function; and, indeed, "harp" playing was considered one of the prime attributes of the hero: The warrior-king, Harold Sigurdarson (Hardrádi), boastfully proclaims:

> Of art-skills, eight have I:
> Ygg's-mead can I brew well,
> hardy am I on horseback,
> at home in the water,
> Skill have I on skis, eke,
> skull a boat well, and am
> handy at shooting, harp with
> my hands, am good at riming.
>
> (Hollander 1968: 200)

In the body of Eddic poetry that has come down to us, there is no example more pregnant in meaning than Völuspá (the Seeress's Prophecy). The eleventh century author, in portraying the coming doom of the old religion, chooses to picture a solo harpist playing as the cock crows (Einarsson 1957: 26f):

> Gladsome Eggthur, the herdsman of giants,
>   sits there in the pasture playing the harp.

The Crimson cock—Thus is Fjalarr called—
crows around him in the wild goose forest.

(verse 36; my trans.)

The mystical quality of the above verse is entirely characteristic of musical performance in the old literature; the affective powers of music are insisted upon: its ability to make persons weep or creatures fall asleep, or even "rafters burst asunder." (Andersson 1930: 145; Felber 1911: 177) It is probably not accidental that the Old Norse work, *gol*, has a triple meaning. Here it obviously refers to the crowing of a rooster (with the usual proclamation symbolism); but the word also means the singing of magic charms; and, in addition, stands for that ultimate symbol of virility: the male sex organ.

The portrait of ancient Norwegian music that has emerged from the old sources appears to bear a number of similarities to that of the hardingfele tradition. "Harp" playing was considered an important skill for the hero to cultivate, and the "harp" player was highly regarded, not only for his ability, but also for certain affective (even supernatural) qualities that were assigned to music. The Harding fiddle, as we have seen, has also been associated with male heroic symbolism, and with a belief in the affective powers of music. The ceremonial function of the "harpist" is not clear, but he was certainly, at least socially, close to the courtly (and highly esoteric) poetic tradition of the skalds. The Hardanger fiddler has never belonged to a courtly nation, but he has maintained a ceremonial function in his society. In both traditions, the music itself is fundamentally solo music in which melody is constantly accompanied by a background of sound, both melody and harmony played by a single person. The bridgeless bowed-harp is paralleled in the Hardanger fiddle by a flat bridge and other features—including sympathetic strings—all functional attributes for this kind of music.

The constant adaptation of features from abroad to remarkably persistent local ideals: In summary, one can so characterize both the art and the music of Norway. In Norway, the inner and outer pulls are so strong that it has been called two nations within one:

> *The two Norwegian 'nations' came close to being distinguished by what is the commonest means of distinguishing one nation from another, namely, a difference in language.*
>
> (Smith 1962: 23)

Arne Martin Klausen has pointed to another dichotomy, one that has recently produced a conflict of ideas in the world of art; as egalitarian principles have been brought down upon the—also—traditional aristocratic values of the artists. (Klaussen 1979) It is impressive that the basic dichotomies of Norway—the combinations of land and sea, male and female roles, urban and rural tongues, egalitarianism and esotericism—cannot be equated with one another. It is their very interrelationships that are fundamentally characteristic of Norwegian culture. These interrelationships are reflected in the Hardanger fiddle, a symbol of the heroic that, at one and the same time, expresses the persistent and individualistic, idiosyncratic musical features of a mountain community.

The main argument of this chapter has concerned the essential nature of a musical instrument. It has been posited that an instrument is far more than its physical embodiment, which indeed is largely determined by a complex of functional characteristics. In this light, the meaning of the instrument is in the mental construct created by the structure of the music together with various kinds of associations brought about either by the sound of the music or the shape of the instrument. Thus, the *hardingfele* is no longer an anomaly: a foreign violin suddenly and inexplicably adopted in Norway; rather, it may now be defined as a highly esteemed, significantly decorated and shaped lyra violin whose remarkable longevity may be explained by a peculiar relevance to its culture. In the following chapters of this book, we will examine this mental construct itself: first, the music as it is structured by the *spelemann*; secondly, the system of rules through which it functions in society; finally, we shall examine its position in respect to Norwegian culture as a whole.

Aural Structuring

*I try to play something typical Telemark, so it's hard to understand.
But—if I can make it . . . Something, something of it I can make
. . . . What do you call it—the water that comes from the moun-
tains —and goes to every place before—it rests.*

Finn Vabø chose to play this tone painting[1] as a contrast to several "easy-
to-understand" pieces—all with symmetrical form and even beat; one
was a wedding march, another a short waltz. He played the example of a
lydarslått (listening piece) in a manner quite unlike that used for dance
music: a tempo rubato and a contemplative style both contributed to the
fantasia-like quality. (Ex. 7)

Ex. 7:   Example of a *lydarslått; Sagafossen:* (beginning)

After his performance, Vabø said:

> That's a fantasy . . . [to be] listened to—but that must be [by] peo-
> ple who know folk music. Because the best komponists who make
> music, they like this. The people who do not like it, they don't play
> anything . . . maybe they play the comb, you know?

While he was talking, Vabø made an excursion into the bathroom to retrieve a roll of toilet paper, which he held high to more dramatically illustrate his meaning.

Finn Vabø proceeded to demonstrate the difference between two varieties of the same traditional dance form: a *gangar* for listening as opposed
to a *gangar* for dancing. (Ex. 8[a], 8[b])

Ex. 8a

8b

   The *gangar* is one of the dance forms grouped under the rubric, *bygde-
dans:*

> The term refers to a category of folk dances, which, in popular per-
> ception, constitute the core of indigenous or national dances of
> Norway. The term belongs to the modern context of folk dancing
> and is a member of a set which also includes references to various
> revivals (mainly song-dances) as well as the more recent figure
> and couple dances of the nineteenth century called turdans and
> gammeldans . . .
>
> Within the geographic area of the hardingfele music . . . there are,
> in terms of rhythm, two main types of bygdedans: a) dances char-
> acterized by a fairly slow, heavy and elastic gait (2/4 or 6/8 meter)

constituting three kinds: gangar, rull and halling/lausdans; and b)
dances termed springar (3/4) which are characterized by 1) light
semi-running steps or 2) uneven ("limping") three-beat steps.

(Blom 1981: 306)

In the present chapter, we shall limit our considerations to the forms of
traditional music stressed by the musicians I came into contact with; they
were in agreement about selecting the *gangar, halling, springar,* and
bruremarsj (wedding march) as the principal forms of Norwegian traditional dance music. They were also in agreement concerning the importance of the slåtts meant for listening. However, their descriptions of the
latter brought to light the existence of several different types. The kind
demonstrated in the above examples by Finn Vabø is generally referred to
as the "old style" *lydarslått* and the seldom heard nowadays. It is associated with the western part of the country, especially Valdres; and the
style is usually—but not always—found applied to pieces that are basically gangars and hallings. Closely related in playing style (although very
different in composition) are newly composed slåtts that make up another
category of listening pieces; these are of an idiom reminiscent of nineteenth-century violin music: romantic tone poems usually depicting rural
scenes. Arne Bjørndal credits Sjur Helgeland with being the first to compose this kind of music (Bjørndal 1960: 131). My introduction to it was
through the playing of Gjermund Haugen (of Notadden, Telemark) who
performed some of his own *lydarslåttar* as a prelude to the church service
held during the 1967 Porsgrunn festival. I later met with Haugen (who,
the reader may remember, gave me my first lesson on the *hardingfele*); he
described his conception of the Norwegian traditional violin as being part
of a world of natural beauty—and indicated that he considered this style
of music to represent the appropriate contemporary idiom. In com-
menting on the increased popularity of the Hardanger fiddle during the
present century, Bjørndal tells us that: ". . . it has no longer the same
function as earlier. From being dance music it has become concert music, or to use *hardingfele*-terminology: the dance slåtts have become
lydarslåtts." (Bjørndal 1964: 170; my trans.) This trend has recently re-
versed itself in the urban areas of the country, where a newly-awakened
interest in traditional dancing has been manifested.

In reference to the great Valdres *spelemann*, Olav Moe, (b. 1872)
Bjørndal tells us:

He united the old dramatic tradition with lyric playing and he did
it well. His versions, for example, of Fanitullen, St. Tomasklok-

kelåten *and* Grihameren, *perhaps the most popular of the newer concert-slåtts, were made with discernment and musical style.*

(Bjørndal 1964: 61; my trans.)

Øystein Odden, for my benefit, dubbed a recording he had made in 1937 of Olav Moe playing *St. Thomasklokkelåten.* A transcription of the opening phrase may be found in Ex. 9a; this passage, thought to be based on an ancient *kulokk* (cow-call), contributes to the pastoral imagery of this piece of program music.

Ex. 9a

Tone-painting, which is so characteristic of listening slåtts in general, is often intimately associated with the tuning of upper and lower strings. Here we have a good example, for the strings are tuned to represent the sounds of bells; the open strings are played pizzicato toward the end of the *slått* in direct imitation of this sound. (Ex. 9b) As the reader may remember from the the preceding chapter, ethical connotations (the direct transference of mood to listeners) have long been an important part of Harding fiddle communication. The power to affect (even manipulate) the assemblage gave the *spelemann* a special role in the lengthy and complex traditional wedding ritual; and different kinds of listening slåtts were designed especially for particular aspects of the ceremony, related to time of day and function.

Ex. 9b

Nowadays, especially in Telemark, one is more likely to hear a kind of *lydarslått* that is performed with the *takt* (rhythm) of one of the traditional dance forms; in other words, it *could* be danced to but is not. The idea of dancing to *Førnesbrunen* (the *slått* associated with the grim legend about the martyred horse who died carrying corpses to the Rauland Church yard) is greeted with incredulity; yet the *gangar takt* is carefully foot-beaten by fiddler and listeners. Another important example of this kind of listening music is the *Kivlemøy* cycle of Telemark (where at least seven such slåtts are known to exist[2]). We shall again quote Johannes Dahle who played:

> . . . *three* Kivlemøy *slåttar, a gangar and two springars. They are very ancient and about the Christian religion. There were once three sisters who, they say, lived in the mountains and played musical instruments—probably the* lur—*on Sundays. They played so beautifully that the people in church were drawn outside to listen; whereupon the priest came out and turned them into stone. I have these slåtts from Knut Dahle, who got them from Håvard Gibøen, who had them from the old tradition.*
>
> (my trans.)

Both *Førnesbrunen* and the *Kivlemøy* cycle are considered, even among *lydarslåttar*, of exceptional difficulty; and the *spelemann* who is capable of performing them well has thus proven abilities of the highest order. It is of special interest that the difficulty of the *lydarslåttar* in general, and of the *Kivlemøy* pieces in particular, is not of the technical but rather of an interpretive kind. There exist, in addition, slåtts demanding a high degree of technical proficiency (e.g., the *Jørn's vrengja*—lit.: *Jørn's Intricacy* —slåtts of Valdres); and the player who executes them receives a different kind of admiration.

The *spelemann* has developed another type of listening music that is directly related to his function as dance accompanist: the playing of the prelude and postlude (*førespelet* and *etterspelet*) as well as segues from one dance piece to another; these may be more or less improvised (according to the skill and ingenuity of the performer) and may or may not use a dance rhythm.

Thus, it seems that the listening pieces themselves can serve at least four distinct functions: 1) to project a particular mood on the listeners for ritualistic or other purposes, 2) to evoke the extra-musical associations (partly through tone-painting) considered necessary to convey the full communication of a traditional legend, 3) to provide a test for the skill of the *spelemann*—either for virtuosity or artistry; and 4) as an integral part of the intricate communicative complex over which the *spelemann* presides as a dance fiddler, whether in resort hotel or for traditional wedding.

As the reader may recall (from the lead quotation of the *Ethnography*), Vabø emphasized the importance of the regional styles and identified them with geographical differences. In response to a request for a musical illustration for different "musical dialects," Vabø acquiesced, but apologetically, as was always the case when he played music from outside his own region:

> *Ja, I can show you a little how they play in Telemark. I cannot play very much—but maybe just a little of the way they play the same music we have here in the West—*

The selection presented for this comparison was *Nordfjorden,* a western springar that has taken root in most of the *hardingfele* territory since it was originally disseminated by the itinerant spelemann-rose-painter, Knut Lurås, of Telemark.[3] (Bjørndal 1952)

Ex. 10a: Fragment from Vesland Springar, Nordfjorden

10b: Same passage embellished in Telemark style

While Finn Vabø, in that initial interview, tried to impress upon me the importance of the regional dialects, I was more interested in discovering how much individual creativity was permitted or expected in this tradition. To the question of: "Could you tell, blindfolded, who was playing?" Vabø immediately replied in the affirmative. (I susequently found this to be true of all who were knowledgeable in the tradition.) Vabø went on to explain that there also exist streams of personal tradition that influence but do not contradict the regional ones. Furthermore a fine individual *spelemann* never simply replicates even his own version. In addition to correctness of regional and personal tradition, "You must add something from the heart." As an example of spontaneous individual creativity, Vabø played *Myllarguten's Siste Slått (Myllarguten's Last Slått),* also the piece he chose for his demonstration of the rubato style of performing listening slåtts. (See Ex. 2.) Of this slått, Vabø said: "There is something crying in it. I believe he *knew* it was the last music he ever played."

How do the *spelemenn* themselves conceptualize their aurality transmitted music? From the remarks quoted alone, we see that a number of lines of distinction are drawn according to 1) easy-to-understand as opposed to difficult-to-understand; 2) basic dance form; 3) function (including several different functions for the listening slåtts); 4) regional style; 5) individual style; and 6) individual performance (referring both to the stylistic traits of the important streams deriving from the playing of the great performers and the spontaneous interpretive traits that make one performance different from another).

Out of this welter of mental groupings can we extrapolate some of the rules that are used by the *spelemann's* head to guide the fingers? We shall begin our study with attributes of the Norwegian *hardingfele* music that have general relevance and later turn out attention to the characteristics that define particular genres within the tradition.

1. *General Characteristics of Hardanger Fiddle Music*

1.1 *Sound*

What are the individual elements that together set off *hardingfele* from *flatfele* music? It seems logical to begin where we left off in the last chapter: with the instrument itself, "a Norwegian lyra-violin with sympathetic strings." There, we posited that the physical shape of the musical instrument was only part of a mental construct produced by a combination of aural and visual stimuli and their associations.

It may be remembered that the term, "lyra-viol" (or its equivalent, "viol played lyra-way"), represented a concept impossible to understand according to the presently-accepted method of musical instrument classification, dependent as it is upon physical type and size. "Lyra-way" referred to features that were unlike in kind—not only characteristics of the instrument itself (flat bridge, small size, drone strings); but also of certain techniques (the simultaneous bowing of several strings and the use of scordatura tunings). Of course, it is clear that all these features, dissimilar though they be, were designed to produce the afore-mentioned thick-textured timbre, a kind of sound ideally suited to the stringed instrument that characteristically plays alone.

1.2 Harmony

The use of a large variety (at least 20) of scordatura tunings merits special attention; because, as Sybil Marcuse has pointed out, they have an important acoustical function to perform (See previous chapter, p. 124.)

In the case of the Harding fiddle, of course, the presence of sympathetic strings further augments this resonant backdrop of sound. As we have seen in the preceding chapter, the sympathetic strings appear to produce physically present bass tones. Thus the vibrating of open strings (and at least one of them customarily sounds as a drone at any moment during the performance of a *slått*) will initiate a thick complementary background to the music; and, to insure this, the sympathetic strings are also tuned variously, to accord with the tuning of the upper ones. The musical significance of this can only be fully understood if one realizes that the choice of tunings for both sets of strings determines the harmonic centers of the piece in question. For example, the most common tuning (*oppstilt*) for the upper strings is:

The matching arrangement for the resonance strings is:

Ex. 11

Slåttar played with this tuning may be expected to revolve around the note, *D*, usually focussing on *A* as a secondary tonal center.

Harding fiddle music is tonal, in the sense (opposed to atonal) that there are in fact pitch centers. It is not tonal, in the sense of tonality versus modality. But a *slått* usually departs from and returns to the original pitch focus, often utilizing an arched contour in so doing. The interim pitch levels frequently consist in the tones that lie two or three fifths from the original on either side; but other intervals may provide focal points, too. Whatever the pitch scheme of the piece is, it is closely related to the open strings (i.e., the tuning) of the instrument. Fourths and fifths predominate in the most usual tunings—for example, in the one we associate with the *flatfele*, *nedstilt* or *nedstilt bass* (lower-tuned bass):

bowed strings   sympathetic strings

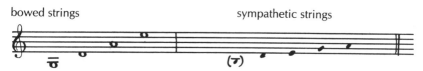

and the one called *kvinten nedstilt* (lower-tuned treble):

bowed strings   sympathetic strings

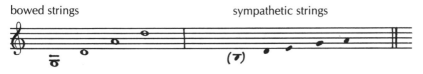

Ex. 12

1.3 *Ethos*

Other tunings include seconds, thirds, and sixths. *Trollstilt* (troll-tuning), to be used only between midnight and dawn, has a major third between the two upper bowed strings; and two minor thirds plus a major second between the understrings:

bowed: sympathetic:

Ex. 13

Again, pieces in troll tuning reflect, in their tonal structure, the emphasis of the major third of their tuning. Troll tuning is only one of a number of tunings that, as we have seen, have extra-musical associations.[4] Thus, it is important to realize that the tuning of both upper and lower strings is a matter, not only of structural harmonic importance to the piece, but also is often credited with producing the particular effect desired.

1.4 Tonality/Modality: Melody

Like the player of the "flat" violin, the *hardingfele spelemann* tunes the instrument by playing more than one string at a time, listening for acoustical beats. This is obviously of the utmost importance for the Hardanger violin; since even the tone quality of the instrument is dependent upon sympathetic vibration which can only occur between strings tuned to pitches that exist within the same harmonic series (just intonation). But just as the mainstream violinist plays tempered (and other) pitches within these focal points (see Chart 2), the Hardanger violinists use a variety of localized pitch systems in which the actual notes differ in frequency of vibration according to locality. It is quite clear that there is in existence no one "pure" scale, based on acoustically correct intervals, as has sometimes been thought in the past. (See Ledang 1974: 107; also Ledang 1969 and 1970) Thus, even the choice of pitch systems is controlled by the *spelemann*, who acts within the bounds of regional tradition.

Reference is frequently made to the fact that Hardanger fiddle music has what is deemed to be an archaic flavor, due to the use of modal scales—particularly the Lydian mode. This is true, insofar as the usual, somewhat superficial, associations with these modal patterns are concerned: However, it is more fruitful to see the music as composed of (disjunct) tetrachords—no doubt reflecting the constructional importance of the patterning of the player's four fingers. Thus, some *slåttar* may use a scale consisting of as many as three tetrachords; and, in overreaching the octave, it is likely to include chromatic pitches:

Ex. 14

The reader's attention is drawn to the first *lydårslatt* excerpt quoted above (Ex. 7), where this tetrachordal melodic construction results in the juxta-

(survey of proportionality in one octave) = temp.			just int.
A*	2,000,000	A	2,000,000
			1,976,423
Ab	1,887,749	Ab	1,897,099
		G#	1,874,736
		G#	1,852,636
G	1,781,797	G	1,799,492
			1,778,279
			1,757,317
F#	1,681,793	Gb	1,686,786
		F#	1,666,902
		F#	1,647,252
F	1,587,401	F	1,600,000
			1,581,139
			1,562,500
E	1,498,307	E	1,517,679
			1,499,788
			1,482,108
Eb	1,414,214	Eb	1,422,623
		Eb	1,405,853
		D#	1,389,280
D	1,334,840	D	1,349,429
			1,333,521
			1,317,802
C#	1,259,921	Db	1,264,911
		C#	1,250,000
			1,235,265
C	1,189,207	C	1,199,830
			1,185,687
			1,171,710
B	1,122,462	B	1,124,683
			1,111,424
			1,098,323
Bb	1,059,463	Bb	1,066,818
		Bb	1,054,241
		A#	1,041,813
A	1,000,000	A	1,011,929
			1,000,000

*This is an adaptation of a table from Eivind Groven's book, *Equal Temperament and Pure Tuning*, 1948.

Chart 2: Comparison of just intonation with equal temperament

position of the timbres of different strings, causing the ear to hear two successive voice parts rather than a single uninterrupted melody line. (Ex. 15)

Ex. 15: Melodic line from Ex. 7:

Also see Examples 8 and 9 for further illustrations of a characteristic kind of melodic dialogue that might be called single line polyphony and has been referred to as "compound melodic line" (Duetsch 1982) and inherent rhythms (Berliner 1978). The contrasting timbres of the strings, combined with the contrasting modal flavors, project the interplay of alternating voice parts that characterizes perhaps the most subtle of contrapuntal techniques—a technique also found in such disparate styles of music as Bach solo sonatas for flute or violin and African *mbira* composition:

> While Shona mbira compositions can be viewed in terms of their harmonic aspects, their most characteristic feature is the complexity of the relationship among the interwoven melodic lines. As mentioned previously, musicians themselves observe that a single mbira can produce the effect of two or more instruments being played simultaneously. One explanation for the apparent complexity of the music lies in a phenomenon known as "inherent rhythms." Inherent rhythms are those melodic/rhythmic patterns not directly being played by the performer but arising from the total complex of the mbira music. For example, in mbira music in which the hands typically play large melodic leaps, the ear does not necessarily follow the precise linear melodic patterns being played; it picks out pitches of a similar level and groups them in separate phrases
>
> (Berliner 1978: 33)

Thus, when one speaks of the polyphonic nature of *hardingfele* music, one is not referring only to its evident thick texture, although the vertical presentation of independent motivic material occurs. One is also making reference to an abstruse approach to melodic patterning. The pitch duality noted above may now be better understood: a tendency to play vertical intervals in just intonation coexists with horizontal melodic passages built up from tetrachordal scales that are not bounded by the octave.

1.5 *Form*

Form is a term that has disparate—even conflicting—meanings. It has often been pointed out that the word is commonly used with two different references: 1) the configuration of a particular piece of music, and 2) one of the particular genres, or types, of music that belongs to a particular tradition. A close study of these concepts, moreover, reveals a far more complex situation; for the first instance actually covers two different concepts: the shape in general (which might be said, paradoxically, to include formlessness) and the skeletal structure of a piece of music (the form of form-and-content). In addition, the word, "form" may also mean "version." When we refer to so-and-so's form of a *slått*, we are focusing on the flexible elements that compose the art of the *spelemann*; on the other hand, when we use the term in the sense of form-and-content, we are concentrating on just the reverse: the inflexible elements that cannot change without changing the very nature of the type itself.

For the purpose of the present study, we are interested in form in the organization of a piece of aurally-transmitted *hardingfele* music as perceived by the greatest authority: the *spelemann* himself. In order to explain the basic constructional principles of his music, Finn Vabø chose a graphic illustration:

> If I play a piece of the music—the old Norwegian music—. Let's say we get things like this—. What do you call that? A painting, ja. If I play the music, maybe, is—You can hear it like that:

Finn Vabø pointed to mountains in a landscape on his wall and drew on paper:

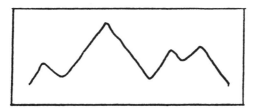

Ja—Like that:

Ex. 16a

And then I take—(pointing to his sketch)—Ja, I do like that—
make it more—

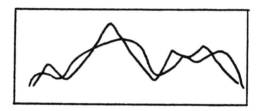

You know, you know what I mean? The point is—You must . . .
understand this . . . and then I put flowers on this—painting—

Ex. 16b

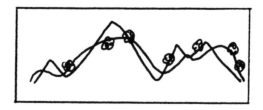

Vabø swung into an embellished version of the entire slått Nordfjorden.
He then proceeded to repeat both outline and finished version. The two
performances were remarkably similar; from these and subsequent ren-
ditions, I was able to extrapolate a number of versions of the opening
phrase—both in outline and embellished form (Ex. 17).

Ex. 17: Different performance by same player (Finn Vabø); comparison of *Nordfjorden*, opening phrase.

Finn Vabø devised the above illustrations to describe the structural form of *hardingfele* music: skeletal outlines embellished by the ingenuity of the individual *spelemenn* and within the traditional styles of particular regions. The melodic outline may be pre-existent (as in the example chosen by Vabø); or it may be part of a newly composed *slått*, which may, in turn, go out into tradition to become a model for infinite transformations by other players. Vabø was careful to explain that he was demonstrating the structure of the music, not showing how the piece might be approached or learned. No player (even a student) would normally play the melodic outline by itself, he emphasized. Thus, his demonstration is far more significant than appears at first; for it is an abstraction by the player himself, and it gives us a rare insight into what he has in his mind when manipulating the total complex of sound on his polyphonic instrument.

But when there was no necessity for keeping the music the same (e.g., for demonstration purposes), Vabø showed his ability to—as he put it—use different flowers; for, within a correct framework one must "add something from the heart." In Ex. 18, we have a comparative tabulation of a phrase taken from *Nordfjorden;* It includes two different interpretations by Vabø, as well as two versions from masters of Telemark traditions, Einar Løndal (Tuddall) and Johannes Dahle (Tinn).

The second Vabø improvisation is of particular interest; for it includes techniques of melodic contraction and amplification—both characteristic methods of traditional variation. For in addition to the more lavish use of ornamentation, the phrase is synthesized in a manner we shall term telescoping: we are presented with the beginning and the end, but the middle is cut short. The Dahle and Løndal examples, while distinct from one another, show a stylistic similarity as compared to the Vestland examples; and we can perhaps understand Vabø's description of Telemark elaboration as "up again and up again." The reader may wish to compare Ex. 10b (Vabø's imitation of Telemark style) with the samples under discussion; for the same phrase is at issue. Other typical techniques of variation are displayed in these examples: e.g. variation achieved through retrograde motion and through bowing change also, sometimes there is exact duplication. Taken all together—the augmentation, diminution, telescoping, and retrograde presentation of ideas—we find, in these short sample phrases, fine examples of the "capacité/anagrammatique" (the property of being "almost infinitely transformable"). (Lévi-Strauss 1971: 578)

The actual number of varied (and non-varied) repetitions of a motive within the hierarchical structure of *hardingfele* music is a matter that is left to the *spelemann's* choice. In his penetrating analyses of *hardingfele*

outline:

Vabø 2

Løndal (Blom 1981: 15)

Dahle (Blom 1981: 14)

Ex. 18: 4 different interpretations of phrase from Nordfjorden

variation technique, Tellef Kvifte has usefully defined the terms relating to components to this musical complex so that their meanings are mutually exclusive (which is not always the case in the natural course of events). In summary form, they are:

| *Slått* | The piece in all its versions. |
| *Fremføring:* (realization) | An actual performance of a slått, which may be divided into 2-4 sections. |

Omgang: (round)	Each section of a *fremføring,* which may be subdivided into at least 2 (and possibly many more) sections, equivalent in length.
Veks (vendslcr)	Subdivisions of the *omgang,* each of which contains a series, all emanating from a single melodic kernel.
Motiv: (motive)	The smallest unit referred to by the *spelemenn.*
Delmotiv:	Part of a motive. (Kvifte 1980: 12: Kvifte 1981: 102)

Kvifte uses concepts drawn from psycholinguistics to describe the possible conflict between playing the tune "the right way" and playing the tune "your way":

> The "right way" refers to a deep "structure" underlying the tune. This deep structure can be realized in many different ways that may differ musically but may be equally "right."
>
> (Kvifte 1981: 102)

Kvifte then proposes "a possible model for such a deep structure," for which the "obvious starting point is to ask the fiddlers how they perceive the formal structure of their tunes.":

> While playing the tune, the fiddler draws on a memory structure containing a) a limited set of motifs, one for each vek of the tune, b) a limited set of variations for each motif, c) a formal structure constructed like a hierarchy and d) a set of general techniques of variation that can be used in any tune.
>
> (Kvifte 1981: 103)

Just as the native speaker draws on more than a vocabulary or grammatical concepts, it is clear that flexibility (and therefore the opportunity for creativity) is built into the code of rules internalized by the *hardingfele* spelemann. To this end, Kvifte has pointed to a source of purposeful ambiguity: the precise line of demarcation between veks is sometimes impossible to draw according to the *spelemann* himself. While terminology can help explain this phenomenon (The term, *elision,* is useful here.), it is important to realize that the principle of flexibility can be (as it has been) incorporated into formal theoretical paradigms: the Indian *raga* system, for example, contains indeterminate, as well as definite, pitches. Kvifte has thus drawn our attention to a prime ingredient of the spelemann's system.

1.6 Rhythm: time

Rhythm is the most inclusive of the musical analytical features; for sound, melody, and harmony cannot exist outside of it (except, of course, in the abstractions presented by theory methods), and formal structure, in essence, is a kind of timing. The humble word, *timing*, used in the old days by music teachers, was appropriate after all; for the patterned manipulation of time itself is what music is about: perhaps the only general statement about music that can be made with any degree of certainty.

Thus, it may be noted that our discussion of the characteristic sound of *hardingfele* music is dependent upon techniques of tuning and playing that determine the tonal centers for each composition; these in turn produce the overall form of each *slått*: the most basic division of time. The comparative demonstration of a danced vs. a listening gangar showed that rhythmic elements can emanate from more than a single perspective —and for more than a single purpose. It should immediately be pointed out that anyone who equates the term, *rhythmic,* with the concept of equally-spaced beats is under a misapprehension. Both *lydarslåttar* and danced *slåttar* are not only "rhythmic"; also, they both can exhibit highly complicated rhythmic structures. Some of the most complex dance forms in the Norwegian tradition are founded on cyclical rhythmic patterns, each of which is composed of unequal beats that bear a subtle relationship to one another; this formulation, which is highly localized, is characteristically played against by polyrhythmic counterpoint in the music. A more detailed analysis of this matter may be found in the following chapter, which deals specifically with this element.

In a *slått* that has a recurrent cycle of beats, both player and audience audibly footbeat this aural foundation to the music—very much the way a Gospel chorus will clap on the off-beats or the Indian audience will keep the *tala*. But the melodic articulations that run counter to the basic *takt* in *hardingfele* music, are not achieved through stressed accents *per se*, but rather through the device of stylized embellishments. The use of musical ornamentation for this basically rhythmic purpose is not unknown; indeed, examples can be drawn from many different cultures: e.g., the Highland bagpipe tradition of Scotland, the Indian classical ensemble, as well as European harpsichord and organ music. In the case of the Harding violin, we could probably list this method of dividing up musical time as another "lyra-way" characteristic, for the relationship of this device to the uninterrupted accompaniment of background sounds is obvious: ordinary stressed accents simply would not be heard.

1.7 Performance Practice

In the foregoing paragraph, reference has been made to aspects of *hardingfele* music that are entirely different from anything usually associated with western European style: the entire rhythmic complex (the elaborate polyrhythmic, largely asymmetrical edifice); but there are also features that are similar to general European performance practice during the Baroque period of music history. It seems that, along with the basic shape of the *hardingfele* body and the "lyra-way" style, a number of features of the Baroque improvisatory style—particularly those related to violin music—have been retained in Norway; these were the aspects that were immediately comprehensible to me, when I first met up with the tradition. First and foremost, is the practice of improvisation upon melodic outlines, a style of improvisation not unlike that used in eighteenth-century European music. More accurately, we should refer to *styles*—for regionalism was an important part of the central European tradition of the time. An excerpt from the Italian Baroque school—written down for pedagogical purposes only—may serve to illustrate the point:

Ex. 19: Model of Baroque improvisation by Corelli (Schmitz 1953: 60)

In mainstream Europe, the practice of embellishing a simple melodic and harmonic structure—the only part of the music that appeared in notated form—began to give way toward the end of the Baroque to a progressive tendency to put more and more down on paper. The German composer, Johann Sebastian Bach, was severely taken to task by a contemporary music critic (Johann Adolph Scheibe, 1737) for being ahead of his time in this respect:

*Every ornament, every little grace, and everything that one thinks
of as belonging to the method of playing, he expresses completely
in notes. . . .*

(David 1945: 238)

There are other indications that certain aspects of Baroque style have
been perpetuated in the mountain pockets of Norway, along with elements that are totally dissimilar. One such feature is the practice of playing uneven subdivisions of the larger note values. The French composer,
Couperin, observed: "We write differently from what we play." (quoted
in Dolmetsch 1916: 53) and this type of rhythmic "alteration" was characteristic, not only of the French, but used to varying extents by the other
principal ethnic schools of the time. In the *hardingfele* tradition, uneven
subdivisions occur both in the short-long and the long-short variety—
with the first form predominating.

Also characteristic of Baroque practice is the on-the-beat accentuation
of ornaments. The typical *hardingfele* embellishment, the *likring,* is a trill
or mordent that is all but unknown today—even by performers of old European musical instruments who try to recreate Baroque performance
practice—but it was carefully described in 17th century instrument
methods. The pulsation of this kind of trill was so rapid as to make it, in
actuality, a kind of vibrato produced by two fingers. Christopher Simpson
gives directions for producing the ornament in his *Division-Viol* (1659):

Close-shake *is that when we shake the Finger as clóse and near the
sounding Note as possible may be, touching the String with the
Shaking finger so softly and nicely that it makes no variation of
Tone.*

(Simpson 1659: 11)

As was the case with the uneven rhythmic subdivisions, this ornament
was not restricted to a single locality, but was prevalent in different parts
of seventeenth-century Europe. Mersenne described it as an embellishment for both viol and violin playing in France; in reference to the latter,
he wrote:

. . . *the strings must be softened by some quavering which ought to
be done by the finger which is closest to that which holds fast to
the stop of the violin, so that the string may be nursed.*

(Mersenne 1636: 256)

We may compare a published description of the *hardingfele* ornament:

> . . . *Likring is an effect peculiar to Hardanger fiddle music. One*
> *starts as for a trill, but the finger does not leave the string . . .*
>
> (Osa 1952: 10)

From an analysis of photographed sound-wave patterns, Olav Gurvin has determined that, in the *likring,* "a tone does not have a stable frequency." (Gurvin 1953: 196) It is virtually impossible to produce this ornament with the left wrist held away from the neck. Thus, when violin technique changed to the vertical, position-playing variety (see Chapter 1), this ornament would no longer have been a possibility. The *hardingfele spelemann* has, of course, continued to use horizontal, across-the-string technique in the basically polyphonic music, and has continued to lock the left wrist against the neck. The right arm is brought down from above in the position we usually describe as the Russian bow·arm. See Ill. 13 for Ola Øyaland's demonstration of this left and right arm position.

2. Genres

> Genres function in culture by means of sets of distinctive features
> which are operative on cognitive, pragmatic, and expressive lev-
> els. The taxonomic features, the conceptual categories, and the
> terms to name them are indicative of the cultural concepts of folk-
> lore forms, and underscore their symbolic meaning. . . . Together,
> all these distinctive features of all three levels, of cognitive, behav-
> iour, and expression constitute a cluster of features which is a set
> of signs and meanings defining the symbolic significance of each
> genre in culture.
>
> (Ben-Amos 1976: 32)

What are the distinguishing features of a particular *slått* according to the *spelemenn* themselves? According to their own accounts, the *slåtts* vary according to: 1) rhythm, 2) melodic outline, 3) modality, 4) regional characteristics, 5) legendary association, 6) motivic structure, and 7) function. Which of these features are distinctive characteristics of the different genres?

A) Fundamental Emic Classification: the Gangar, Springar, Halling, and Bruremarsj

The most fundamental classification of this material to the *hardingfele spelemenn* is its grouping into the genres named for the *bygdedansar*. Scholars have assumed that the characteristics of these genres have been derived from their dance function. Even though Alver and Bjørndal documented the prevalence of listening slåtts at their time, they nonetheless stated:

> *The* slått *music is, first and foremost, dance music. . . . Considering that the* gangar, halling, *and* springar *are tied to dancing. Eivind Groven thinks that they are most probably designed by it. A better formulation would probably result if one were to substitute "for it" for "by it."*
>
> (Bjørndal 1966: 99; my trans.)

Thus, the various *slått* forms are commonly defined in terms of their rhythmic nature, which is assumed to be derivative of their dance function. However, recent research has uncovered a far more complex picture. Egil Bakka has pointed out that, while: ". . . it is natural to reckon *bygdedansar* and *gamaldansar* as two *genrar*," (Bakka 1982: 227) it is not so easy to point objectively to the distinctive characteristics that distinguish the individual *bygdedansar* from one another: (Bakka 1982: 227)

> *In the areas where we found both springar and gangar in a certain tradition, the two dance-types have the same construction and the same motives and are separated from one another only by unlike music and dance rhythm.*
>
> (Bakka 1982: 228; trans.)

The *gangar* (from the word, *gang*, "walk") is a stately ceremonial dance that lends itself to transcription in either 2/4 or 6/8 meter, according to whether the subdivisions are of the duple or triple variety. The 6/8 *gangar* is usually characterized by a horizontal oscillation of three and two-note groupings (hemiola). These patterns are superimposed over evenly-spaced foot-tapping in a duple meter. The rhythmic counterpoint between bowing rhythm and foot-tapping thus produces vertical combinations of threes and twos as well.

The springar (from *spring*, "run" or "bound") is lively and usually defined as possessing triple meter, although actually the form exhibits even greater diversity than does the gangar:

> *Springar dances can display a significant amount of variation within the four-part organization on a regional basis. Whereas one dance may feature a lengthy and varied vendingsdel (as found in springar dances from Hordaland, Sogn, and Sunnfjord), another may involve little more than the woman making one or two turns beneath the man's uplifted arm (as in springleik from Vågå, Gudbrandsdal). Dance meters are equally diverse, falling into one of three categories: 3/4 time, asymmetrical 3/4 time (in which one or more beats are of slightly unequal length according to a fixed pattern per measure), and no measure divisions. . . .*
>
> (Beal 1984: 240)

Moreover, it may be remembered that the *hardingfele* slåtts are not only used for dance purposes: *lydarslåttane* are designed for listening, not dancing at all. Furthermore, when a *gangar* (or other form) appears as a listening *slått*, its rhythmic nature may be essentially different. In the old style, the characteristic rhythmic patterns are not apparent, and there is a meandering, fantasia-like exposition of the material, sometimes presented in *tempo rubato*. Particularly interesting, then, is the fact that a close inspection of a representative selection from each *genre* suggests, a third distinctive feature in three of the four *genres* under discussion. The *gangar, springar*, or *halling* meant for listening each seems to have retained its peculiar type of motivic construction. Thus, it should be interesting to investigate the extent to which the symbolic significance of these genres is restricted to functional necessity. With this idea in mind, I would like to discuss the three distinctive features (function, rhythm, and motivic structure), as they relate to each of the *slått* forms under consideration.

The rhythmic structure of the *springar* and *gangar* is intricate and very different in character from that found in any other European tradition. Characteristic are abrupt shifts from vek to vek accomplished through the elision of the last motive of the first vek with the first motive of the succeeding one, Footbeating by performer and audience is used as a background—a foil—against which the complex counter-rhythms may be felt. As mentioned above, subdivisions of the beat are performed unevenly; ornaments mark off the counter-rhythms in the melody and are usually accented on the beat, taking time from the principal note; again,

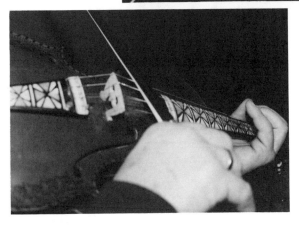

13. The mind directing the fingers. Ola Øyaland demonstrates playing position.

as noted above, the syncopated bowing style lends still another element to the total complexity of the rhythmic scheme.[5]

The acrobatic halling has none of these complexities and consistently utilizes a duple rhythmic structure. Elision between phrases is not uncommon, however, sometimes effecting syncopation between footbeating and music-accents that may continue throughout an extended period of time. The only form based on a completely even and symmetrical beat structure is the wedding processional; and, even here, there may be a hidden suprise. It is characteristic of the wedding march to have an abrupt shift of accent through the occasional addition of an extra beat. No one seems to know the reason for this (although some have guessed it to be a trap for the unwary marcher); if it occurs, it always occurs consistently at the same point of the march.

Motivic structure can best be studied through the use of analytical graphs; for these diagrams, I have used a free interpretation of the Jan LaRue timeline system. Ex 20(a) gives the opening melodic line of a gangar that was transcribed from the playing of Svein Løndal and published in *Norsk Folkemusikk* (Gurvin I: 154). Underneath is a timeline representing the motivic development of the same 13 measures.

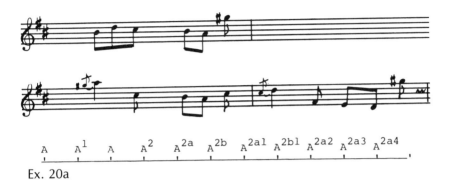

Ex. 20a

The method of motivic development observable in this example seems to be the generating principal behind *gangar* construction as a whole: new motivic elements are added successively to old material from the preceding phrase in a chain-like formation. Thus, the last element may well have grown into something entirely unlike the first; in this particular example, the opening motives (A, A'):

Ex. 20b

develop logically into very different motivic material:

Ex. 20c

to conclude, at the very end of the *slått:*

Ex. 20d

For this technique, I have selected the term, "growth". (Hopkins 1978)

For an example of a *springar,* I have chosen *Rakstejenta,* as composed and played by Johannes Dahle (my recording and transcription). This illustration is again presented as typifying its kind. While chain-like motivic growth occurs to a limited extent, it is subordinate to the more customary phrase variation technique. As may be observed in the example, phrases are commonly defined by musical rhyme and presented in a parallelism reminiscent of the medieval sequences, often with open and closed endings. Motivic material from the opening theme may be drawn upon later for new development or transformation, as happens in the stretto-like concluding section (where motives clearly derive from the third measure of the opening line). The over-all effect is of a patterned design that is in complete opposition to the principle of organic growth that characterizes the *gangar*. (See Ex. 4 and Ex. 21)

Ex. 21

In the motivic structure of a *halling*, one may observe only the suggestion of chain formation in the background of what is predominantly new material. (See *Tåkatind: Ex. 5*) The Bridal march shows the patterned type of variation technique we observed in the springar but presented in simple and more symmetrical form; note especially the "open and closed" endings of Example 3.

B) *Legend Cycles*

Hardingfele music, as we have seen above, can be, and has been, classified in different ways for different purposes. The *spelemenn* refer to cycles of *slåtts* based on individual legends, and these groupings may be set off from one another by more than this single distinctive feature. The reader's attention is again drawn to the *Kivlemøy* cycle of Telemark.[2]

C) *An Etic Classification*

Morton Levy, the Danish ethnomusicologist who has made a specialty of studying the Setesdal *hardingfele* tradition, has noticed that the group of *slåttar* using *gorrlaus* tuning share a number of characteristics in common. *Gorrlaus* (loose string) tuning is unique to Setesdal and all the slåtts that utilize it are gangars.

> *In Setesdal today are found three different* gorrlaus slåttar. *That is to say, they are known by the local people as three different* slåttar, *but for scientific systematization and analysis of them, it is better to call them three* slått *types. . . . One of these three types has its own name. . . .:* Norafjells. *Each of the gorrlaus slått-types has its own rhythmic foundation and it is possible to separate them from one another. They can unequivocally be defined in relation to each other by the rhythmic beginnings, while the tonal foundation is the same in all* gorrlaus slåttar. *By this common tonal ediface, which is constructed over the bottom F string, one can, on the other hand, separate them from all other Setesdal* slåtts.
>
> (Levy 1974: 82; my trans.)

Gorrlaus tuning is as follows:

bowed strings: sympathetic strings:

Ex. 22

Morton Levy, from the analytical point of view, has noticed some interesting correspondence amongst these pieces, not only in regard to tuning system, but also in respect to rhythm and tonality (ibid.); they also share, of course, the same regional base. (See *Chart* 3 for a comparison of different kinds of *genre* groupings.) The players do not deny the existence of these relationships, but simply attach no significance to them. To the outside researcher, who is trying to understand all musical associations, the existence of this grouping may be enlightening.

For the description of general characteristics of *hardingfele* music, I have kept as close as possible to the data supplied by the fiddlers themselves; concerning these features, there is general agreement among the *spelemenn* of the different regions in which I worked (Hordaland, Telemark, and Hallingdal). The analysis of musical structure presented by Finn Vabø himself, as noted above, gives us an insight into the mind of the performer of non-written-down music and clearly demonstrates the purposefulness that can exist in an aural musical tradition. It is particularly significant that Vabø chose a visual analogy for his presentataion. European "art" (i.e., mainstream) music has become so closely involved with an elaborate system of pictorial representation of music (Hopkins 1966) that it is often defined by it; and Vabø who, we may remember, did not feel that his music could be learned by notation (See Part I), himself chose a visual means of describing its structure.

Conscious control of his resources may also be observed in a spelemann's use of scordatura tunings for his instrument; a matter, as we have seen, that affects not only the *timbre* but also determines the tonality of the music. The complexity of this tonal material is further evidenced by the coexistence of two different determining factors; (the tendency to play acoustically correct intervals vertically along with horizontal passages showing tetrachordal construction).

In the fundamental *genre* grouping, the rhythmic nature of the danced and listening *slåtts* is highly diverse. Therefore, it seems that the distinctive character of each *slått* type is partly maintained through motivic organization. Motivic organization, rhythm and function—as distinctive features in *hardingfele genre* differentiation—point to the existence of a cluster of genre determinants (not necessarily related). (See Chart 4)

This notion is very close to the position of Lévi-Strauss who speaks of flexible molds that are constantly being transformed by individuals. In reference to music, he is particularly explicit: Composers use "the works of their predecessors as a point of departure for creating works that none-

Fundamental genres

	DG	LG	DS	LS	DH	LH	B	K	G
Function	+	+	+	+	+	+	+	+	+
Rhythm	+		+		+		+		+
Legend								+	
Mode									+
Melodic outline								+	
Region								+	+
Motivic structure	+	+	+	+	+	+	+		

DG	. . . .	danced *gangar*
LG	. . . .	listening-*gangar*
DS	. . . .	danced *springar*
LS	. . . .	listening-*springar*
DH	. . . .	danced *halling*
LH	. . . .	listening-*halling*
B	. . . .	*bruremarsj*
K	. . . .	*Kivlemøy* cycle
G	. . . .	*Gorrlaus* cycle

Chart 3: Distinctive features of the different genre groupings

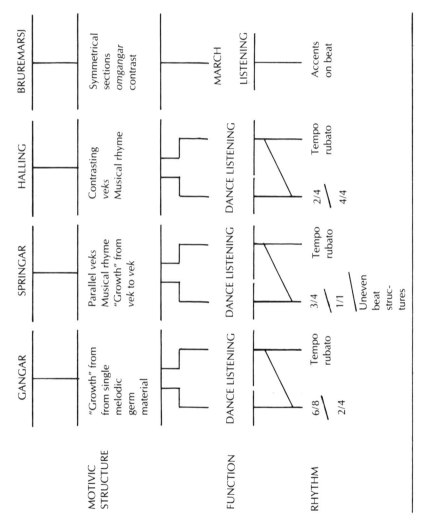

Chart 4: Distinctive Features of the Four Fundamental Genres

theless have marked individual styles impossible to confuse with one another." (1971: 578; my trans.) Alan Dundes expresses a similar point of view in his introduction to Propp's *Morphology of the Folktale:* "And how precisely is fairy-tale structure learned from hearing many individual fairy-tales? Do children become familiar enough with the general nature of fairy-tale morphology to object to or question a deviation from it by a storyteller?" (1968: XV) Perhaps this explains why our cowboy stories must have good and bad characters (but none in-between)—and why it is possible to write an "anti-cowboy story"; or why novels almost invariably concern themselves with persons in their youth.

Hardingfele players do indeed learn their tradition through memorizing a large number of individual pieces. Only when they have completely mastered such a body of material are they permitted to add anything at all of their own. This long apprenticeship system, which is characteristic of musical instruction in a number of different cultures, serves (as Dundes suggests) to transmit concepts of *genre* from one generation to another.

But this agreed-upon cluster of distinctive features sets off the material in its most fundamental fashion, the same material may be divided meaningfully in other ways for different purposes. Thus, the picture that emerges of *Hardingfele* fiddle music is of a body of aural tradition that is structured, classified and transmitted according to elaborate rules that are tacitly acknowledged whenever the *spelemann* plays, or the knowledgeable listener responds appropriately.

Aural Thinking

I shall never be able to dance to the playing of my husband; for he was born and brought up in Hallingdal, while I was brought up on Telemark music.

Dagne Groven Myhren

Magne Myhren agreed. The discussion, concerning regional characteristics of the springar dance form, took place in 1967. More than 15 years later (in 1983), Dagne Myhren reaffirmed the truth of the statement: ". . . even though I have danced to Magne's playing":

> *In fact, just recently, I danced the* hallingspringar *in public. but my dancing the* Telespringar *and the* Hallingspringar *are two different things; it's not the same. The point made is correct; and it says something important about the essential nature of our tradition.*

The high degree of significance accorded these subtle differences may be inferred from the point of view expressed in the above quotations, a matter Jan Petter Blom has drawn to our attention: "It is the quality, not the amount of variation that matters, a fact that accounts for the observation that fiddlers and dancers, objectively speaking as well as according to native theory, have difficulty in achieving competence in more than one local tradition." (Blom 1981: 310)

I The Problem

The extremely esoteric nature of the *hardingfele* tradition demonstrates the necessity of having specialized knowledge (and that acquired early in life) in order to perceive this music as it is meant to be perceived. In more general terms, it highlights the problems involved in approaching any unfamiliar music. To what extent will our understanding be impeded or enhanced by previous knowledge and experience? Our attention is thus drawn to the cognitive component in music perception; and this may be seen as crucially important in understanding the nature of the difficulties involved in attempting to acquire what Mantle Hood has called "bi-musicality":

> Perhaps it is not necessary to remind the reader that we are speaking of the world of music, that training in basic musicianship of one order or another is characteristic of cultivated music wherever it is found and to some extent is unconsciously present in the practice of ingenuous music. It may be some comfort to the music student of the West to realize that the Chinese, Javanese or Indian student also must jump through a series of musical hoops. But if this kind of training is indeed essential, the Western musician who wishes to study Eastern music faces the challenge of "bi-musicality."
>
> (Hood 1960: 55)

Aurally transmitted and unattached to any formalized theoretical system, the Hardanger violin tradition is undoubtedly the kind of tradition that Hood had in mind, when he referred to "ingenuous music." Just how much, and what kind of, training (unconscious or not) is necessary for an intelligent understanding of this kind of music is an important (and so far unanswered) question. The attitude expressed in Dagne Myhren's comment (see head quotation, above) indeed indicates the presence of a strong cognitive component in this Norwegian folk tradition. Yet, many have refused to acknowledge the existence of thinking without a verbal manifestation:

> The writer for one, is strongly of the opinion that the feeling entertained by so many that they can think, or even reason without language is an illusion. . . . Once more, language, as a structure, is on its inner face the mold of thought. . . . It is doubtful if any other cultural asset of man, be it the art of drilling for fire or of chipping stone, may lay claim to a greater age. I am inclined to believe that it antedated even the lowliest developments of material culture, that these developments in fact were not strictly possible until language, the tool of significant expression, had taken shape.
>
> (Sapir 1921: 15, 21f, and 23)

More recently, an author has expressed the commonly-held view: that aural tradition implies something other than a deliberately structured art form, something that needs to be "fixed" in a notational system:[1]

> *Among such peoples (West African) a drummer may, either*
> *alone or in combination with others, create incredibly complex*
> *contrapuntal rhythms, which disappear at the moment of inven-*
> *tion; they are not fixed in any system of notation.*
>
> (Diamond 1974: 298)

The above words were offered to refute the opinion of Lévi-Strauss: that music is one of the prime manifestations of thinking (1971: 577 and 581f); the author was drawing attention to the fact that Lévi-Strauss has focused on European art music which he assumed to be highly organized because of the existence of a system of notation.

But John Blacking has defined music, whether improvised or not, as "humanly organized sound" and further suggested ". . . that a perception of sonic order, whether it be innate or learned, or both, must be in the mind before it emerges as music." (1974: 11) Thus, it would seem that a detailed study of how skilled musicians from outside the Norwegian *hardingfele* tradition initially perceive, and then try to understand, the esoteric rhythmic component described above may give us a significant insight into the nature of this music; by extension, it may tell us something about the cognitive element in aurally transmitted music in general. The musical feature chosen for this study seems especially well suited to the subject, for it happens to be a feature that defies notation of any kind.

Linguists, aided by the development of information theory, have done interesting work on the influence of phonological systems upon the perception of speech patterns (see Fry 1970 and Fudge 1970). However, it is the perception of non-verbal patterns of communication in which we are interested. The intangible qualities of musical perception make this study far from straightforward; as has recently been observed;

> *The optimistic view of classical neurology that musical func-*
> *tions are clearly localized has not been verified. Not only are fixed*
> *anatomical representations unattainable for the various aspects of*
> *musical perception, memory, or performance, but even basic mu-*
> *sical operations—such as chord or melody perception and identi-*
> *fication, music reading, or vocalization—seem to be fairly com-*
> *plex processes that are manifested with considerable individual*
> *variability. . . .*
>
> (Deutsch 1982: 469)

In music (as opposed to language):

> . . . we are dealing with a system of communication in which each
> piece of music consists of a few non-referential items that are com-
> bined according to the prevailing stylistic "syntactic" rules of har-
> mony, melody, timbre, rhythm, or musical form. Music is thus a
> game of combinatory acoustical constructs that the brain of the
> composer can conceive and that the listener should be able to
> learn or discover. For the latter, the intelligence of the communi-
> cation resides in processing the musical message in such a way as
> to gain conscious or unconscious access to the rules and its forms
> . . . .

> (Deutsch 1982: 471)

The art historian and psychologist, Rudolf Arnheim, has drawn an
analogy between abstract art and music: "In a successful piece of abstract
art or music, a pattern of forces transmit its particular blend of calmness
and tenseness, lightness and heaviness—a complete transubstantiation
of form into meaningful expression." (Arnheim 1939: 10) In another
work, the same author has made a detailed study of what he has termed
"visual thinking," an interest that stemmed from his extreme dissatisfaction with the status of the arts in academic institutions:

> The arts are neglected because they are based on perception,
> and perception is disdained because it is not assumed to involve
> thought. In fact, educators and administrators cannot justify giving
> the arts an important position in the curriculum unless they under-
> stand that the arts are the most powerful means of strengthening
> the perceptual component without which productive thinking is
> impossible in any field of endeavor. The neglect of the arts is only
> the most tangible symptom of the widespread unemployment of
> the senses in every field of study. What is most needed is not more
> aesthetics or more esoteric manuals of art education but a con-
> vincing case made for visual thinking quite in general.

> (1969: 3)

Arnheim has compared the historically "high esteem of music" with "the
disdain of the fine arts" (1969: 2); but, as Charles Seeger has pointed out:
"It was communication in speech about music, not communication in
music itself that had a place in the quadrivium." (1961: 78).[2]

Arnheim's work examines—and indeed builds a powerful case for
—the intellectual component in the visual arts; but certain of the conceptual tools he uses have proven themselves to be useful for a somewhat

analogous study of aural perception. In this chapter, I am going to describe the method I have used to obtain the reactions of skilled musicians trained in different musical cultures, when they are presented for the first time with a sample of music from the totally unfamiliar—to them—Hardanger fiddle tradition. For the particular musical component to be tested, I have chosen the *springar* rhythmic structure.

II *The Experiment*

Described by Finn Vabø as "the soul of Hardanger fiddle music," the *springar* has a special significance to the *spelemenn*; and a student is considered to have reached a milestone, when he is ready to learn his first *springar*. It is danced to a lively tempo in triple meter, and it may also occur as a *lydarslått* (listening *slått*)—not intended for dancing at all. It is the normal, danced *springar*, with its recurrent, three-beat cycle, that we shall be concerned with here in this study. The rhythmic composition of this dance is extremely complex and may be characterized as consisting of the following features:

1. Several large sections, usually of contrasting tonalities that result from the utilization of different open strings as tonal centers.

2. A number of equal-lengthed phrases within each section. Each phrase is often repeated literally or close to literally and usually contains two or more occurrences of the basic three-beat pattern.

3. The beat pattern, which differs both as to stress and as to duration according to locality. In several regions the beats are of the unequal variety more commonly associated with Bulgarian dance music.

4. The subdivisions of the beat, which are characteristically uneven (usually of the short-long variety).

5. Ornaments, containing odd numbers of little notes; they are usually accented on the beat and consequently must take time from the first of the uneven units:

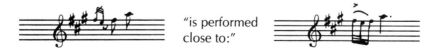

"is performed close to:"

6. The bowing style, which involves a characteristic slurring across the beat, a factor that produces syncopated articulations in the drones and polyphony of the lower voices.

Superimposed upon all this, there may be abrupt shifts from one phrase, or one section, to another. This is sometimes the result of elision (the last beat of a phrase coinciding with the first beat of the new one); and sometimes the result of cross-rhythms in the melodic line.

Fundamental to this rhythmic edifice is the three-beat pattern which is of such structural importance to the totality that not only the fiddler but also the audience foot-beats while the music is playing (much in the spirit of the Indian audience keeping the *tala*.) Indeed, the full effect of deliberately contrasting accentual patterns in the melodic line of a particular section (and their resolution) can best be felt by the listener who is experiencing this foot-beating. I have delimited the scope of my experiment to this element in the Hallingdal and Telemark versions of the *springar*. In Telemark, the second of the three beats receives the accent and the last is somewhat shorter than the other two (which differ even less from one another). In contrast, the *Hallingspringar* has a short, accented first beat and longer second and third beats which are nearly equal in length and stress to each other.

Record companies have not understood the inherent importance of the foot-beaten pattern and have taken care to dub out this sound from their commercial recordings. I have been able to take advantage of this omission and thus chose five springars from RCA *Norsk Folke-musikk* discs for my taped examples, which include:

1. *Jon Vestafe,* played by Kjetil Løndal (Tuddal, Telemark) after Svein Løndal. (FEP 46)

2. *Hallingstuga,* played by Odd Bakkarud (Nes, Hallingdal) after Knut Tuen. (FEP 32)

3. *Rjukanfossen,* played by Johannes Dahle (Tinn, Telemark) after the composer, Knut Dahle. (FEP 22)

4. *Igletveiten,* played by Kjetil Løndal (Tuddal, Telemark) after Leif Sandsdalen. (FEP 46)

5. *Vrengja,* played by Odd Bakkerud (Nes, Hallingdal) after Knut Tuen. (FEP 32)

The demonstration tape contains lengthy portions from the beginnings of the examples (in the order listed above). Each of the selections is long enough to include several sections and, in each case, represents more than half the entire slått. In the three interviews that have been made thus far, each musician recorded his or her perceptions of the basic structure during an hour to an hour and a half long work session. They were informed beforehand that there was a regularly recurrent cycle of beats and that the beating of this pattern would be audible in a live performance of the music. The three musicians consulted in this project were:

1. *L. Shankar, who is a well known virtuoso both in his native India and in this country. He has made numerous recordings, has taught Indian violin playing at Wesleyan University and has written a doctoral dissertation on that subject. He holds a Ph.D. in world music.*

2. *Michael Kaloyanides, who plays bouzouki, lyra, guitar and percussion instruments. He has performed in rock and Greek bands, has made field trips to Greece and Turkey for ethnomusicological research, and learned to play the lyra while living in Crete. Kaloyanides also holds a Ph.D. in world music from Wesleyan University where he wrote a dissertation on Cretan music; he is now a faculty member of the University of New Haven.*

3. *Blanche Blitstein, who majored in violin and in music education for her Bachelor and Master of Music degrees. She has done orchestral work under such conductors as Jonel Perlea and Leon Barzin and is at present a string specialist in the Long Island school system.*

It may be noted that the musicians participating in this project are players of fiddle-type instruments; all had extensive applied and theoretic training in music, and all have functioned professionally both as teachers and as performers.

In studying the response of these musicians to previously unknown music, we have been interested in ascertaining to what extent their perception is a passive reception of the material and to what extent it is dependent upon (and inextricably involved with) active cognitive operations. To this end, we have asked five basic questions:

A) Was the music meaningfully transmitted immediately? (*The Initial Perception*)

B) How did the perceptions of the three interviewed musicians compare with one another? (*Three Different Perceptions*)

C) Upon finding their original perceptions of the music to be unreliable, how did the musicians proceed? (*Search for Appropriateness*)

D) What features came to light during the restructuring process? (*Aural Concepts*)

E) How did the musicians themselves sum up their experience? (*Judgments*)

In evaluating the responses of the musicians, I have made use of a number of terms and concepts that have been derived from the work of Rudolf Arnheim. These include: active exploration, focusing, selection, completion, correction, synthesis, combining, separating, simplification, memory, comparison, abstraction, concept formation, putting into context, learning, reappraisal, confirmation, deepening of understanding. (Arnheim 1969)

The role of the consulted musicians (as will become evident) is one of active participation in the project. This study is essentially a collaborative enterprise. The original ideas grew out of my own experience with the *hardingfele,* especially in striving to play the instrument idiomatically from instructions of the *spelemenn* in Norway.

During the working out of the project itself, I have benefitted from an active correspondence with Norwegian musicians and scholars. At each stage of my work, they have provided me with intellectual feedback and other assistance—including tapes made expressly for the project.[3]

III *Mechanical Measurement of the Beat Pattern*

In order to obtain a machine's eye view of the beat pattern, I worked with the equipment of the Mason Laboratory, Yale University.[4] To produce a graphic representation, we used a variable band pass filter to screen out all high frequencies and a level chart recorder to produce a visual pattern on paper. (See Chart 5) I have used this method to analyze the beating on a tape especially prepared for this purpose in Norway; it consists of a re-recording of the five *springars* represented on the demonstration tapes.

The wave pattern pictured in Chart 6 provides impressive proof of the

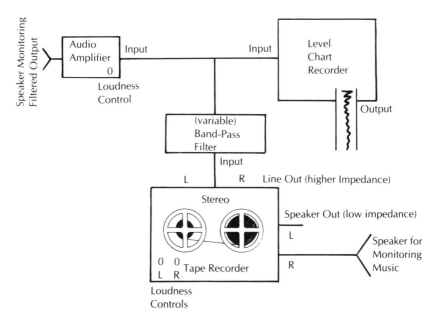

Chart 5: Apparatus used for analysis of foot-beaten patterns.

regularity of the uneven beat cycle. This design was produced by the beginning of Jon Vestafe (Ex. 23), the first example on the demonstration tape. One should realize that the ratio 18-15-10 is maintained at a lively tempo.

Eivind Groven, who some years ago analyzed foot-beaten structures of the *hardingfele* music through hand pricking rolls of moving paper, similarly found examples of astonishing consistency. (Groven 1971: 99ff) The fact that such consistency can exist is important evidence of the purposefulness and control of musical execution in this tradition. Perhaps even more important to the theme of this paper, however, is the large area in which mechanical representation of the beat structure does not convey the (nevertheless communicated) intentions of the musicians. The individual expression of a particular performance must include the special inflections, ritards, and accelerandos that result from the articulations of personal communication. Even more impossible to deduce from the mechanical record is a perceived beginning or ending. Indeed, no slått will actually be performed so rigidly that a ratio like the one in our first exam-

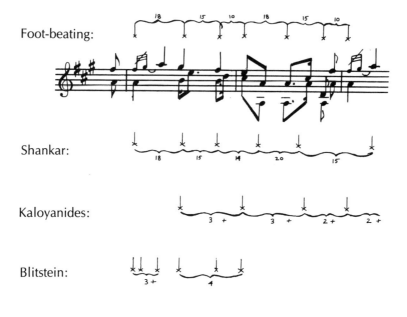

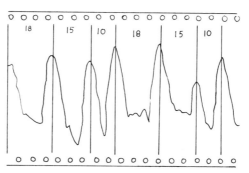

Example 23: Comparison of Pattern Perception. *Jon Vestafe* (after Knut Dahle), played by Kjetil Løndal (Telemark) Structural rhythmic pattern as perceived by Shankar, Kaloyanides, and Blitstein, followed by a mechanical representation of the actual foot-beating (where comparative distance-comparative time).

ple will be maintained throughout. It is interesting to note the findings of the psychologist, Carl Seashore, in respect to this matter. Not understanding the important area of interpretive license (that has to exist in any musical tradition that includes performance), he expressed amazement that

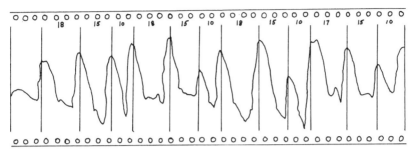

Chart 6: Mechanical representation of *Jon Vestafe* phrase

the measurements of sound wave patterns made by famous pianists, violinists, and singers, showed great areas of divergence from musical notation. (Seashore 1938: 288; see *Notes on the Transcriptions.*) Thus, it turns out that the machine's eye view, while extraordinarily useful for analytical purposes, is—in respect to significant communication—a completely uninitiated observer.

IV *The Taped Interviews*

A) *The Initial Perception:*

All three musicians listened silently to the five taped examples and then requested at least three hearings of *Jon Vestafe* before offering any comment whatsoever. It was clear that, in each case, the initial perception of the music did not include a recurrent beat pattern. This is especially noteworthy; because (as mentioned above) the listeners had been informed of the existence of such a structure at the onset of the interview, and their attention was focused on this matter. It is clear that the musicians, like the machine, were uninitiated observers.

B) *Three Different Perceptions:*

A second phase of the investigation began when the musicians sought means for uncovering that which was not readily apparent. Shankar continued for some time to express skepticism concerning my reiterated assertions that there was, in fact, a rhythmic cycle:

Shankar: Well, I don't think it's in any tala.

Hopkins: I should say that there is a regular beat structure that re-
           peats—that is, that is repeated over and over again.

Shankar: No, no what I mean is: it is not based on any particular
           cycle.

Hopkins: Yes, it is.

Shankar: Is it?

Hopkins: Yes, yes—and—and this cycle is important as a back-
           ground and it is—

Shankar: Yes, I can see the opening theme (sings)—but the thing is,
           it's not like—similar—following strict beats, you know,
           compared to South Indian—so—they might go a little
           faster and slower, or sometimes it's like 6 at the beginning,
           then it gets like 5 1/2 or 5, you know.

Hopkins: Do you think you could tap that out? While it's playing?

Shankar: Yes, definitely. So, that's what I was trying to get, but—

(Shankar tapped beats while first springar was played through. See Example 23 for a transcription of the beginning through the first beat of
the second phrase.)

Shankar: But the pattern changes.

Hopkins: Actually, they don't perceive a difference. They perceive it
           as the same pattern all the way through.

Shankar: Yes?—Yes, kind of hard. (Laughs) I don't know the music,
           you know.

The similarity of the overall rhythmic design to the Indian tala system
(characterized by periodic returns to a reference point) has already been
mentioned; and Shankar seems to have been using a cognitive structure
that was already familiar to him when he focused on the larger components (the phrases) before attempting to isolate the groupings within
them. He remained skeptical of the existence of a beat cycle and contin-

ued to perceive an unsteady pulse. His spoken beats were as even as the melodic figuration would allow them to be; thus he over-reached the beginning of the new phrase. (See Ex. 23.)

Kaloyanides, in complete contrast to Shankar's approach, attempted to build up to the larger components through tying together small clusters of twos and threes:

Kaloyanides: Oh, I get a sense of it as being—Well, I'm trying to get the number of beats, and I sense it in groups of twos and threes—off-hand. With all the material I sense it as being —hearing twos against threes quite often—a matter of structure. In a lot of it, give me the sense of a triple meter; but then I hear, rather than three beats in each major division, I hear two.

Like Shankar, Kaloyanides perceived the music through known constructions, as he tried out a 13-beat sequence whose component parts $(3 + 3 + 3 + 2 + 2)$ represent an uneven beat structure. The concept (if not the proportion), as we have seen, is applicable to Norwegian music: but Kaloyanides assumed the accented second beat of the measure to be the beginning of the cycle. He does not begin clapping until the seventh measure of the piece: thus, in Example 23, I have transposed his beating of an analogous phrase for comparative purposes. After finding that the pattern could not be kept up, he commented: "Very complicated!"

Predictably, Blitstein's perception of the rhythmic structure shows the influence of the European violin tradition, a music in which melodic and harmonic considerations have customarily determined rhythmic character. (Hopkins 1967) Hence, she alone of the three musicians analyzed the rhythm principally through singing (and later, playing) the melodic line.

Blitstein: Could I reproduce that much? If I think I can?

Hopkins?   Yes, sure.

Blitstein: OK.

(Blitstein sang the opening motif in the rhythm.)

Blitstein: So it could be: 1, 2, 3. Then a measure of 4—a measure of 3 and a measure of 4—or a measure of 7 with a strong—

> (*sings again*) . . . Could I hear that much again?

Hopkins: Yeah, let see—

Blitstein: See if I'm right?

Hopkins: And tap while it's going on? Is that a good idea?

Blitstein: Ok. Let's see if—it fits.

> (First two phrases played, then)

Blitstein: Back to beginning—I'm lost. What I'm doing is not *that*.

> (First three phrases played, then)

Blitstein: Now I get 8—4, 5, 6, 6, 8 (*sings*)

Hopkins: OK, try tapping it while it's going on—

The initially perceived rhythmic pattern, 3 + 4, quite apparently reflects the melodic contour; very likely, it is also influenced by harmonic factors, since Blitstein carries her pattern through the first half of the fourth beat—up to the change of register (see Example 23). This perception of the rhythm, which (like the other perceptions) has been constructed out of previous experience and completed through factors of expectation, is unlikely to prove meaningful in an unfamiliar context.

The different precepts were logically (indeed, skillfully) constructed according to the musical system familiar to the particular listener, but it was obvious to each musician that the conclusion arrived at did not agree with the musical scheme; the others would have concurred with Blitstein when she exclaimed: "It doesn't fit at the end of each measure or phrase. I cannot figure out the rhythmic pattern."

C) *Search for Appropriateness:*

> *What do we mean by intelligence? There is no agreed definition; and psychologists are apt to confuse processes leading to intelligent solutions with what it is to say that a solution is intelligent. But it is confusing to equate, say, good memory or concentration,*

or any such, with intelligence—even if these characteristics are necessary for deriving intelligent solutions. It is confusing because we should be clear about what it is to say that one solution is intelligent, another not, irrespective of how the solution is obtained. To judge that a solution is intelligent we do, however, have to know what data and what previous solutions were available, or we will be in danger of attributing intelligence to something that merely copies. Clearly a necessary criterion of intelligence is novelty. Novelty alone, however, is not enough, for what is novel may be arbitrary, or downright misleading. Evidently, to be appropriate is also a necessary condition for intelligence. I shall proceed to define an intelligent act or an intelligent solution as any act, or solution, which has appropriate novelty.

(Gregory 1974: 630)

We recall that Shankar observed: "Kind of hard. I don't know the music, you know." This kind of "knowing" can only be arrived at through a search for what is or is not appropriate, and this search for appropriateness, in accordance with the above definition, must be acknowledged as an immensely important cognitive operation.

In our experiment, of course, the opportunity for mere imitation is not present. But the striving for an appropriate response was at the root of each musician's investigation. Now it is apparent that this searching for appropriateness (or should we call it "meaning?") can only be understood in a cultural context.

Rudolph Arnheim, who has applied Gestalt principles to the field of aesthetics, has demonstrated that these principles do not involve minimizing "the role of learning and experience in perception." (See Gombrich 1960: 262) In Arnheim's words:

Gestalt psychologists . . . while pointing out that the capacity to see shapes is not brought about merely by repeated exposure to the stimuli, have no reason to suggest that a gestalt shows up with automatic spontaneity.

(Arnheim 1969: 30)

In Gestalt terms, past experience, knowledge, learning, memory are considered as factors of the temporal context, on which Gestaltists have concentrated their attention during the early development of the theory: the temporal context influences the way a phenomenon is perceived. An object looks big or small depending on whether it is seen, spatially, in the company of smaller or larger objects. The buildings of a middle-sized town look tall to a farmer, small to a New Yorker, and correspondingly, their expression differs for the two observers. . . Such examples do not demonstrate that there is no intrinsic connection between perceptual patterns and the expression they convey but simply that experiences must not be evaluated in isolation from their spatial and temporal whole-context.

(Arnheim 1966: 67)

I have dwelt on this point because it is not easy to be aware of the extent to which the obvious may be a perception organized by matters of expectancy—matters that are derived from previous knowledge and experience. To again borrow an analogy from the visual field: "We do not always realize that the theory of perspective developed in the fifteenth century is a scientific convention; it is merely one way of describing space and has no absolute validity." (Read 1956: 66f)

It is as true for aural thinking as it is for visual thinking that perception consists in the grasping of relevant generic features of the object—and that a conception of structure must be present before abstraction can take place. Thus, concept formation must be acknowledged to be present in aural forms, just as it is in visual shapes (see Arnheim 1969: 153, 173, 27ff). In reference to rhythm it has recently been pointed out that:

The principle underlying the spontaneous organization of sounds into definite patterns appears to be similar to pattern perception in other areas, and seems to resemble what is known as the "figure-ground" relationship. . . . It is this ability to differentiate between figure and ground which is at the heart of rhythmic ability; . . .

(Davies 1978: 198 and 199)

The musicians in our experiment, having found that their original attempts at abstraction were not appropriate to the situation at hand, expressed perplexity, as we have seen. Then they proceeded to set about the task of restructuring in order to solve the problem that had been set before them. At times they verbalized about the difficulties encountered in purposefully shifting their orientation. Blitstein, for example, explained: "It's the end of the thing that really throws me . . . The end of that figure. I can't differentiate between the ornamentation and the beat." And later: "Now the beginning of each thing—I'm not sure whether it's an up-beat or whether it's the first beat or if it's an introduction. . . . Now I don't know if that's the start. I'm very confused; and I think that's one of the, one of the many things that's throwing me."

Kaloyanides, while working on the first example, remarked: "That's one way I hear it. Sometimes I hear it differently—." And, again, in reference to the following *springar:* "Well—I listen to it different ways, the different times I hear it. Sometimes I get a steady pulse, sometimes I tend to group it different ways—. But . . . sometimes I feel four strong beats, sometimes I feel three." Later, during the third example: "In looking for the cycle, I have a lot of trouble in recognizing where a phrase will end and begin, if there is such a concept." At the end of the entire session, Kaloyanides summed up some of these problems as follows: "What sort of complicates it for me is the lack of an introduction and a resolution of a phrase; that's more of a musical continuum that I hear. And it sure would take numerous listenings of the material to be able to develop a sense of the pattern. You could discover where people see the beginning of a phrase."

D) *Aural Concepts:*

The restructuring process resulted in the trying out of new and different possibilities—mental templates that might be called "aural concepts," to adapt Arnheim's terminology (1969: 27). It is especially significant that this restructuring process was carried out, in the case of each musician, according to the path already established in his or her initial responses to the material (and determined, of course, by experience): it is most interesting to see certain features come to light in aspects that were similar enough to the familiar tradition for enlightenment to take place.

Shankar continued to envision the aural scheme in terms of the phrase lengths and their division. In the second example he found:

> *Two different themes. Yes, two different themes. The first . . . is like four times. Then the second theme is reproduced four times.*

In the third *springar* (Ex. 24), he begins to concentrate more carefully on the subdivisions of these periods:

> *It starts with 6 beats, you know. Triplets, but let's beat it:*

> *. . . See, he improvises on 6 beats. . . . After 6 cycles, he goes to a different register, and the same thing — .*

During the playing of the fourth *springar*, I noticed that Shankar was clapping a specific South Indian tala:

Hopkins: *You were tapping rupaka?*

Shankar: *Yes, yes, rupaka. Rupaka tala. And it is not extremely strict, but — at the same time, it goes:*

> *Of course, it varies, also; so it's triplets also within the three beats — Yes, sometimes.*

I was impressed by the analogy to rupaka tala, for, although it certainly did not fit completely (as Shankar implied), this tala contains the heavy second beat and light third beat that are characteristic of the Telemark *springar*. Shankar continued in his analysis of the fifth and last *springar* to proceed to, and then concentrate on, the smaller dimensions of the rhythmic structure — and to find patterns in them somewhat analogous to patterns in Indian music.

Kaloyanides, continuing to conceive of the music as being built up from small groups of twos and threes, began to experiment in the fourth example with more intricate configurations; he also extended his analysis to the larger dimensions:

Kaloyanides: *I also have the sense of — triplets. Six groups of triplets there.*

Hopkins: *Which you felt in the last one?*
Kaloyanides: *Yes, the same as the last one. Also, the two against three is there. . . . Sometimes, the phrases run 3 groups long, sometimes 6 groups long. . . . Also I hear like a — slight delay before the one. . . .*

Hopkins: *Could you express that slight delay in a —*

Kaloyanides: *Metrical frame? Yeah. I'm trying to figure how much of*

> *a delay it is. (Listens to examples) . . . Hearing it in 6*
> *groups of 3, it would beat like 18. I hear a 19th beat.*

Hopkins: *. . . Would that correspond to any Greek rhythm? Do*
                you know?

Kaloyanides: *Something with 19 beats? No. Anything that's in Greek*
                music, anything that's really complex—and that stan-
                dard over a long period, it's usually slow. . . . So you
                won't get something that quick.

It is important to realize that Kaloyanides had determined, not only the number of phrase subdivisions (6) but also the amount of irregularity; however, the beats are intended to be perceived in groups of 3, and the ratio between them is an even more subtle one (close to $4 + 4 + 3$).

Blitstein, at the conclusion of her work with the third *springar*, recognized and articulated the problem she was up against:

> *Let me tell you, I have a great deal of trouble isolating the beat pat-*
> *tern from the melodic pattern.*

Unlike the other musicians, who eventually found certain mechanisms in their own musical systems that provided some insight into the problem at hand, Blitstein was working from knowledge of a tradition whose principles in respect to rhythm are almost antithetical in nature to those of Norwegian fiddle music.

> *Music in the Western classical tradition, although tonally very*
> *complex, is usually rhythmically simple. There are two possible*
> *reasons for this. Firstly, as stated earlier, the rhythm of a piece*
> *tends to be carried by the notes themselves, whereas, in rhythmi-*
> *cally more complex music, the rhythm is to a greater extent ex-*
> *pressed independently of any tune. . . . Secondly, Western music*
> *has confined itself largely to the use of meters involving units of*
> *two, three, or four beats. (The term "metre" is used here to de-*
> *scribe the basic, underlying pulse of a piece of music around*
> *which the different rhythms are fitted.*
>
> (Davies 1978: 178)

After realizing that she was being misled by the melodic figuration, she began to concentrate on the lower voice lines, the contrapuntal motives and drone patterns—and to experiment with uneven beat patterns. It is interesting to note that the style or melodic elaboration found in *harding-fele* music is remarkably similar to that found in Baroque violin music. (Hopkins 1967) Blitstein's adroitness in dealing with the melodic and harmonic aspects of the music were undoubtedly due to her experience with this Baroque tradition; but the familiarity of this aspect of the music necessarily made the rhythmic dissimilarity more difficult to accept:

> *No. . . . I miss that ornament every time. See, the ornament comes where I don't think it's going to be.*

In one instance (the third *springar*), melodic contour influenced all three musicians into a period of general agreement, but this lasted only through the first two sections (see Example 24). The musicians perceived an even beat and triplet subdivisions, although the beats actually exhibit the typical Telemark configuration (the ratio averages out to 15/14/10), and the notes in question are not of exact triplet length (But close to ♪♪ or ♪♪♪). The ear, influenced by the 3-note groupings of the figuration at a lively tempo, heard in each case, what was a familiar relationship. Section three begins on the last measure of section two (a beautiful example of phrase elision); there is no help from the melodic figuration, and all three listeners were lost:

Blitstein: Now what happened? Where did it go?

The sound wave pattern is also blurred at this point; for there is a change of tempo at the beginning of the new section, and, indeed, it takes some time before the new tempo becomes stabilized.

E) *Judgments:*

The musicians expressed great respect for the Norwegian tradition in their judgments offered at the end of each interview. Shankar pronounced it "very intricate," and added: "I think it will be most difficult for musicians trained in western classical music with no experience of Indian or other non-western musics." Blitstein agreed and thought that even a non-musician, whose brain "doesn't fit into all these cubbyholes" would probably have an easier time.

Kaloyanides summarized his impressions as follows:

Foot-beating:

Ex. 24: *Rjukanfossen*

> *Very confusing stuff. Let's see—any general things. I get a very polyrhythmic sense—a combination at the same time. . . . This is very—foreign to me . . . My first impression is to grab at something familiar. Very tricky stuff!*

It is of major importance that, in no case, did the initial perception in-clude a cylical beat pattern—even though the consulant-musicians were all advised before hand that such a pattern existed. We should realize that the first (and considerably lengthiest) portion of each interview passed without comment while the examples were played a number of times. In each instance, the musicians had to deliberately devise a method for discovering what was not readily apparent. An examination of their own words (as quoted above) reveals the existence of the significant features derived from Arnheim's study of "visual thinking." (see above, p. 190) Their search for understanding necessitated an active exploration that involved focusing on specific aspects over others—a simplification of the total musical construction. The selection of certain elements was influenced by the memory of learned knowledge (carry-over from the familiar tradition). Shankar's skepticism derived from his expectation concerning the nature of a recurrent beat pattern; where he preceived an arbitrary unsteadiness (that would probably accord with the mechanical representation), the *hardingfele spelemann* perceives articulations within a consistently recurrent pattern. Blitstein, inhibited by the nature of her tradition from considering certain possibilities, made a synthesis that was logical according to her own experience but not logical in the context of the Norwegian tradition. It is also important that all the musicians soon became aware that their solutions were not meaningful within the appropriate context; their reappraisals resulted in the restructuring of "mental templates" that resulted in some deepening of understanding—although in no case, of course, was this understanding complete.

It seems clear that aural perception (like visual perception) involves the grasping of structural features; in applying these ideas to cross-cultural study, this abstraction of cognitive elements is influenced by concepts of appropriateness that are themselves determined by previous knowledge. Restructuring of the original aural concepts was, as we have seen, consistently and logically accomplished according to whether this predetermined train of thought was or was not in some way analogous to the relevant thinking process.

"No one borderline separates a purely perceptual image—if such there is—from one completed by memory." (Arnheim 1969: 84) In a very real sense, Arnheim's completion by memory is a comparison—a process that must, it appears to me, go on constantly and automatically. Some years ago, I suggested that the old name for the discipline we now call "Ethnomusicology"—"Comparative Musicology"—was more correct than the later term, for "Every time we transcribe a piece of ethnic music into our notational system we compare it with our music." (Hopkins 1966: 312) Perhaps it would be closer to the truth to enlarge this concept to: "Any time we hear a piece of unfamiliar music we perceive it automatically through comparisons with familiar music."

Now, it is apparent that (according to the predispositions analyzed above) comparisons can occur with appropriate or inappropriate mental images. It is also true (although not so apparent) that appropriateness is a matter that has been decided by the in-group and cannot be measured mechanically. For example, a correctly perceived triplet rarely consists of a precisely equal group of three notes, and notes of different vibration frequencies within a scale system may be perceived as both identical and "in tune." Indeed, a note that is identical in pitch with another may be perceived as "out of tune" because of its contextual position in the musical scheme. Yet, none of these things are matters of chance, for they can all be accounted for (and will be expected) by those in the know. We remember that Seashore, not understanding this last matter, was shocked when he discovered that his measurements of sound wave patterns made by famous performers showed great areas of divergence from the musical notation.

Scholars interested in structural analysis have often become aware of the importance of non-verbal systems of human communication. They frequently turn to musical analogies to describe this concept (e.g., see Leach 1973: 40); since they have noticed that music, considered thus as one of a number of manifestations of thought, more closely approximates the permutations of mental patterning than does verbal communication (which is fairly limited to linearity). Lévi-Strauss, of course, was especially impressed by this circumstance (what he terms the *capacité anagrammatique*) and deliberately utilized formal musical structures to describe mythological thought patterns in his monumental work on that subject (1964-71; also see Hopkins 1977) He has explained that he refused to abandon himself to "that form of mysticism that proclaims the intuitive and ineffable character of moral and aesthetic sentiments and even at times maintains that they illuminate the consciousness independently of all intellectual apprehension of their object." (1971: 596) He is probably thinking of such criticisms of his theories as those made by the author who recently complained that they would not be tenable for an aural, improvised tradition (see above quotation).

But neither the West African drumming nor the Norwegian Hardanger fiddle tradition would be more intellectual (nor would they be more permanent), if either were associated with a written notation; for the structure itself is an aural structure and individual elaborations on that structure have meaning when the aural tradition is no longer extant (as those who do research on the performance practice of past styles well know).

The *hardingfele spelemann*, Finn Vabø, pointing to the monumental volumes of published transcriptions for that instrument, had remarked that new pieces could not be learned from them, because: "The music is not there. He made it quite clear that he had the utmost respect for the editors (all of whom were outstanding both as players of the instrument and as scholars) and for the edition (which has a place of honor on his bookshelf). Vabø, was simply calling attention generally to the limitations of musical notation for prescriptive purposes in respect to the intangible aspects of his tradition—those factors that must be learned by ear. Thus in this chapter, we have limited our study to an examination of a single characteristic of *hardingfele* structure—one that cannot be adequately represented visually by notation but one, nonetheless, that is freely acknowledged by the musicians themselves to be of prime importance. The demonstration described above has indeed pointed to a strong cognitive component in even the initial percept of this un-notatable rhythmic feature.[5]

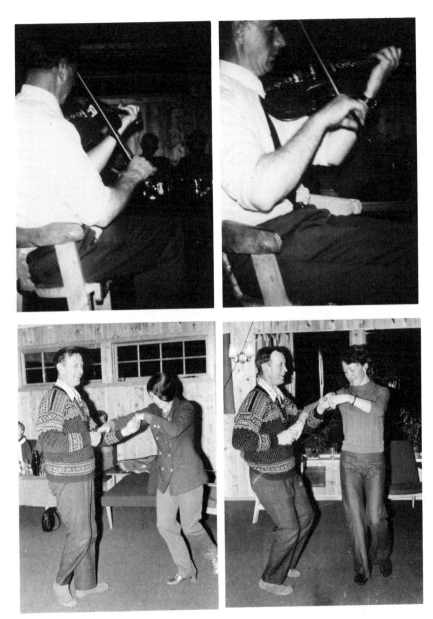

14. *A musical form of situational code switching took place in the Kostveits' living room, when the serious audience for the playing of Trygve Vågen (a) and (b) gave way to informal singing and dancing (c) and (d).*

Musical Codes

It is only that I think the world should know about our special tradition here in Tinn.

Johannes Dahle

 Thus, Johannes Dahle expressed both his belief in the unique value of his tradition and his conviction of the importance of its dissemination. In the present chapter, we shall consider the character of this transmission: how it operates (or is made to operate) within the complete cultural picture. We are concerned here with both the maintenance and development of co-existent and highly localized systems of communication. It is of particular significance that Norwegians themselves refer to these different local styles as "musical dialects"; for in this sense (as a meaningful and highly stylized system of cultural communication) there is an appropriate analogy to linguistic usage. Musical codes, like their counterparts, are "basic controls on the transmission of culture"; and they are of no less importance as creators of social identity. It might well be expected, then, that changes in musical codes may involve changes in role relationships and in procedures of social control. (see Bernstein in Gumperz 1972: 494) Furthermore, the individual choices that effect musical changes are meaningful in themselves. (Blom 1972: 408)

However, there is an important difference between the way language and music (particularly instrumental music) operates in society. Instrumental traditions, by their very nature, are specialist systems of communication—a matter not generally recognized for its full significance. The code system is far more complicated, since it is acquired over an extended period of learning and since it generally recognizes a variety of different levels of understanding and expertise.

In considering the character of the transmission of Hardanger fiddle music, we shall focus upon the extent to which, and to what purpose the individual player is permitted to, is able to, and does, affect the transmitted material. In this discussion, the term, "change," will be used in all-encompassing sense to include notions I have elsewhere introduced as "permanent" and "temporary" change; the former referring to the development into a new style from which there is no return (alteration of the code itself) and the latter expressing both the practice of musical variation and the process of musical code-switching (changes legislated by code rules).

> It is evident that musical code-switching, like its linguistic counterpart, implies control over temporary change. The linguistic analogy may be carried further: one could say that a musical kind of metaphorical switching occurs when the Beatles borrow from the style of Indian music or from the European Baroque, and that situational switching takes place when a concert virtuoso introduces the encore piece after a formal concert. As is also true with languages, appropriateness is an obvious delimiting factor in code choice; such sociological notions as setting, social situation, and social event would certainly prove useful tools in any attempt to deal logically with this matter. Both individual choice and socially established rules (expressed, for example, in the concept of "domain") must have an effect on musical choice. For it is also true of musical communication, as linguists have said of languages, that these concepts "represent an attempt to explain the natives' conception of their behavioral environment in terms of an ordered set of constraints which operate to transform alternative lines of behavior into particular social meanings."
>
> (Hopkins 1976: 451; Blom 1972: 433)

From Finn Vabø's demonstration tapes, I would like to present four direct quotations—statements that admirably summarize the basic values of the tradition:

1) "You must understand the geography of Norway to understand its music." (i.e., *regionalism*: shared identity, the acknowledged reason for the existence of musical codes)

2) "One must first learn many *slåttar* as they were made up by others or passed from person to person in the tradition. Only when one has

mastered all this music, is one able to compose new compositions." (i.e. *knowledge and skill*: code acquisition)

3) You must have the right bowing and note skeleton, and then you must add something from your heart." (i.e., *individualism*: the power to go beyond the code as well as to create within the code structure)

4) Those who don't like this music—Well, they play no instrument—or else, perhaps, they play the musical comb." (i.e., *esotericism*: recognition of levels of quality)

Those who understand their regional traditions, if they undergo thorough training on the *hardingfele*, will have the appropriate knowledge to be permitted to add new material (if they can), showing individual inspiration; the result will be understood and appreciated by the initiated. We shall examine each of these four elements in turn, from the point of view of its relationship to the occurrence or non-occurrence of change in the Norwegian tradition.

I *REGIONALISM:* SHARED IDENTITY

Finn Vabø expounded upon the relationship between geography and music in the following terms:

> *An undulating countryside inspires a similar type of music. In the West,* hardingfele *music is close to that of the ordinary violin and the music of Scotland. . . . In Hardanger, they have the purest tradition. . . . Some of the most difficult to understand* slåttar *come from Telemark, where they take the melody up again and up again —very much like their mountains.*

Some years after I first met Finn Vabø (and long after he had received considerable recognition as a *Vestland* fiddler), he applied for, and received, a grant for study in Telemark. It was his obvious admiration for the Telemark tradition that sent me to that region on my next and subsequent field trips. The particular data for this chapter thus is drawn from my experiences in Telemark.

The *bygd* of Rauland in Telemark (see Part I) is a widespread community of farmers who raise animals (principally sheep) on the spectacularly beautiful—but not overly productive—mountain slopes. It is an area known throughout Norway as the heart of the Telemark (a region, as we have seen, particularly renowned for richness of folk arts and crafts). Without exception, every person I met was highly skilled in some specialty (silversmithing, fiddling, singing, weaving, woodcarving) in addition to the farming or other work that was his or her principal means of subsistence. It is of special significance that the citizens of Telemark are no less proud of their abilities in farming than they are of their skills in these occupations (which form a natural part of their daily routine). There is absolutely no line drawn between the two kinds of things.

A quiet conviction of self-worth has long characterized the Telemark *bonde*—and tended to elicit some astonishment from visitors accustomed to a more materialistic kind of competitiveness:

> *"You have been in Thelemerken?" inquired the lieutenant. "That's the county for old Norsk customs and language . . . some of the bonders are very rich, and proud of their wealth. I remember being at a farm some miles above Kongsberg, where I saw a number of copper kettles ranged on a shelf, as bright as bright could be; I found that these were the gauge of the bonder's wealth. For every thousand dollars saved a new copper kettle was added. You have no idea how tenacious these people are of their social position. . . . And yet even the wealthiest of them live in the meanest manner."*
> (Metcalfe 1858: 300f)

Today it is just as true that the residents of Telemark are both a prosperous and a proud people, proud of their artistic reputation and way of life. In regard to their language, Einar Haugen calls the vocabulary of Telemark "one of the richest of all the rural dialects and one of the most conservative." (Haugen 1962: 171) He describes the regions of Telemark and Voss as "homes of folk poetry" and states that they are "greatly admired by the advocates of folk culture." It is interesting that Haugen found that their feeling of self-worth stayed with immigrants to the United States from these areas and manifested itself in the retention of their dialects in the new country. (Haugen 1962: 353) The recent interest in folk music among urban Norwegians has brought the different regional styles into close proximity in the cities: and one hears a new term (no doubt enviously) applied: "Telemark imperialism."

Socially, the citizens of Rauland are tightly knit; husbands and wives from other communities (especially if they come from urban areas) experience difficulties in being accepted. There are legends and fiddle pieces (generally humorous in tone) about single women who move into the community from a city or town—and a special term (*fenta*) with a perjorative connotation that translates to "tramp." The accompanying legend to the *slått, Møsvannsfenta* (after Johannes Dahle who received it from Knut Vågen, ancestor of Trygve), has a surprise ending that can only be appreciated by those who understand the generally low expectation for the urban invader. In this case, two sisters—described as *flink* (clever) and from the town of Skien—eventually married Møsstrand boys and settled down contentedly in that isolated area for the rest of their lives. It is significant that the "ancestral farm" remains of paramount importance, even to members of the family who have moved far away from the area. They continue to refer to it as "our farm" and always try to return at harvest time—to help with the work and share in the bounty. There is a commonly known folk song concerned with the meeting of a farmer and his ancestral spirit, *Haugebonden.* (Ex. 25)

Ex. 25: *Haugebonden.* Sung by Eivind Øvgarden (my recording: Rauland, Telemark, 1972).

As might be expected under these circumstances, rivalry amongst the peoples of different mountain valleys is great—in fact, often acrimonious, to judge from a certain genre of competitive song. In the *stevleik* (literally, *stev*-play), two singers alternately improvise insults to one another much in the manner of the Spanish-American *decima*. Each singer uses a short, pre-existent melody as a vehicle for the improvised text in this song competition.[1] Sometimes the participants vie with one another as male and female; but often, they represent two mountain valleys, each regarding the opponent as a personification of the foreign community. In the past, anger engendered by this musical rivalry has led to more physically violent forms of combat, particularly during the explosive atmosphere of an after-wedding party. In an example I transcribed from the singing of Eivind Øvgarden, the initial challenge is presented as follows:

> Yes, you will *stevjast*[2], then I shall answer
> and the whole evening, so shall it be!
> Oh, you will *stevjast* with me in the evening,
> You shall not die before you go pop!
> O, it was the sacred Christmas Eve,
> When the farmer went seeking melodies,
> And when he came upon the grove,
> There he heard the haugebonde rhyming in the frost.
> Greeting, to you, that's what he heard in the icy grove.
> Haugebonden, dancing and rhyming.

The challenger answers:

> Yes, I shall *stevjast* you for a long time,
> so you'd better be ready for a great many!
> Oh, I'll *stevjast* with you today;
> then you'd better be able to go in thousands!

Later on, the insults become more vindictive:

> Oh, you who have been so scared of my rhyme,
> you shall have a nozzle to wear on your nose!
> Oh, it will be made from the hide of a cat,
> with all of the claws turned outside in!

Frequently, as in "the dozens," the Harlem, New York, *genre*, members of the immediate family are insulted:

I know your father, I know your mother;
I know your sister, I know your brothers;
I know you and the whole house,
you squealing fleas and deadly lice![3]

The *stevleik* has become within recent years a thing of the past. But strong feelings of identification with the family, the ancestral farm, and the mountain valley are as present today as they used to be. Thus, it is not surprising that the people living in these communities have firm convictions concerning the retention of their musical and linguistic traditions.

The cultural geographer does not neglect landscape molded by human hand or plow from consideration; thus, it is important to view regions as created by human beings as part of their own environment, not separate from it. The social institutions of human beings usually involve established meeting places; these "domains," as they have been called (Fishman in Gumperz 1972: 435) are as important in determining musical as linguistic code, for it is just as relevant that: "They attempt to summate the major clusters of interaction that occur" in a pluralistic setting (Gumperz 1972: 441). As an example, we may consider the various domains of the mountain community in Rauland.

The Rauland, *spelemennslag*, we remember, meets in the folk mural-decorated room of the *Kommunehus (Rauland Huset)* situated out in the farm land. The weekly dances, on the other hand, take place in the secondary school auditorium (which serves as a comunity center). This building (contemporary style with a sod roof) houses formal events of both national and international culture: folk music competitions in the summer, but also weekly movies (usually American). Music teaching in the school curriculum, however, consists of instruction in plastic flutes; and the playing and singing from the typically homogenized kind of song books with which we are all familiar. National music is only approached in high school music appreciation classes—in other words, as a cultural duty. However, very recently, the high school has been offering evening courses in musical instrument instruction; both guitar and *hardingfele*, significantly, are especially popular. Yet, these same people continue to sing, play, dance (and teach) their national music informally at home (a third domain); and some of them take part in regular meetings of dancing or fiddling groups.

Directly across the street from the school used to be the Rauland Kafeteria, favorite gathering spot for the local teenagers who played the juke box and bought sodas and snacks. Nowadays, with access to cars, they can travel further afield. The church is a fifth domain, the setting of another, also entirely different, musical code: the organ and vocal music of Bach and other Lutheran composers. The fiddler, leading the bridal procession at a traditional wedding, must, as we have seen (Part I), halt at the front door.

A person born in the bygd of Rauland or of Tinn in Telemark will identify with the Rauland or Tinn variety of Telemark culture: the rules that are relevant to each locality. We have seen that this heritage also involves knowledge concerning the appropriateness of specific musical styles to different "domains." Within each of the domains that are appropriate to *hardingfele* playing, the social situation itself may or may not be appropriate to the tradition—or to a particular style within the tradition. Thus, our hypothetical person's inheritance includes an awareness of the specific social situations that require particular styles of *hardingfele* music: listening, dance, and the various categories of wedding music, for example.

II *KNOWLEDGE AND SKILL:*   CODE ACQUISITION

> One must first learn many *slåttar* as they were made up by others or passed from person to person in the tradition. Only when one has mastered all this music, is one able to compose new *slåttar*.
>
> (Finn Vabø)

It will be remembered that, when Finn Vabø was asked about early *hardingfele* instruction, he drew attention to the importance of the musical milieu; just a as a young child learns the complexities of his/her native tongue more readily than a language can be acquired later in formal class instruction, so the firmest foundation for understanding a musical system is laid early in life, within its own environment:

> Not everyone can start to play. He (a young student) must have it from his father. They must live in it; then they have the music—a little bit of it—in their heads, becuse they live in it, the family. . . . Well, that is not an easy question to answer. It depends on—We use a French term; do you know it? The milieu. The musical milieu. And then they take not so long to learn. . . .
>
> (Vabø)

Many years after these words were spoken, Vabø pointed out, in another interview, that it was not necessary for a student's parent to be a player:

he or she can still learn from the milieu: ". . . if they listen to others when they play—take something from one player and something from another —and then give something special from their own heart." He then described the circumstances surrounding his own son's learning process:

> When he was a little boy, he would come in to me at bedtime and ask me to play so he could go to sleep. He takes things I play— things he's heard around, since he was this high—. . . . If he come to me and says, "I want to play Myllarguten's Siste Slått, I play, slowly, and then we start together.

It is interesting to compare the above with a description of Myllarguten's early environment:

> The father had a good understanding of the fiddle; and he was able to play many of the old slåtts. He would take the boy on his knee and rock him, singing slåttar. "Father crooning for Møllaren: That was the nicest thing known," said Ingebjørg Pilodden (Myllarguten's half-sister). And the old one taught the quiet child.
>
> (Berge 1972: 4f; my trans.)

As we have seen in the preceding chapter, even the initial perception of musical elements is conditioned by cultural learning. Leonard Meyer has pointed out that:

> . . . while recognizing the diversity of musical languages, we must also admit that these languages have important characteristics in common. The most important of these, and the ones to which the least attention has been paid, is the syntactical nature of different musical styles. The organization of sound terms into a system of probability relationships, the limitations imposed upon the combining of sounds, and so forth are all common characteristics of musical language.
>
> (Meyer 1956: 62f)

To follow his train of thought further; the tension that can be produced in a piece of tonal music by a continual evasion of perfect cadences is achieved in *hardingfele* music through a similar perpetuation of counter-rhythms against the recurrent cycle of beats: the effect of surprise, achieved in tonal music, for example, through the deceptive cadence, can be transmitted in a *slått* through the avoidance of a definite phrase

ending by elision. Meyer points out that what he calls "designative behavior" (our affective responses, the doctrine of *ethos*) is also a cultural
phenomenon:

> *This is important as it takes most of the sting out of the criticism
> that music which attempts to designate emotional states depends
> for its effect upon the learning of conventional signs and symbols.
> For this fact isn't peculiar to music but is characteristic of all emo-
> tional designations.*
>
> (Meyer 1956: 22)

Some one and a half centuries after Myllarguten's childhood, I observed a three-year-old child in Hallingdal being bounced on her father's
lap to the uneven beats of a *Hallingspringar;* the young listener was not
only being introduced to the complicated rhythmic structure and particular pitch system of the locality, as well as other general characteristics of
the style, she was also being introduced to rules of appropriateness established by the community—that this kind of music is appropriate to this
social event (a national folk music competition, in this case) and to this
setting (the auditorium of a secondary school building). This is an example of what Merriam called "enculturation" (1964: 145f), and it is similar
in nature to the initial acquisition of one's native language.

Those who wish to become instrumentalists should ideally have this
background, but the ability to put the code of appropriateness into effect
is part of the mastery of the instrument learned by a *spelemann* during a
long period of apprenticeship. This learning does not always take place in
a formal atmosphere; it has always been an important part of the business
of the players' organization (*spelemannslag*)—a chapter of which exists
in every locality where the Hardanger fiddle is played. A renowned
player usually presides over the local group and will give special attention to especially interested and able students; nowadays, providing tape
recordings to be studied. Recently, the increased interest of young people
—and the consequent necessity of teaching a large number of beginners
at the same time— has resulted in the setting up of special courses of instruction, usually under the auspices of the local *spelemannslag*. Both
Finn Vabø and Knut Buen reported an overwhelming response to announcements that such courses would take place and Vabø described
other results: the need for inexpensive instruments, simple pieces to play,
and group playing experiences. However, the instructional atmosphere is
still informal (see Ill. 5). This learning period consists in the memorization
of a body of set pieces, note for note, ornament for ornament, and bow-

ing for bowing. Just as the student of Indian music learns the concepts of *raga* and *tala* through the acquisition of numerous individual pieces, the student of *hardingfele* music learns the skill of improvisation on stock Norwegian melodic outlines and rhythmic patterns in this manner.

Finn Vabø had included in his demonstration tape an illustration of his own method of teaching a student his "first *springar* of the big ones" (*Star yguten*); there was meticulous attention to intonation and to the correct execution of embellishments:

Ex. 26

The precision of instruction that had so much impressed me in my personal experiences with Gjermund Haugen and Johannes Dahle (Part I) is apparently not a new feature of the tradition; for we are told that Knut Dahle, as an apprentice to Håvard Gibøen over a century ago, was never able to satisfy his master:

> He was time after time with him; time after time, he thought: Now, you've got everything; But, no, thank-you.
>
> (Berg 1972: 222; my trans.)

Gibøen was ". . . like a schoolmaster; he went over the most important slåtts with Knut again and again, correcting them beat for beat. . . ." (Berge 1972: 222)

The "first *springar*" was obviously chosen for its simplicity of ornamentation and harmony, the latter almost entirely limited to the simple droning of open strings. As is apparent from the above example, the student learns correct ornamentation along with the melodic line. It is also apparent that he/she is not expected to play the skeletal melody by itself; as pointed out in an earlier chapter, it is not easy to play a single melodic line on this polyphonic instrument. Vabø, however, did this for my benefit, and the larger notes in the above transcription reflect his performance. Thus, a large body of slåtts must be learned with the utmost precision, from the "first long piece" (usually, the Seljord *Bruremarsj*) through the "first *springar* of the big ones" to the final crowning achievement of such a virtuoso feat as the *Kivlemøy* cycle. There is no doubt that these pieces have a significance beyond their technical difficulty. As we have seen, the melody upon which the *Kivlemøy* slåtts are based is one of the oldest in the *hardingfele* repertory, the legend is also ancient, and the pieces are *lydarslåttar*, meant for listening purposes. When a *spelemann* has passed this test, he is at liberty to invent new music of his own. Many players who meet for lengthy work sessions in the local *spelemannslag* every week never intend to reach this point and are satisfied to remain amateurs, as they refer to themselves.

It is especially significant that the pieces considered the greatest tests of musicianship are the listening pieces, which are not usually the most technically difficult. In a tradition that makes great technical demands, I have frequently heard a *spelemann* described as not great because, although he could play all the notes, "there was nothing more."

III *INDIVIDUALISM:*   CODE-SWITCHING AND INNOVATION

> You must have the right bowing and note skeleton, and then you
> must add something from your heart.

The aim of this exhaustive system of training is not, then, simply to preserve the old; rather, its ultimate goal is the creation of new music: ". . . then you must add something from your heart." As we have seen in an earlier chapter, the *spelemann* who has reached this point is credited with special powers: a concept that is well known to Europe in the "genius" idea.

In considering the *hardingfele* as a musical instrument (Chapter 1), we have discovered that it reflected certain contradictory features in Norwegian society. We are once again faced with a seeming dichotomy: an intense conviction that the regional dialects must be maintained accurately, with—nonetheless—the highest esteem given to individual inspiration and creativity. Both the values of individualism and of cultural preservation have been considered characteristic of lands that share mountain and sea cultures; they are usually characterized by different male and female cultures and, often, by transhumance (the removal of animals and personnel to highland farms in the summer).

> *Wherever transhumance is or has been practiced, it is associated with difficult environments and marginal conditions, where it has provided opportunities for escape from authority and served as a means of preserving and transmitting ancient traditions.*
> (Evans 1957: 27; also see Evans 1958: 10)

The early 19th-century Scottish economist, Samuel Laing, considered the qualities of individualism and egalitarianism to be particularly pronounced in Norway, a country he described as the "Highland fens without the Highland lairds." He attributed this peculiarity to the traditional equal inheritance of land: "In Norway . . . every man has Odel's right, or as I understand the term, is feudal superior of his own lands . . ." (Laing 1854: 40).

Ironically, it was the peripheral political position of Norway during more than 400 years of domination by Denmark (1397-1814) that allowed this economic system to be perpetuated in the highlands. The Norwegian humanist, Absalom Pederssøn Beyer, writing in early 17th century Bergen, complained:

> *From the day when Norway fell under Denmark . . . it lost its virile strength and power and became old and grey and heavily weighted-down . . .*
> (quoted in Storm 1895: 21; my trans.)

Absalom reminded his readers of the far-reaching exploits of their ancestors and was especially bitter concerning the trading monopoly established by the Hanseatic merchants who had long since founded an outpost for themselves in Bergen. Norway had indeed "lost its virile strength" and become "old and grey and heavily weighted-down" *as a political power;* without a court of her own or opportunity for official trade relations, she had actually become remote to her neighbors in Europe. Two centuries later, the Scottish economist, Laing, called Norway ". . . the most unfrequented tract of land in Europe." (Laing 1854: 62) and observed:

> *It appears extraordinary that three millions of people, so near to our coast, require all the articles which we manufacture, and hav-*

*ing commodities which we specially require,—wood and iron,
—should have so little correspondence with Britain.*

(Laing 1854: 13)

He found the country to be ". . . evidently rich and well cultivated" and
seemed to feel that the inhabitants might not have suffered unduly from
". . . being removed from all foreign influences." (Laing 62f) Indeed,
these matters were of little moment to the majority of rural Norwegians,
who continued to live in their mountain communities as generations had
lived before them, and to maintain firm confidence in their manner of interpreting and dealing with the world.

From the foregoing, it would seem that all idiosyncratic characteristics
of the isolated mountain valleys of Norway could be neatly explained by
geographical, political, and sociological determinants—from the con-
ventionalized communicatory structures represented by domains to individualism itself. However, functionalist explanations prove far from adequate for events that unfolded after Norway regained a large measure of
autonomy in 1814. There were two immediate results of independence
form Denmark: 1) a strong nationalistic fervor that manifested itself most
dramatically in the institutionalization of a new written Norwegian language—one that reflected the speech patterns of the rural dialects, and 2)
increased ease in communication with the rest of Europe. These two ten-
dencies might well seem to be in direct conflict with one another. Yet, we
have interesting evidence from a contemporary journal that Norwegians
did indeed take advantage of the increased ease of transportation at the
very time nationalistic ideals were in ascendency:

*Note, 1876.—During the twenty years that have elapsed since my
first visit, the development of tourist traffic between England and
Norway has been very remarkable. Instead of a vessel of notorious
unfitness for passenger traffic, such as that in which I sailed from
Hull in 1856, there are now some excellent vessels sailing from
that port to the same destination. Instead of carrying six or seven
saloon passengers and two in the forecabin, they are now all
crowded at every trip during the summer. . . .*

*The still greater and really astonishing increase of steampacket
communication on the coast, fjords, and lakes of Norway, will be
described as I proceed.*

(Williams 1876: 17f)

The increased availability of convenient modes of public transportation
and the increased amount of travel for reasons other than necessity were

preceded by a sudden increase in national prosperity and population growth. The above-quoted economist, Laing, associated these circumstances with Norway's new political state of independence (Laing 1854; 122). Finally, in this century, the building of the railroad from east to west, through the formidable mountains between Oslo and Bergen, and, recently, the prevalence of motor vehicles, has resulted in a complete breakdown of the old social order.

With eyes awakened to the new possibilities, one can view Norway's pre-independence history in deeper perspective. Indeed, there exists documentary evidence that traffic between the outside world and even the rural districts of Norway never in fact came to a complete standstill. It seems that during these centuries of foreign domination—while Norwegian culture remained an unknown quantity to most European peoples—there was always some commercial activity on the part of Norway. The Danish rulers saw to the construction of a system of roads; and, we know that, even during the most difficult years, a trading network had to exist to procure, for all parts of Norway, at least one necessary commodity: salt. Salt was used to preserve herring, the staple food for all social classes in the "Atlantic Ends." The salt way had to be kept open, and that became a popular saying.

Even the mountain barriers that surrounded the pockets of settlements in the highlands were not so impenetrable as generally supposed. There were constantly traveling tinkers, weavers, and peddlers of wares who managed to deal with them; and an art historian has found that:

> Telemark, a culturally rich district in south central Norway, has fostered a number of capable rosemalers. Though their own district was economically unable to support many artists, they found eager patrons in the adjacent districts of Numedal, Setesdal, and Rogaland. Their urge to create and beautify must have been unusually strong, for the barriers between their home district and their neighbors were tremendous. Mountains cover all but the coastal region, and swift running streams and huge lakes are too numerous to count. To reach any other part of Norway from Telemark it was necessary to go on foot over the mountains, and often over not just one range but several. Even now there are only a very limited number of roads through the district and just a few miles of railroad.
>
> (Stewart 1953: 100f)

Thus, the seaman, the tradesman, the craftsman, peddler, and artist all seem to have traveled across the mountain barriers, when it was necessary to do so. The *hardingfele spelemann*, as has been remarked upon in passing, was also itinerant. Very often, the fiddler would leave his farm and his family behind him—sometimes for a period of years—while he wandered from community to community, applying himself to his exacting, although unremunerative, art. He played at weddings (where he served a ritualistic function) and dances; and, in the old days, competed with other fiddlers at the fairs. Thus, he could, and often did, build up a reputation. Today's *spelemann* travels constantly to folk festivals for very much the same reason. Indeed, the Harding fiddler's lengthy absences from home have become such an important part of the tradition that a number of *slåttar* are said to have been given to fiddlers by *fossegrimen* (the waterfall sprite) to insure a welcome reception after a lengthy absence from home.

All indications show, then, that the linguistic and musical dialects have never been maintained for the reasons of necessity alone; traffic in and out of settlements in the highlands was not so infrequent as has been assumed; yet the desire to hold on to local identity remained. It was reflected in the attitude of an eleven-year-old schoolboy to a teacher native to another locality of Norway. The teacher (as may be remembered from the *Ethnography*) had been hired, after studying and passing examinations in the dialect; but, during the first day of classes, the incensed student walked out on him and shouted: "You have the pitch wrong. I will not stay to hear my dialect insulted." This action on the part of the Rauland scholar is an example of a deliberate effort to impede the occurrence of any change in his linguistic dialect. It exemplifies the same kind of will that is implied in the quotation heading the previous chapter: "I shall never be able to dance to the playing of my husband; for he was born and brought up in Hallingdal, while I was brought up with Telemark music."

It seems that preservation is not the result of passivity or stagnation but, to the contrary, it is willed by individuals, an active force controlled by those who are able. Just as the schoolboy was guarding his form of speech, the skilled *hardingfele spelemann* insists upon the utmost precision in maintaining local styles—and even individual interpretations.

As we have seen, the *hardingfele* tradition is by no means an anonymous one. Two great 19th-century virtuosi from Telemark, Håvard Gibøen (1809-1873) and Torgeir Augundson, better known as Myllargulen, (1801-1872) have not only become household names, but they have also been accorded a permanent place in national history. Indeed, the centennial anniversary of their deaths was commemorated in 1972 by a formal concert to which the king lent his presence and gave the keynote address. Notwithstanding substantial differences in individual style, these two master *spelemann* are both considered to be prime disseminators of

Telemark tradition. Eivind Groven, in making a comparative analysis of their music, has pointed out that even though ". . . they were often together and learned from one another. . . . this did not prevent each from possessing a repertoire that belonged to his own temperament. Therefore, we can today speak of Myllar-playing and Håvard-playing." (Berge 1972: 234; my trans.)

Johannes Dahle is a quiet proselytizer for the Tinn tradition, always generous with his time for those who are sincerely interested in publicizing it. In recording Dahle's playing at different times over a period of years (1967-1979), I found that he was quite able to reproduce with exactitude his own compositions, those of others, and even particular improvisations of well-known *spelemann*. (See Chapter 5 for a detailed example.) This ability existed side-by-side with his creative ability, for he continued to invent new music.

We have here evidence for the deliberate prevention of change for reasons of maintaining self identity—an example of the individual musician's control over permanent change. Moreover, the ability to change from one musical code to another (to code switch) implies a control over temporary change. A further adaptation of sociolinguistic concepts proves useful to show the interdependency of musical meaning and social situation, as may be illustrated by the following examples:

1) *Situational code switching:* Trygve Vågen brought about a redifinition of situation when he switched from virtuoso to dance accompanist. (*Ethnography*) Upon the appearance of refreshments in the Kostveits' living room, he led the persons present to change from respectful listeners to participants in the dancing and singing. (Ill. 14)

2) *Metaphorical code switching:* When I asked Vabø if he could demonstrate on his instrument the difference between the music of his own region in the west and that of Telemark, he responded: "Ja, I can show you a little how they play in Telemark. I cannot play very much—but maybe just a little of the way they play the same music we have here in the west—" It is interesting to note that Dagne Myhren was also willing to *illustrate*—even to perform—dance steps from other regions. However, she maintains that there is an essential difference between this and dancing her native idiom. (See preceding chapter) In both cases, there is a musical quotation, no change in situation.

3) *Situation, Setting, and Domain:* At the Tuddal Festival, we remember, Knut Buen felt equally at home in the rarified, dedicated atmosphere of the "invited day" and in the informal atmosphere of the previous day

15. *Knut Buen*

Knut Buen hosting the invited *spelemenn* on the second day of the Tuddal Festival.

KONSERTER,
MUNCH-MUSEET

Sommerkonsertene i Munch-museet, Tøyengt. 53,
finner sted *hver tirsdag kl. 20.00*. Entré kr. 10,—.
Billetter selges i Munch-museet fra kl. 14.00.
Arrangementene administreres av Oslo kommunes kunstsamlinger på vegne av kulturutvalget.

JUNI
Tirsdag 12. juni kl. 20.00
    Irma Urrila, sopran, Geir Henning Braaten, klaver. Verker av Mozart, Schubert, Bergman og Mahler.
Tirsdag 19. kl. 20.00
    Oslo Trio: Stig Nilsson, fiolin, Aage Kvalbein, cello, Jens Harald Bratlie, klaver. Verker av Haydn, Grieg,
    Sæverud, Halvorsen og Dvorak.
Tirsdag 26. kl. 20.00
    Eva Knardahl, klaver. Verker av Grieg.

JULI
Tirsdag 3. kl. 20.00
    Erik Niord Larsen, obo, Hilde Ringlund, klaver. Verker av Hindemith, Poulenc, Britten, Debussy og
    Dutilleux.
Tirsdag 10. juli kl. 20.00
    Bjarne Fiskum, fiolin, Einar Henning Smebye, klaver, Verker av Brahms, Webern og Strauss.
Tirsdag 17. kl. 20.00
    Ole Jørgen Strømberg, klarinett, Geir Tore Larsen, cello, Helge Myhren, klaver. Verker av Beethoven,
    Brahms og Schumann.
Tirsdag 24. kl. 20.00
    Torkil Bye, fløyte, Helge Myhren, klaver. Verker av Blavet, Franck, Martinu og Poulenc.
Tirsdag 31. juli kl. 19.30
    Knut Buen, hardinfele, Einar Steen-Nøkleberg, klaver. Verker av Grieg.

AUGUST
Tirsdag 7. kl. 20.00
    Anne-Eline Riisnes og Eline Nygaard, klaver. Verker av Grieg, Haydn og Chopin.
Tirsdag 14. kl. 20.00
    Knut Skram, baryton, Robert Levin, klaver. Verker av Schubert, Sparre-Olsen, Sinding, Ives og Copland.
Tirsdag 21. kl. 20.00
    Knut Skram, baryton, Robert Levin, klaver. Verker av Schubert, Sparre-Olsen, Sinding, Ives og Copland.
Tirsdag 21. kl. 20.00
    Egil Hovland-konsert. Medvirkende: Den Norske Blåsekvintett: Per Øien, fløyte, Erik Niord Larsen, obo,
    Erik Andresen, klarinett, Odd Ulleberg, waldhorn, Torleiv Nedberg, fagott, Geir Henning Braaten, klaver.
Tirsdag 28. kl. 20.00
    Gunnar Sønstevold-konsert.
    Medvirkende Norsk Strykekvartett: Ørnulf Boye Hansen, fiolin, Mette Steen, fiolin, Oddbjørn Bauer, bratsj,
    Marie Strøm, cello, Gunnar Sønstevold, tasteinstrumenter, Mai Sønstevold, tasteinstrumenter.
Søndag 5., 12., 19. og 26. august kl. 14.00:
    Teatergruppen Ensemblet presenterer forestillingen «Edvard Munch — painted words». Medvirkende:
    Ineke Brinkman, Gry Enger, Rolf Iversen, Bjørg Vatle. Musikk: Magni Wentzel, Regi: Karen Randers
    Pehrson. Entré kr. 20,—.

Omvisninger i Munch-museet
I tiden 20/6—26/8
Tirsdager kl. 18.00:
    Omvisning på norsk.
Onsdager kl. 12.00:
    Omvisning på engelsk.
Torsdager kl. 18.00:
    Omvisning på engelsk.
Fredager kl. 12.00:
    Omvisning på engelsk.
Lørdager kl. 12.00:
    Omvisning på engelsk.
Søndager kl. 13.00:
    Omvisning på norsk.

Knut Buen

Torkil Bye

16. Knut Buen is just as much at home in the formal setting of the recital hall;
public service calendar of events in Oslo (summer, 1981).

when anyone was welcome to get up and perform, another example of situational shifting (Ill. 15). Both situations took place on the grassy open lawn of the folk museum; but the atmosphere was just as intensely serious on the second day as if it had been a concert hall. Buen showed himself able to cope expertly with the concert hall domain; although the atmosphere was similar it brought with it certain additional forms of communication: e.g., formal dress, and printed announcements, programs and calendars with formal pictures (Ill. 16).

The significant thing about the existence of various kinds of musical code switching is that it illustrates the manipulaton of resources within conventionally established boundaries. Control over temporary change, I have termed it; and this ability is manifested in another way by the technique of improvisation on stock melodic outlines. Constraints placed by geographical factors (region or locality) or social convention (domain or situation) are not passive determinants after all but challenges to the skill and ingenuity of the player.[4] The greatest players, in addition, have the power to create new pieces within the old framework and even to add new elements that can remain permanent features.

IV ESOTERICISM: CODE SECRECY

> Those who don't like this music—Well, they play no instrument
> —or else, perhaps, they play the musical comb.

The Hardanger fiddle tradition functions both as a symbol of cultural pride and as a secret code that is fully understandable only to the fiddlers themselves. Most of the residents of Rauland share this code to a greater extent than might be imagined; they understand the rhythmic patterns, recognize the tunes upon which the slåtts are based, know the folklore surrounding players and music, and have for this tradition the same kind of nationalistic veneration that makes them esteem, rather than disparage, their local language dialect. But Finn Vabø, we may remember, emphasized the difference between easy-to-understand and difficult-to-understand pieces, and he maintained that those who did not appreciate the most difficult pieces were those who did not play themselves. Only the *spelemann* can instantly recognize the player on a strange tape recording by individual style. Unknowledgable listeners, at the other end of the spectrum will say: "It all sounds the same; you can't tell one piece from another," or·complain that: "There is no melody anyone can sing."

Harding fiddle communication on its most esoteric level is from one fiddler to another; it exists informally in the back corridors of festival halls or at the weekly meetings of the local *spelemannslag*—or, competitively, on the festival platform itself. The *hardingfele spelemann* performs three principal functions within his community: he leads the bridal processional at traditional weddings, he plays for dancing, and he plays to be listened to. Being a good dance accompanist is an art in itself, and certain fiddlers are esteemed for being clever at it. But the greatest glory goes to the virtuosi of the tradition, and the most highly regarded slåtts are *lydarslåttar*. Thus, the concert situation is of central importance to the tradition; it is always a formal affair, to some extent at least, for the mere presence of a skilled Hardanger fiddler will turn an informal gathering into a respectful audience—as happened when Trygve Vågen played at the Kostveit farmhouse. Even later in the evening, when he switched from virtuoso to dance accompanist (and caused a redefinition of situation), it was quite clear that he was in complete control of the social as well as the musical organization of the evening.

Showmanship has a place in any virtuoso tradition and serves to further identify the musician as endowed with special powers. Per Bolko, the Hardanger virtuoso whose shoulder was bitten by an ardent fan—and who named a fiddle *slått*, the *Shoulder-Bite*—is credited with putting into effect a Paganini-like scheme. Bolko, it seems, devised a stratagem for getting the better of his competitors at a wedding to which a number of *spelemenn* had been invited. He would previously tune his strings so high in pitch that the other players, trying to match their leader's brighter intonation, would find their strings breaking, one by one. The general consensus was "*trolldom.*" (Bjørndal 1966: 137)

Myllarguten himself was explicit in stating that he wanted his music to be listened to, not danced to; his biographer does not hesitate to call him a genius (Berge 1972: vi). Both Myllarguten and Gibøen were child prodigies, and they performed many of the same kinds of feats as boy wonders that we associate with 19th century virtuosi of the standard violin tradition. At a very tender age, they amazed unsuspecting relations who mistook their playing, usually heard from behind doors, for that of the finest *spelemenn*. They competed successfully with the best adult virtuosi of their time when they were so young that they had to be lifted to a table to play, stools provided for their tramping feet.

Myllarguten's fame spread so that by the time he was fairly well on in years, he received a command-invitation to play for the king of Denmark in Copenhagen. We do not know the royal reaction to Myllarguten's playing, but we do have a newspaper criticism of one of several performances in the Tivoli concert hall. According to this account, his playing struck the Danish newspapermen—among other things—as formless and unmelodious, his instrument's sound as raw. Most interestingly, he was faulted for "tramping so hard" with his feet (Berge 1972: 79). The response from the Norwegian urban establishment was scarcely more knowledgeable, when Myllarguten, at Ole Bull's invitation, took part in a program of folk music in Bull's newly acquired Bergen theatre. (Smith 1943: 84) But up and down the west coast of Norway, as well as in all parts of Telemark, Myllarguten left a lasting mark—both in the form of a style of playing and a body of pieces. Similarly, the Tinn inheritance, developed by the creative will of Johannes Dahle, has become a predominant influence in all of Telemark. It seems that the esotericism of the tradition, while leading to gross misunderstandings among outsiders, does not stand in the way of perpetuation and development by those who have the ultimate power, the *spelemenn*.

It is interesting that special magical powers were attributed not only to the swashbuckling Myllarguten, but, just as frequently, to the sober Gibøen. Johannes Dahle, like Gibøen before him, stayed close to home, drawing disciples to his isolated farm house and sending tape recordings out. He avoided competitions, even though he used to be asked to judge them; the reader may remember that his listening-piece celebrating the antics of the wild stallion, Tåkatind, was composed as a rebellion against the atmosphere of a national competition from which he was returning. Despite his retiring nature, he received exceptional recognition during his lifetime: the King's medallion (a national honor) and his bust placed in the Tinn secondary school entrance, not to speak of the more than 400 pieces recorded by the National Broadcasting Station. (See Appendix for a listing of his repertoire, as compiled by Magne Myhren.) The verneration he received was for his knowledge and development of the Tinn tradition, certainly one of the richest and most esoteric traditions in the world. (See Ill. 17)

In summary, then, we can say with some conviction that the *harding-fele spelemann* is able to change code according to audience, social setting, or situation; he is able to persuade, preserve, and to innovate. Strong feelings of social identity, as well as great respect for the achievements of certain individuals, has resulted in great preservative powers —both as to styles and to particular pieces. At the same time, an equally strong respect for the creative abilities of the great *spelemenn* invites innovation.

> *The emphasis on individual choice must not be construed as an argument that minimizes societal influences: . . . social factors, whether pertaining to the culture at large or to particular groups of musicians, are reflected in the way musicians decide to pursue their craft. However, a realization of the nature of a musician's control over his resources may well answer questions that are totally inexplicable now, especially in regard to sudden and unexpected shifts in style.*
>
> (Hopkins 1976: 462)

It may also explain the seeming dichotomies of Norwegian traditional culture; why it is possible to have the co-existence of the ancient and the new, the far-away with the close at hand in this nation that has been called "two countries in one." (See Part II, Chapter 1) This evidence of the individual musician's control over his resources implies, for the sphere of musical performance, the same kind of "aural thinking" that we have found to be an integral part of even the initial perception of a musical structure (Chapter 3). It may further be seen in emic genre differentiation (Chapter 2); for genres seem to be classified, not only in accordance with obvious similarities of sound patterns, but also with reference to a cluster of associative features known only to those within the tradition.

Jan Vansina has found that, in attempting to determine the historical veracity of nonliterate sources, the character of each genre must be taken into consideration. Precise re-telling, for example, must be an ingredient of magic formulas, he points out (Vansina 1961: 143f). John D. Smith has described a religious epic tradition in western India that is not improvisatory, even though it exhibits the basic features noted by Lord for epics in general (Smith 1977: 141). Vansina and Smith were describing for their fields the effect of individual control over change.

Indeed, no mechanistic interpretation can account for the striking success of intentionality to preserve, reject, vary, innovate, or alternate between traditional styles or elements. Melville Herskovits has isolated selectivity as ". . . an important feature of culture change; that is, no group accepts innovatons from other cultures wholesale, but rather accepts some items and rejects others." (1948: 5) Alan Merriam has discussed for music the point made by Vansina for oral history: i.e., one may expect less change to occur in religious music than in social or recreational music. (1964: 3007) And the musicologist, Gustave Reese, has provided an impressive example, citing a chant melody that appeared in manuscripts dating from the ninth to the eleventh century (Reese 1947: 115f)[5]. The important point, however, is not the religious nature of the music but the desire to preserve it intact.

It seems that every approach we take to the study of meaning within the Norwegian *hardingfele* tradition leads us back to the same dichotomies —contradictions that have been noticed for the other aspects of Norwegian culture by analyzers in other fields. However, there is one common factor that overrides these differences, and that factor is the control of change—a cognitive matter.

The existence of aural thinking bears out the opinion of Lévi-Strauss that music (like language) is one of several manifestations of human thought. Some years ago, he complained to an assemblage of anthropologists and linguists:

> . . . we have been behaving as if there were only two partners —language on the one hand, culture on the other. . . . But we have not been sufficiently aware of the fact that both language and culture are the products of activities which are basically similar. I am now referring to this uninvited guest which has been seated during this conference beside us and which is the human mind.
>
> (Lévi-Strauss 1963: 71)

This analysis of "aural thinking" as it operates within the context of Norwegian society may have more general relevance for understanding the skilled musician's cultural role; it should be fruitful to compare with information from other cultures. To this end, it has been necessary to ask: why should an individual *spelemann* determine to preserve this characteristic or to change that one? Given the existence of aural thinking, change and non-change need no longer be seen as opposites; rather, they may be viewed as different aspects that are available to the *spelemann* for his manipulation. In this light, the consistent co-existence of preservation and innovation within the tradition must be considered a distinctive feature of it. But we still must consider how this esoteric code is viewed by outsiders to the tradition.

Emergence of the Classical

I nearly fell off the piano stool, when Knut showed me how the Telemark springar should really be played. I injected the Tele-springar rhythm into the Grieg piano arrangements whenever I could; sometimes a full bass line makes it impossible.

 Rehearsal sessions for the LP recording of the Knut Dahle pieces that had once—nearly a century ago —introduced Grieg to notated examples of Norwegian indigenous music had yielded an unexpected result: an attempt to graft onto the Grieg arrangements the original performance style. Einar Steen-Nøkleberg spoke of his new knowledge as a revelation. I could not help contrasting his enthusiasm with the attitude of the cellist who had warned me in Bergen eighteen years ago:

The way they hold the bow, with the little finger often raised above—not even touching—the wood. You'll see they can't develop right arm technique: never learned to hold the bow correctly.

The professional cellist—a member of a visiting symphony orchestra —prepared me for my first personal encounter with Hardanger fiddle music. Finn Vabø's deft manipulation of the bow, however, provided me with a very different picture from the one I had thus been led to expect; and it was, moreover, a first impression borne out by later experience. In contradistinction to the opinion quoted above, the bow arm position used in *hardingfele* playing is not an incorrect, or ineffectual, one; indeed, it is almost identical with the position used to advantage by the Russian school of violinists.

The cellist's remark is significant for our purpose because it serves to demonstrate a typical misunderstanding of the rural violin tradition by a fine player of symphonic music—a tradition knitted to the courtly centers of central Europe. During the eighteen years since this incident took place, the *hardingfele* tradition has become increasingly important in the cities of southern Norway. Most unexpectedly, it has recently manifested itself in the southern port city of Stavanger—a piece of news that made the headlines and a featured article in *Spelemannsbladet*, the official organ of *Landslaget for Spelemenn (The Players' National Association)*:

> Stavanger is not the first city that comes to mind in connection with folk music. Earlier, many associated it with herring in oil. Nowadays, it is only oil. Herrings are gone. But, during the last 5-6 years, there has existed a spelemannslag in Stavanger—of all places—under the name, Vibå Spelemannslag.
>
> (Hovda 1979: 12; my trans.)

Stavanger seems indeed an unlikely place for germination of interest in traditional culture. The Harding violin had never gained a foothold in this part of Norway, a region associated with that brand of pietism that saw the fiddle as an instrument of the devil; and Stavanger long ago began to assume a cosmopolitan status—first as a seaport, more recently as a hub for air travel. In 1979 (the same year as the publication of the Hovda article), the Norwegian-American weekly, *Nordisk Tidende*, devoted a front-page story to the subject of the newest Stavanger industry. Under the headline: OIL ACTIVITIES HAVE NOT LED TO UNCONTROLLED DEVELOPMENT IN STAVANGER, we read:

> It is 15 years since the search for petroleum first began on the Norwegian Continental Shelf. In the course of these years, most of the firms taking part in the exploration have located their headquarters in Stavanger.
>
> A total of 6,500 foreigners from altogether 80 countries have taken up residence in Stavanger. They represent half of the population growth in Stavanger for the period after oil activities began. . . . Stavanger's American school. . . . is one of the largest in Europe. There is also a French and a British school.

Most interesting for the subject at hand is the following remark:

> The mayor believes that the cultural influence of the influx of foreign nationals has had an enriching effect on the local community.

These influences can also give the district an increased realization
of its own identity and a desire to preserve local traditions. . . .
(*Nordisk Tidende* 9/13/79:lf: my trans.)

The presence of a chapter of national fiddlers' organization in an area
that has been so inhospitable to this tradition—and at a time of such a
dramatic influx of foreign personnel and capital is thus explained: the result of an increase in feelings of self worth, brought about by the very existence of ethnic diversity.

It is important to realize that Stavanger is only one of the most recent
areas to be newly receptive to the Hardanger fiddle, a gradual encroach-
ment upon the *flatfele* territory began as far back as the end of the last
century:

A charasteristic feature of the Norwegian spelemanns-tradition the
last couple of hundred years is that the land, so to speak, is divided
into parts: one where hardingfele *is the dominant instrument, and*
one where the ordinary violin has ruled. During the last century,
the boundaries between these two kingdoms have had a tendency
to shift: the hardingfele *made an impasse into traditional* flatfelle
districts. What are the reasons for this?
(Ledang 1974b: 317; my trans.)

The desire to solve this puzzle led to the development of a remarkable aural history project conducted by the University of Trondheim in 1972-3.
The information gathered in *Musikklivet i ei bygd,* (*Music Life in a Town-*
ship), is relevant to our present topic of study, especially interesting in
juxtapostion to the Stavanger news stories detailed above.

The subject of focus in the Trondheim project similarly concerns the
penetration of the Harding violin into an area previously outside its domain, but this time the locality in question, the township of Meldal in the
region of Trøndelag, lies at the northern, rather than the sourthern, pe-
riphery of *hardingfele* territory. The time period under scrutiny occurred
at the extreme other end of the chronological spectrum—at the time
when the Harding fiddle was beginning to assume an extra-regional importance. Ledang tells us:

In Trøndelag, from the old days a typical flatfele *kingdom, the*
hardingfele *has become used in cities during the last generations.*
It is striking that Meldal (a township with rich local culture-tradi-

tion, having, among other things, a line of celebrated spelemenn *from 1800-1900) is remarkable in this connection. Here the* hardingfele *was introduced at the turn of the century and is today used by the most acclaimed* spelemenn.

(Ledang 1974b: 317; trans.)

The basic information gathered for this project was obtained through tape-recorded interviews and old newspaper articles. These materials demonstrate that the strongest influences upon the citizenry of Meldal were public concerts and *kappleikane* (the competitions). Concert-giving *spelemenn* from the *hardingfele* regions of Norway included Meldal and neighboring townships on their itineraries from 1896 to the second World War. *Kappleikane* not only provided an opportunity to bring music from Hardanger fiddle territory, but also (according to sometimes quite critical remarks in contemporary newspaper articles) imposed the authoritative opinions of judges who apparently were not averse to withholding awards from *flatfele spelemenn*, and sometimes even advising them to purchase Hardanger violins. Hallvard Ørsal, denied a first prize in the 1905 *kappleik* on this account, bought himself a Hardanger fiddle forthwith; in later years, he not only won several first prizes as a Hardanger fiddle player in national competitions, but his concert tours took him to America, as well as, on many occasions, to Meldal. Critical voices were raised in contemporaneous newspapers; for example:

> *It bothers me much that judges of Kappleik tell the players to switch to* hardingfele. *What is going to happen when people from some such valley hear such talk:* Hardangerfele, Hardangersom. Hardangerdragt! *Do you see pest-contagion? . . . the peculiarities of the* tronderske *are disappearing with the* fela *which is made for them and to which they reasonably belong.*
>
> (*Fjellposten* 2/1/17; quoted in Ledang 1974: 322; trans.)

It seems that an elite *hardingfele* tradition was being imposed upon those who had been brought up on the less esoteric style of dance music with broad European ties—the waltzes, rheinlanders, polkas, etc. of the flat violin, which was defined according to its dance function. The Hardanger violin, on the other hand, played lydarslåtts and "high prestige dance slåtts from the *hardingfele* territory." Thus, the intrusion of the new instrument brought with it "wide-reaching consequences for the playing style," and the *hardingfele* began to assume the role of national symbol. Ledang points to the national-romantic "set into an actual political connection:

the striving for national autonomy and for national identity. Its concert-function identifies the urban bourgeois music-milieu" as opposed to the "local milieu" of traditional music:

> *The appraisals that appeared in the local press depend on such a view. . . .* "And so we had the pleasure of hearing a section of old *slåtts and other national music from his (Lars Nordvolds) harding-fele.* Lars is a master spelemann, *has been involved with concert-participation and plays constantly in festivals and stemner."* (Ork-dølen *13, Aug. 1918)*
>
> (Ledang 1974: 327)

As Ledang points out: "The central thing is that this acceptance refers to a certain framing tied to the performance: a concert situation." (Ledang 1974: 327)

These symbolic associations of the *hardingfele* invite the veneration of some who think they ought, rather than actually do, understand and enjoy the music [also documented by the Meldal project; see Ledang 1974: 325]—not unlike some who attend symphonic concerts.[1] Among members of the in-group, of course, the special, almost religious-like awe that accompanies the concert-virtuoso function of this music is, as it has been, sincerely felt. I have experienced this aura in many diverse settings; as we have seen, it turns informal situations into formal ones—whether in farm house or city apartment, sheep meadow or recording studio. The extra-musical connotations, including the genius-talent concepts, are present today as they were during the nineteenth-century and possibly earlier. Recently, a new and important strain of interest in traditional music and dance has manifested itself among urban young people. An American graduate student who spent a year in Norway studying the Hardanger fiddle made a valuable analysis of the contrasting atmospheres of *flatfele* and *hardingfele* parties in Oslo. The former, she reports, were characterized by lightheartedness, informality, and all-inclusive participaton; technical proficiency in the dancing was not sought after. The music, of course, continued to be the so-called "gammaldans" style: the polkas, waltzes, rheinlanders, and other central European dances of the late nineteenth-century. In comparison:

> *. . . the* Hardingfele *parties were solemn affairs. The meal was eaten in almost complete silence, and then the dancing began. Only one fiddler played at a time, as is the tradition with the har-dingfele. . . . The fiddler at such parties is always an expert, usually*

a visiting professional from the country. The dancers were also excellent, executing the dance steps with great skill. The dancers didn't talk much and tended to select their partners from a close group of friends. There was little mingling and I was conscious of being an outsider.

The formality of the hardingfele *party was evident both in the emphasis placed on technical proficiency in both dance and music, as well as in the presence of small closed social groups. Another formal aspect was the dress of both musicians and dancers. To a greater extent than at the Østerdal* flatfele *parties people wore the costumes of their districts.*

The most striking aspect of the hardingfele *party was the extent to which both dancers and fiddlers seemed to be "in another world."*

Alcohol is served at these parties, with the fiddlers being among the more conspicuous consumers. However, instead of making people louder and more outgoing—as was the case at the flatfele *party—it seemed to have the opposite effect on those at the* hardingfele *party, making them moodier and more introspective. I believe that the alcohol may have been in order to gain an increased sense of being in a different world. . . . Hardingfele parties are . . . similar to participating in a religious ritual.*

(Neal 1978: 4ff)

Despite the constancy and the significance of the cultural role played by the Norwegian indigenous tradition, a recent historian of Scandinavian music utterly ignores its existence:

Norwegians are by no means deprived of creative genius, but political and economic reversals conspired to punch a hole in their country's history. During the baroque and classical eras the cultivation of music depended on a leisured aristocracy; but no Esterhazys lived in Norway. (Yoell 1974: 12)

While the traditional music of Norway remained invisible to the above author, it has more commonly been regarded as raw material for nationalistic composition by music historians. An early expression of this point of view (dating from the last quarter of the 19th century) was articulated by Rikard Nordrak—the composer who, during a short life span, greatly influenced Edvard Grieg:

They talk of carrying rocks to Norway but we have enough rock.
Let us use simply what we have. Nationalism, in music for exam-
ple, does not mean composing more Hallings and Springars such
as our forefathers composed. That is nonsense. No, it means build-
ing a house out of all these bits of rock and living in it.

(quoted in Lange 1958: 31)

An English news item that made reference to both the time and the place
of the Meldal project (the Trondheim area around the turn of the century)
provides us with an illustration of the outside view of Norwegian music:

The coronation of King Haakon and Queen Maud at Trondhjem
last month, the recent visit of Dr. Edvard Grieg to this country, and
the death of Hendrik Ibsen . . . call attention to Norway, the ro-
mantic land of mountain and fjord. The history of its art, as op-
posed to its folk music, almost begins with Grieg, whose composi-
tions, although he studied at the Leipzig Conservatorium, show the
strong influence of Norwegian national melodies and rhythms.

(*Monthly Musical Record* XXXVI 1906: 427)

Edvard Grieg had long been recognized in Europe and America as a
"nationalist" composer when an English critic in 1879 complained rather
illnaturedly that: "Grieg's mania for nationalism stifles the impulses of his
genius"; and more generally asserted that: "the importance of folk-music
for an already highly developed art-music is generally overestimated
. . . ." (*Monthly Musical Record*; July 1: 98f). Sometimes these anti-na-
tionalist opinions were given an ethnocentric bias:

To understand the artistic character and work of this composer,
Englishmen must do what is for them a somewhat difficult thing,
put themselves in sympathy with the intense feeling of nationality
which often inspires the inhabitants of a poor country when made
conscious of its inferiority by political connections with a more
powerful and dominant state. We, whose concerns are as world
wide as the British Empire, who know no masters and no superi-
ors, can hardly be expected to understand such a sentiment. . . .

(*The Musical Times*, Feb. 1888: 73)

More characteristic, however, were comments demonstrating a curious combination of ideas: a characterization of Grieg's music as being

facile, ("easy-to-understand," Finn Vabø would say) with a genuine interest in the innovative idiosyncratic aspects of his style. Thus, Daniel Gregory Mason wrote: "To the musical amateur no contemporary composer is better known than Grieg. Every school-girl plays his piano pieces . . . ." (Mason 1903: 201). The Russian composer, Peter Ilyitch Tchaikovsky, commented in a diary entry (1888): "Grieg is probably not by any means so great a master as Brahms. . . . apparently in Grieg the inclination toward obscurity is entirely absent; nevertheless, he stands nearer to us, he seems more approachable and intelligible because of his deep humanity." He continued to detail the reasons for his admiration of the Norwegian's style:

> Hearing the music of Grieg, we instantly recognize that it was written by a man impelled by an irresistible impulse to give vent by means of sounds to a flood of poetical emotion, which obeys no theory or principle, is stamped with no impress but that of a vigorous and sincere artistic feeling . . . a perfect simplicity, far removed from all affectation. . . . It is not surprising that he should be popular everywhere—in Paris, London and Moscow—that his name should appear in all concert programs, and that visitors to Bergen should deem it a pleasant duty to make a pilgrimage to the charming though remote haven where Grieg retires to work and where he spends most of his life.
>
> (Mason 1903: 200)

The skyrocketing of Grieg to international fame must have warmed the hearts of the Norwegian intelligentsia who, since the severance of Danish rule in 1819, had succeeded in developing *Nynorsk* and subsequently engaged themselves in the promotion of Norwegian indigenous culture in other realms. Small matter that, with the inimitable pidgeon-holing techniques of the culture analysts, Grieg has been stamped officialy as a "genuine minor master" (Abraham 1948: 16). Grieg had become a cornerstone of Norwegian formal culture—the guarantee, so to speak, of a place in history. Grieg, it is evident, took his role of cultural leader seriously; he was personally active in various official capacities as a promoter of contemporary Norwegian music. He arranged concert programs for the purpose of giving young Norwegian composers an opportunity to be heard, including the establishment of the National Music Festival in Bergen. At the same time, he favored a less parochial outlook on the part of Norwegians; for, we are told that "in the face of narrow-minded local patriotism, he insisted that one of the finest European orchestras should be engaged." Thus, the Dutch *Concertgebouw* orchestra under Mengelberg was invited to Bergen. (Abraham 1948: 11)

Now for our purposes, it is interesting indeed to reflect upon the fact that the activities of Grieg, as well as the printed views on his cultural role in Norway, occurred at the same time as the *hardingfele* of the southern highland area was being rather aggressively promoted, the period during which the national "folk" tradition of Norway was functioning through the concert circuits as a tradition associated with an "urban bourgeois music-milieu." (Ledang 1974: 327). Since the springars and hallings, in contradistinction to the prediction of Rikard Nordrak, have in fact continued to be played and to be composed to this day — indeed, to function as viable pieces of musical communication on their own, it is clear that we are dealing with more than a single body of music and more than a single perspective on the different musical traditions involved.

An important and dramatic meeting of the two (we might term "inner" and "outer") musical worlds in Norway occurred through the strenuous and persistent efforts of a fine *spelemann* from Telemark. In 1888, the same year that Tchaikovsky entered the above-quoted analysis of Grieg's music in his diary, Grieg received a letter from Knut Dahle. It is worth quoting in some detail:

> I am an elder national Hardanger violinist and have learned accurately to play after the fine old spelemenn Myllarguten, Håvard Gibøen, and Hans Hellos from Bø. I have long brooded over whether it could be played from notation and not get buried with the artist; therefore, I presume to send you some lines, since I have heard from newspapers and magazines that you have become the lands greatest musikanter . . . I began to play the violin when I was 10 years old and learned from my grandfather [Knut Synnstaut]. Later I visited these musician-spelemenn, and I recall many times travelling 6 [Norwegian] miles on my skis to obtain a single fingering. Therefore, I think it would be deplorable if it should completely die out.
>
> —Will you be so good as to respond . . . with the information of whether you or some one else is interested in preserving the tradition that for 100 years stood highest here in the valley. . . . I await your answer with yearning.
>
> (Anker 1943: 72f;
> Recently reprinted in Buen 1983: 72; my trans.)[2]

Grieg's response is not extant, although there was such a letter, according to a reference in another communication from Dahle to Grieg dated August 8, 1890. Here, Knut Dahle repeated his request and appended a list of slåtts that he had obtained from the great 19th century Telemark *spelemenn*. Three months later, Dahle wrote again:

> *Since I see that you have returned to your homeland, I have taken the liberty of writing you a few lines to wish you welcome back. I wrote a letter to you last fall but didn't know that you were abroad, but addressed it to Kristiania and that is probably the reason why you have not received it. My request concerned whether the national music could be preserved—the good Telemark slåtts which after my understanding stood on a much higher plane than they do now. Now I am approaching my sixtieth year and it is not certain how long I can continue to play; and there is no one in Telemark who is playing the old ones as I do.*
>
> *I have been visited by many spelemenn who are now doing their best to hold on to the past, but no one has learned my slåtts from end to end, but they are satisfied with anything. . . .*

Dahle followed this with a note just one week later:

> *I am waiting with yearning for some lines from you—I have nearly come to a disagreement with myself over whether to send this letter, when we do not have the least knowledge of each other.*
> (Buen 1983: 76; trans.)

This rather one-sided correspondence was initiated during a period of sadness and disillusionment in Knut Dahle's life. Dahle's wife, Ingeborg, had died in 1888, and this was a time especially notable in Telemark for religious revivalism:

> *Especially, they cracked down on the spelemann and the fiddle. It was sinful to play. . . . It was fiddle playing that tempted the young people to gather together and do what was bad, they thought.*
> (Buen 1983: 66; trans.)

Johannes Dahle told me that it was his grandfather's unhappiness that led Knut Dahle to journey to America in 1896, originally with the idea of emigration in mind. In America, Knut Dahle was warmly received by the

Norwegian-American community; he played *hardingfele* concerts, actually made instruments to sell, and composed at least one *slått* in commemoration of the New World (*Dakota Prairie*), which I have heard Johannes play on more than one occasion. In time, however, Knut Dahle decided to return to Norway and he arrived back in Tinn, Telemark, on July 18th, 1901. In 1901 (more than ten years after the original letter), Dahle again wrote to Grieg: "Today I noticed in the *Varden* that you have given a concert in Bergen and that you have also come home from abroad. I want to let you know that I also have been to America and come home." Dahle goes on to tell Grieg that many of his slåtts— particularly the Myllarguten ones—have been preserved through transcription in America; but:

> . . . I so fervently want a composer here to do the same thing and write them down. . . . When I am gone, the slåtts also will be gone. What is played now is in every way different. Will you have the goodness to write me again with the information concerning whether you have an interest in the old slåtts or if you know some one else.
>
> (Buen 1983: 76f)

Significantly, Knut Dahle enclosed with this letter a note from "Professor Hansen in Decorah, a great *Musikanter.*" This letter got an immediate and positive response from Grieg. Grieg, a keyboard player, pointed out that the slåtts should be transcribed by a violinist" . . . for bowings, tunings, fingering and matters of tone quality." He thanked Dahle for writing and concluded:

> I feel . . . that something might, ought, and shall be done. I shall today write to Kristiania about the matter. If a violin player can be found there who understands transcription and has the interest for this work, then he must either travel to you . . . or you must travel to him in Kristiania. . . .
>
> (Buen 1983: 77)

Grieg wrote to the violin-conductor, Johan Halvorsen, the same day as the above; and arrangements were made in short order for Dahle to travel to Kristiania and stay near Halvorsen while he transcribed the slåtts, Grieg acceding to a request by Dahle for travel money, Finally, on November 17, 1901, Halvorsen wrote Grieg:

Knut Dahle has come. Today rescued 2 slåtter *from oblivion. They are not so straightforward to transcribe. Small explosive charges that are like a little sandbar on a river rapid. . . . Knut Dahle is an intelligent and solid* spelemann.

(Buen 1983:83)

The early correspondence between Knut Dahle and Edvard Grieg has been quoted in some detail, because it has been given virtually no publicity even though it was made available to the public by Øyvind Anker almost 40 years ago. The significance of the fact that it was Knut Dahle who approached Grieg seems to have escaped most historians; those who mention it at all usually ignore Dahle's participation in this communication altogether (e.g., Lange 1958: 60). In point of fact, the evidence shows that Dahle persisted for more than 10 years before eliciting any real interest on Grieg's part; even then it seems clear that Norway's most celebrated composer was finally propelled into action by the news of Dahle's success with his project in America—as well as, of course, the letter of recommendation from the *musikanter* in Decorah, Iowa.

The letter Grieg wrote to Halvorsen detailing his reaction to the transcriptions has, on the other hand, been quoted frequently but selectively. Especially popular has been the following paragraph:

That, I call a Saturday evening, dear Halvorsen. Outside southerly gales are shaking the house, while a regular deluge pours down from the heavens above. But in this room it is cozy. I have just received your slåtts and have right now read them through again, making me actually chuckle with delight.

(Buen 1983: 88)

Grieg went on to lament that: ". . . I am not a fiddle player. How I hate this Leipzig Conservatory." Like Halvorsen, he comments on the characteristic use of the tritone—a feature, he said, that made him "wild and craxy in the year 1871—I stole it straight away for my *Folkelivsbilleder* (Folklife Pictures)." This interval, he called a spectre ". . . from one or another ancient scribe," and offered, with some indignation, a further comment:

It is inconceivable that no one here is taking up national music research when we in our folk music have such new sources for those who have ears to hear with, hearts to feel with and the intellect necessary to transcribe.

(Buen 1983: 83)

It is difficult to take seriously Grieg's much-quoted protestation that it would be "sinful" to arrange the slåtts for keyboard. Not only does he immediately follow with: "But the sin will sooner or later be committed. It is too tempting"; less than one paragraph later, he asks: "Do you want me, at this point, to attempt to get both your work and mine published at Peters?"

These last remarks have not been widely quoted—nor have the following sentences:

> It was good you sent Knut Dahle home again before he did some stupidities. This evening I received a divine letter. He was hurt in Kristiania, he said, he, because he could not fathom how he had lost . . . 40 kroner: "On trips, I never keep money in one place but set aside a little here and a little there . . . I came home and newly scrutinized my hiding places and found them in the inner jacket pocket; thus, I lost nothing on the trip . . ." So you see, he has fantasies; yes, one makes excuses for the old one, only to be glad of the result.
>
> (Buen 1983: 89)

Both Halvorsen's transcriptions and Grieg's arrangement of them were eventually published by Peters. Knut Dahle's name does not occur in either, although Grieg does mention "an old gleeman" in the preface to his edition:

> These Norwegian "Slåtter" ("Slått" is the usual Norwegian name for the peasant's dance), now for the first time brought before the public in their original form for the violin (or for the so-called Hardanger-fiddle) and re-arranged for the piano, were written down after an old gleeman in Telemarken. Those who can appreciate such music, will be delighted at the originality, the blending of fine, soft gracefulness with sturdy almost uncouth power and untamed wildness as regards melody and more particularly rhythm, contained in them. This music,—which is handed down to us from an age when the culture of the Norwegian peasant was isolated in its solitary mountain-valleys from the outer world, to which fact it owes its whole originality,—bears the stamp of an imagination as daring in its flight as it is peculiar.
>
> My object in arranging the music for the piano was to raise these works of the people to an artistic level, by giving them what I might call a style of musical concord, or bringing them under a

Ex. 27: (1965)

Ex. 28: (1967)

Ex. 29: (1975)

Ex. 30: (1979)

Ex. 31 (1979)

Ex. 32: (1979)

Ex. 33: (1983)

system of harmony. Naturally, many of the little embellishments, characteristic of the peasant's fiddle and of their peculiar manner of bowing, cannot be reproduced on the piano, and had accordingly to be left out. On the other hand, by virtue of its manifold dynamic and rhythmic qualities, the piano affords the great advantage of enabling us to avoid a monotonous uniformity, by varying the harmony of repeated passages or parts.

The meeting of the inner and outer national schools of Norway was not accomplished without friction. The flagrant lack of respect and lack of sensitivity to the artistry of Knut Dahle on the part of Grieg is difficult to countenance; after all his stock in trade was the presumed Norwegian character of his music, and Dahle was ". . . considered to be a master-spelemann by the bygdefolk who paid him great respect." (Hølje Dale, Rjukan, during an interview concerning his childhood memories in *Spelemannsbladet*. Nr. 3, 1981: 24; my trans). Curiously, there is genuine interest in the musical novelties at the same time contempt is expressed toward the musician who played them; and it is quite clear that both Grieg and Halvorsen are encountering the tradition for the first time —6 years before Grieg's death and a quarter century after his acceptance by the outside world as a nationalist composer. It is also ironic that, since the publication of the piano arrangements of Opus 72, analysts of Grieg's music have reserved their highest praise for the originality and intricacy they have found in these piano pieces. Quite typical is the following comment: "Of all the Norwegian folk music Grieg has taken up for artistic treatment, this is the most individual, that which stands most sharply in contrast to ordinary European musical feeling in respect both to har-

Ex. 34

Ex. 35

mony and rhythm." (Monrad-Johansen 1938: 348) Characteristically, they single out for special praise: ". . . the combination of 6/8 and 3/4, frequent use of augmented fourths . . . (and) skillful employment of ornament." (Abraham 1948: 64) Yet, Grieg himself clearly states:

> The few passages in which I consider myself authorized as an artist, to add to, or work out the given motives, will easily be found, on comparing my arrangement with the original, written down by Johan Halvorsen, in a manner reliable even for research-work, and published by the same firm.

In actual fact, the Halvorsen-Grieg versions of Knut Dahle's material show their lack of knowledge of the tradition. One of these pieces, *Jon Vestafe*, is already known to the reader, who may remember the measurements of its foot-beaten pattern (Ex. 23). The title, *Jon Vestafe*, refers to a *spelemann* who was closely associated with this *slått*. Jon Kjos (1754-1826) lived west of Tinn in Åmotsdale; hence, the name, Vestafe used by Tinn *spelemenn*. Whether Jon Kjos was the composer of this *slått*, or whether it was so called simply because he was fond of playing it, is not known. But we do know that Kjos was an early teacher of Torgeir Augundson, more commonly know as Myllarguten (the Miller's Boy). During the time Myllarguten was a young herdsboy in Åmotsdale: "Jon taught Torgeir many good *slaatir* that he was very fond of and which he often played. He called them 'Kjos-slaattine,' after Jon." (Berge 1972: 8; my trans.)

It should be interesting to compare what has survived in printed form (the Halvorsen and Grieg editions) with what continues to be transmitted aurally; we can refer to a number of recorded performances (from 1965-1983). Finn Vabø used this piece as his example of a *Telespringar* in the demonstration tapes he recorded for me in 1965, and Example 27 is a transcription of the first phrase of his performance. Two years later, during my first visit to Tinn, I recorded Johannes Dahle and Øystein Odden playing *Jon Vestafe* together (see Example 28). Despite the similarity between these two performances, there is substantial difference in another Johannes Dahle version of this *slått* recorded by Ola Kai Ledang in 1970 — also at Dahle's cottage (see Example 34). Both versions were received by Johannes Dahle from his grandfather, Knut. The considerable dissimilarity between them is due to the fact that they derive from two different strains of Telemark tradition (that of Rauland as opposed to that of Tinn).

Thus, Example 28 and Example 34 represent two different versions of the same phrase, recorded in the same place by the same player who learned both examples from the same source (Knut Dahle). I have heard many performances of the first version; they have been remarkable for their similarity to one another, whether performed on separate occasions by the same player or whether played by different Telemark *spelemenn*. Transcriptions 29 through 33 are all taken from performances of this first, more common, version. Example 29 represents the recording made by Kjetil Løndal for the perceptual experiment described in Chapter 3. (Also see that chapter for the machine's eye view of this passage.) Examples 30, 31, and 32 are taken from recordings made on my 1979 field trip. Examples 33 and 35 were written down from a tape recording made in November, 1983, when Ola Øyaland, leader of the Tinn *Spelemannslag*, found no difficulty in responding to my questions on the subject by playing *both* (Rauland and Tinn) versions of the *slått* under discussion: another skilled example of code-switching. Altogether, these examples attest to the reliability of this tradition throughout an eighteen year span.

Now we shall return to the Halvorsen transcripton of *Jon Vestafe* (Example 36). It may readily be noticed that the structure of this Telemark *springar* was distorted through incorrect barring. The Grieg arrangement (Example 37), which was based on Halvorsen, naturally had to be equally incorrect.

Now we have a clue to the peculiar brand of Norwegian-ness that belonged to Grieg and other nationalist composers who actually had little or no contact with "The Folk." Johann Vaa, writing in a recent issue of *Spelemannsbladet* suggested a term for this kind of music: kluss. Grieg's music, he wrote, is " successful kluss." (Vaa 1981: 15) When I asked Mr. Vaa to give an English definition of this word, he responded as follows: "to change a thing that ought not be changed. If you still do it, it is not so good as originally or it is quite another thing." In a book on Norwegian contemporary music, we are told that the nationalist composers:

> . . . *tried to immerse themselves in the old traditions, partly by becoming absorbed in the old collections of Lindeman and Landstad, partly by studying the results of contemporary research, such as O.M. Sandvik's transcriptions of folk melodies, and partly by observing traditions as they were still practiced.*
> (Hamit 1981: 10f; also see Gurvin 1940: 45;
> Huldt-Nystrøm 1966: 259)

It is clear that Grieg successfully used (insofar as his audience was concerned) ideas drawn, not from the folk tradition, but from the pale reflection of it found in published transcriptions: collections that did not differ-

Ex. 36

Ex. 37

entiate between *hardingfele* and *flatfele* styles, let alone regional styles, and made no reference to pitch system, uneven beat ratios, ornamentation, or improvisation. From the evidence found in contemporary references, we can deduce that the uninitiated public would have found it more difficult to deal with the real thing; for example, in a 1902 issue of a New York City music review, under the column heading, "This Week in Brooklyn," we read:

> On Tuesday evening, Mr. Thomas Witney Surette gave his last lecture on Folk Song, his subject for this week being Norse Music. Mr.

Surette was assisted by Miss Rebecca Mackenzie, soprano, who sang a number of the weird, haunting melodies in the original tongue. . . .

(The Concert-Goer #209, Nov. 14, 1902)

Some years later, an author refers to the "uncouth wildness of the dances themselves, as well as the rustic quality of the native instrument" (Abraham 1948: 66) More hostile was the response of urban Norwegians to the introduction of rural singers on Groven's radio program in the early part of this century; there was an outraged demand for singers who could "sing in tune" and who were properly accompanied by the piano. As we have seen, the pianist, Einar Steen-Nøkleberg, has experimented with injecting the *Telespringar* rhythm into the Grieg piano versions of the Dahle *slåttar*. Working with Knut Buen and Gunnar Dahle, he became aware of the subtle complexity that is part of the performance of the music in aural tradition, now as then.

Even today, one comes across the identification of traditional music with the past; e.g., see the Hamit quotation above. It bears witness to the fact that the evolutionary view of music continues to be as strong as the indigenous musical tradition continues to be vigorous. In the final section of this book, I would like to draw attention to what I find significant about the evidence from both sides of the folk-art confrontation.

CONCLUSION

Johannes Dahle echoed the spirit of his grandather when he replied to my expression of gratitude with: "It is only that I think the world should know about our special tradition here in Tinn." One can only imagine how surprised Knut Dahle would be if he could know that the outside public has readily accepted a distorted representation of his music in notation, while the *spelemenn* have continued throughout this century to transmit the Tinn slåtts aurally with astonishing accuracy.

It seems that the viewpoint of Grieg's public, on the one hand, and of the esoteric circle of "folk" musicians on the other, represented different comprehensions of the definition of history itself. In order to explain what I mean, I shall digress—and refer to an entirely different field of study: the history of science.

The historian of science, Thomas Kuhn, has pointed out that what he calls "normal science" draws a straight line of progress to the present. He compares the typical mentality of this kind of science to the "typical character of Orwell's *1984* : ". . . a victim of history re-written by the powers that be." (Kuhn 1962: 167) Most interestingly, he points out that:

> *Science education makes use of no equivalent for the art museum or the library of classics and the result is sometimes a drastic distortion in the scientist's perception of his discipline's past.*
>
> (Kuhn 1962: 167)

Those ambiguous words, *classics* and *classical* were apparently not used in European music history until after the style period known as "classical" in the narrowest sense. Perhaps this was occasioned by the fact that music had long been considered a science, not one of the humanities, and therefore it was expected that music also should proceed by accumulation of knowledge. At any rate, it seems that it was dissatisfaction with the new style that caused a changed viewpoint on the part of contemporary spokesmen for nineteenth century music:

> *Only from Romantic music's "taking the upper hand" and from the opposition it met (to which many important musicians of the 19th century belonged) did the need arise to find a name for that which would serve as an esthetic norm and a bulwark against what was felt to be an exaggerated individualization; only then did it become customary to speak of a "classic" beauty in contrast to what were considered "excrescences." Whereas for literature Schiller was already using the expression "classic" and Goethe applied it as contrast to "romanticism," in music the word "romantic" was apparently used earlier than "classic."*
>
> (Blume 1970: 8. Also see Bukofzer 1947: 410)

It is seldom realized that the European concept of classicism in music is of such recent vintage. Most important of all for our purposes is the fact that it brought with it a new interest in musical styles of the past. (Einstein 1947: 10; Grout 1960: 411ff)

Today, the term, "classic," is confusedly used in a number of different senses. Almost always, however, it carries with it the idea of ideal monuments that continue to be viable through time. When we speak of the Indian classical tradition or of *piobaireachd* as the classical music for the Highland bagpipe, we are referring to—as Peter Cooke aptly phrases it—a tradition with a pedigree. (Cooke 1979: 93) This is another way of saying: a tradition with a history. The reader may recall that Norwegian music has been regarded by some to be history-less, a matter explained by the fact that the country was, for many years, politically impotent.

The term, *history*, continues to be used with ambiguity. While the chanter who perpetuates knowledge of genealogical and other significant facts from the past is commonly known as an "oral historian," the phrase, "historical record" is usually assumed to involve the kind of written-down documentation upon which a "history of Spain," for example, might be written. The events detailed therein are assumed to have occurred far enough in the past to have become "historical"—i.e., of epic importance. To "make history": this contains the ideas of "epoch-making." To "have a history": implies the state of possessing the perspective of past events, whether or not they are of epic, or epoch-making proportions. Yet, "historical" can involve the idea of truth, accuracy of being objectively correct. A fourth meaning has been admirably described by the philospher, Martin Heidegger:

> . . . the totality of those entities which "change in time," and indeed the transformations and vicissitudes of man, of human grouping—their "cultures," as distinguished from Nature . . .
>
> (Heidegger 1962: 430)

It is in this sense that we say we should consider people in their historical context, and it is from this point of view that we can see anthropology, sociology, and history as requiring equivalent techniques of approach. Thus, to "put into historical perspective" means that we must uncover the relevance of the thing within its time context.

It is important to realize that any understanding of culture change must also involve an understanding of cultural non-change (or perseverance). To once again quote Heidegger:

> The "antiquities" preserved in museums . . . belong to a time "which is past"; yet they are still present-at-hand in the Present. How far is such equipment historical, when it is not yet past?
>
> (Heidegger 1962: 380)

George Kubler has developed this line of thought:

> The historian's special contribution is the manifold shapes of time. The aim of the historian, regardless of his specialty in erudition, is to portray time. He is committed to the detection and description of the shape of time.

> *Time, like mind, is not knowable as such. We know time only*
> *indirectly by what happens in it: by observing change and perma-*
> *nence; by marking the succession of events among stable settings;*
> *and by noting the contrast of varying rates of change.*

Perhaps the intimate association of music and history in many cultures may partly be explained by what Langer has described as the ". . . most important and novel revelation of music—the fact that time is not a pure successon, but has more than one dimension." (Langer 1942: 174)

Paradoxically, it was the art composer, Grieg, who proceeded according to the same perspective as "normal science"—accumulation of knowledge, using what he deemed folk music as raw material; while it was the folk musician, Dahle, who fought to preserve, disseminate and achieve a place in history for the classics of his tradition of Tinn, Telemark. Grieg's music—"a victim of history re-written by the powers that be"—must now be regarded, by those who consistently follow his own line of thinking, out-of-date music. Knut Dahle's music (now that music fashions have changed) is no longer considered raw material by any composer, but that does not mean that evolutionary doctrine in reference to Norwegian folk music has disappeared.

Surprisingly, we still find scholarly references to "levels of culture"; and we still come across the opinion that some musical systems are more culturally bound than others, a view similar—it would seem—to a belief that some persons can be a little more pregnant than others.

However, the theory that some music can be understood outside of cultural context is important for us to consider at this point. Both the concept and the fact of its being held up as an ideal came into European thinking not long after the "classic" idea with its concomitant interest in the past:

> *Most Western music has been "about something." . . . Within in-*
> *strumental music itself, the critical enthusiasm for the pure and ab-*
> *solute is the product of a very recent aestheticism. It belongs*
> *mainly to the second half of the nineteenth century; and judging*
> *from the theorizing about the other arts, it appears as part of the*
> *hostile reaction to the modern world, as an expression of distaste*
> *for objective reality and common emotion. "Pure form" in all the*
> *arts is meant to reinstate spirituality in the teeth of vulgar material-*
> *ism and practical life.*
>
> (Barzun 1980: 6; also see Meyer 1956: 3)

Curiously, the international court style of the 18th century was admired for the same reasons as the national idioms of "The Folk;" both were considered to belong to the past and to derive from a purer, simpler, and more orderly manner of life. Thus, this dissatisfaction with the past was expressed by what Alan Dundes has termed "the devolutionary premise." —a conviction that technological progress must necessarily be accompanied by cultural loss. In reference to folklore, Dundes asks: "Are folklorists doomed to study only the disappearing, the dying and the dead?" (Dundes 1969: 131)

The point Dundes is making is relevant to our study. For the classical music of Tinn, as well as the newly composed slåtts, are communicating today; indeed they are present-at-hand, both to performers and listeners. Grieg's music seems objectively to have little, if anything, to do with Norwegian folk music; but there is no doubt that it continues to be meaningful to those who understand its extra-musical, as well as musical, significance. Indeed, the continuance of this present-at-handness for any tradition whatsoever depends upon the continuance of this kind of knowledge.

What is fundamentally at issue, of course, is the ability to control the accumulation of knowledge, the transmission of culture (history itself) from one generation to the next. From this point of view, an understanding of aural transmission may be seen as a prelude to the study of culture change, which has been described as: ". . . a problem of cultural, social and mental survival, a problem which may be more crucial to man than mere physical survival." (Munch, 1956: 4)

It is the *spelemann* who has control for the Harding fiddle tradition over ". . . the totality of those entities which change in time." To paraphrase Heidegger rather loosely: the *spelemann* wields power over the transformations and vicissitudes of his system of musical communication —a highly cognitive operation performed upon complex cultural symbols by a trained specialist. All of this can be hidden from the historian who forgets, as Kubler has phrased it, that:

> *Written documents give us a thin recent record for only a few parts of the world.*
>
> (Kubler 1962: 12)

17. *Recognition received by Johannes Dahle during his lifetime; his bust prominently displayed in the entranceway of the Tinn secondary school (a); the King's medallion among his decorations (b).*

Postscript

Perhaps because it seems so obvious, the assumed dichotomy between researcher and researchee still remains largely unquestioned; if the latter uses an unwritten mode of transmission, the gulf seems wide indeed. But despite the popular slogan, the medium may not be the message after all. We have seen that in the aurally-transmitted Hardanger violin tradition, the musical message is carefully controlled to represent the ideas of the *spelemenn* according to an elaborate intellectual system. The fact that this musical system is invisible to the thin, recent record of the music history books only demonstrates the insularity of the authors of these books.

It is important to realize that the retention of culture can be an active, not a passive, process; and that admiration of a knowledgeable group for the abilities of a particular individual within a cultural circle gives such a person the power of a cultural leader whose determination to retain or not to retain must be respected. Furthermore, it is often forgotten that the desire to have such power (whether for its own sake or for the sake of a cultural ideal) is just as likely to occur within a non-formalized as with a formalized tradition. Johannes Dahle, who accepted this power for the sake of his inheritance, stayed quietly close to home; yet he received more recognition during his lifetime than do most artists. (Ill. 17) We know that Knut Dahle, during a bleak time for traditional music, gave recitals that were held in Telemark farmhouses; three years after his death, ". . . there was an unveiling of his monument in the church-yard." (Dale, 1981: 24)

In other words, the artist figure, with all its associations, can and does exist outside the prestigious social structure. We can easily relate to the *hardingfele spelemann* a description of what the sociologist, Arne Martin Klaussen, has termed, "this elite comprehension of art and artists": a charismatic figure that is above everyday trivialities of administration and routine. The reader may remember that the *spelemann* has a reputation for leaving farm and family to their own devices while he either stays

18. *Sketch by Chris Lagaard; a rendering of the art mystique.*

close to home, oblivious to what goes on around him, or leads an itinerant life, travelling from fair to fair, or competition to competition. (See Ill. 18 for an artist's rendering of this conflict.) Klaussen has analyzed the confrontation that occurred between egalitarianism and the "art myth," when the boundaries of the welfare state were extended to include artists in Norway's new culture policy (Klaussen 1979); although little attention seems to have been paid to the traditional musician in the official arguments, the new ideas eventually forced a more inclusive definition of traditional music, and many *spelemenn* at first did not find it easy to open the doors of their organizations to other instrumentalists. Within a surprisingly short time, however, we find the pages of the spelemann's newspaper reflecting the new multicultural point of view (Ill. 19); without doubt, this acceptance was facilitated by the active perpetuation of the diversity of the *bygde* traditions, whose continued existence has been willed long past functional necessity.

Many fear new occurences because, believing in the evolutionary (or devolutionary) premise, they assume that the new must inevitably extinguish the old. But they leave the individual out of their consideration. Those who assume that the opening of the doors of the conservatory of music to the *hardingfele* would weaken the traditions of piano and vioioncello, would be just as much in error as those who unjustifiably feared that the presence of accordion and guitar in the *spelemannslag* would diminish the importance of the Hardanger violin. The *hardingfele* has not only continued to flourish in Norway, it has also been receiving much attention in the United States within the past few years (Ill. 20). In response to this new enthusiasm, two dedicated men from Minnesota, Thorwald Quale (son of the *spelemann*, Joger Olson Quale) and Carl Narvestad, organized the Hardanger Fiddle Society of America in 1983. The Meldal Project, described above, brought to our attention the interesting circumstance of a so-called "folk" instrument being aggressively promoted as the national instrument of Norway to the point of causing *flatfele* players to give up their instruments. Even this has not turned out to be a permanent debilitation of the tradition, however, for—also recently—there has been a newly awakened realization of the relevance of this instrument to the music of the *flatfele* communities.

The national romantic imagery associated with the *hardingfele* needs a little of our attention at this point. The candy-box portrayal of national identity has done a disservice to the *hardingfele*, and even more to the sæter, tradition, promoting the yearning for a past utopia that has been discussed above. There are some today who have been drawn to the tradition at least partially for these reasons; like their nineteenth-century

19. *New acknowledgement of diversity in Norway. Tonje Marie Eike dancing the halling (a); accordionists Oddman Haugen and Willy Raustad (b); squib from Norway Times/Nordisk Tidende (c); Dagne Groven Myhren accompanied by a reconstruction of a 14th century lyre made and played by Sverre Jensen (d); Rolf Bjøgan dancing the halling on a stretch of freeway and accompanied by the flatfele played by Jan Vesenberg (e); and Sinding Larsen playing reconstruction of the medieval fiddle (f).*

Society for Preservation
Of Hardanger Fiddle
Music to be Organized

Plans are underway to organize a
society for the promotion and
preservation of Hardanger violin music
in America.

There will be an organizational
meeting immediately following the
Valdres Samband business meeting and
memorial service at the stevne at Mt.
Horeb, in the afternoon of June 18. The
society will be independent of the
Samband and other Norse groups but
will be cooperating with all. The site was
chosen because a great number of
Norsemen, including many Hardanger
music lovers, will be present at that time.

The promoters point out that there is no
longer an influx of fiddlers of the rare
eight-stringed violin from Norway and
that if the music of Norway's traditional
folk instrument is to survive in America
something must be done to encourage it.

Already an interest in the proposed
organization has been expressed by folk
from a wide area. Two of the instigators
of the organizational meeting are
Thorwald Quale, Duluth, and Carl T.
Narvestad, Granite Falls, Minnesota.

20. *The hardingfele tradition in the United States. Anund Roheim (Montana)
has exerted a major influence for many years (a); Tore Heskestad (extreme right)
with his New York group, Trollungene (b); instruments played at a meeting in
Brooklyn, including one recently made by Joe Baker in Massachusetts (third
from left) (c); news squib on the formation of a national hardingfele society at a
meeting of the Valdres Samband, Mt. Horeb, Wisconsin (d); Loretta Kelly (California) (e)., and Andrea Een (Minnesota) (f).*

predecessors, they are searching for a simpler, more wholesome existence than the chaotic industralized ways of life they find around them. Indeed, there is much to admire in *bygde* society, especially in the acceptance of musical communication as a natural and important part of life (as described in Chapter 4); and it would be impossible to imagine any interested child denied the opportunity for this kind of experience, relegated to the "listener" status on the basis of a talent test. But those who ignore the specialist—and the virtuoso—genius—magic element of this tradition are, I believe, making a serious mistake, because they are refusing to acknowledge the power that can emanate from human creativity, quite apart from social status and the established forms of propriety.

In the United States, bondage did not prevent the profound impact of African and African-derived musical traditions through the influence of individual musicians in their roles as children's nurses or plantation workers. Gilbert Chase, in setting about the task of writing a book on the history of American music, found himself confronted with the problem of describing the culture of a country that possessed: "No European courts for the cultivation of art music." (Chase 1955: ix) and Chase chose a focus that resulted in a radical departure from other views of music in the United States:

> *I make no apology for devoting so much attention to types of music, such as the revival hymn and ragtime, that have hitherto not been regarded as "important" or worth the serious attention of the music historian.*
>
> (Chase 1955: xix)

The *hardingfele spelemann*, similarly invisible to most historians, continued to cultivate and promote the esoteric and diverse traditions of Norway. (Ill. 21) It is well to remember that the original significance of national identity in Norway had nothing to do with the imposition of a single culture or way of life; it was related to the appreciation and cultivation of what was uniquely Norwegian—necessary, as the mayor of Stavangar succinctly said, so that Norwegians would have something to give in return for what they took from other foreign nationals. *Nynorsk* was never intended to represent a single spoken language, but rather to provide an umbrella that would permit the diverse verbal communication systems to continue to flourish. In the same spirit, the *hardingfele*, reflecting a complex of musical and extra-musical mental imagery, represents the diversity that has been, and continues to be, an outstanding characteristic of Norwegian traditional music. As such, the symbolism of the

Hardanger violin can be taken more generally to represent the concept of multipluralism as an abstract principle.

A "thin recent record" does not permit visibility to the numerous modes of communication that are happily coexisting in the world today. Indeed, such a perception not only makes invisible the classics of the Tinn tradition but also the classics of the Viennese symphonic music-grammar: a system of musical communication that is being held in a contextless academic strangle hold called "common practice harmony." Knut Dahle was insulted and exploited by the powers that be; as was, in his day, Mozart (another transmitter of family tradition) when, after he had composed a number of his major works, he was advised by a leading authority in Vienna to enroll in the conservatory and study the rules of counterpoint. Knut Dahle and Wolfgang Mozart were no more unwelcome to the inner circle than are today most of the accomplished young musicians who knock on the doors of music departments and conservatories. Whether virtuoso performers on electic guitar, *hardingfele*, or *bandura*—or skilled composers for *reggae* bands—they are likely to be unwelcome for their very expertise. Indeed, they are feared by those who believe in the inevitability of cultural progress.

In today's world, the actual existence of mortals who communicate through traditions is threatened by the stupidity of experts-in-all-things. The many blossoms will continue to grow on their own, so long as the gardener does not forget that the roots and the buds on the tree are both independent and dependent on each other—and all today in the present.

21. Carrying on a family tradition: Finn and Øivind Vabø.

Appendix

Johannes Dahle and His Slått Art

by Magne Myhren

Sources and abbreviations:

I-VII = Gurvin *et al* 1958-1965 and Blom *et al* 1979-1981 vols. I-VII. Numbering system used for the transcriptions in these volumes forms the basis for this listing. The few slåtts that have not been included in these volumes have been listed here in their appropriate groups without number. The use of a parenthesis around a number or letter indicates that the transcription in *Norsk Folkemusikk* (Gurvin and Blom 1959-1981) was written up after another *spelemann* but that Johannes Dahle did play that version of the slått.

NRK = Norwegian Broadcasting Company Archives (434 slåtts, the earliest recorded in 1942).

RB = Rikard Berge collection (114 slåtts on wax cylinders recorded in 1912).

Td = *Norsk Folkemusikksamling Arkiv* (Archive of the Norwegian Folk Music Archive housed at the University of Oslo).

a. = after

d. = ditto

****

Note: This is an abridged English translation of the original by the author of this book. For the wealth of bibliographical and musicological information supplied in the original, the reader is directed to Buen 1983.

Gangarar: 6/8

[*Gurvin I and Blom VII (II)*]

(16)	*Knut Dahles farvel. NRK Magn* 2074; *Td* 1734; *RB* 48.
(19)	*Gangar* a. Knut Sønnstaul. *NRK Magn* 2072; *Td* 1736.
(20)	*Gangar* a. Knut Lurås. *NRK Magn* 2073; *Arkiv* 52985; *Td* 1728; *RB* 46.
(21)	*Gangar* a. Mosafinn, learned from T. Haugerud. *NRK Arkiv* 52986.
(23)	*Helg. NRK Magn* 954 (2 recs.); *Td* 1725; *RB* 39.
(24)	*Friaren* (F-c-a-e), learned from Jon Dahle. *NRK Arkiv* 54001.
30	*Lurås-stubben. NRK Magn* 2073; *Td* 1728.
31	*Torgjeir Brynjulvson. NRK Magn* 2073; *Td* 1729; *RB* 49.
(32)	= 173.
(67)	*Meeglaren* (A-e-a-e). *NRK Magn* 954; *Td* 1731; *RB* 72.
(70)	*Hardingjenta. NRK Magn* 952; *Td* 1735; *RB* 37.
73b	*Pål Løytnantsdreng. NRK Magn* 1986; *Td* 1727; *RB* 6.
(75)	*Skardsnuten,* learned from Torkjell Haugerud. *NRK Arkiv* 52985.
(76)	*Heiloen. NRK Magn* 954; *Arkiv* 52986; *Td* 1724.
(77)	*Sindroen. NRK Magn* 1980; *Td* 1726; *RB* 24, s.
(79)	*Gangar* a. Myllarguten. = *Gamle Jakop. NRK Magn* 2073; *Td* 1734, Halvorsen.
(80)	*Helloslått,* learned from T. Haugerud. *NRK Arkiv* 52985.
84a	*Saeterjenta under Gaustafjell. NRK Magn* 2074; *Td* 1732; *RB* 29.
(87)	*Gangar* a. Knut Sønnstaul. = *Bjørtuften. NRK Magn* 2072; *Td* 1736; *RB* 82.
(90)	*Nøringen* (A-e-a-c#), learned from Lars Istad. *NRK Arkiv* 52986.

(91)   *Gangar*, learned from Håvard Gibøen. *NRK Magn* 2073; *Td* 1727; *RB* 38.

(92)   *Lydarslått* a. Mosafinn, learned from Haugerud? = *Flatbøen*. *NRK Arkiv* 52986.

(93)   *Vårlengt*. *NRK Magn* 2807; *Arkiv* 52985.

98c   *Kivlemøygangar* (F-c-a-e). = *Systerslått*. *NRK Magn* 1986; *Td* 1738; *RB* 95 & 96, Halvorsen.

(101)   *Kviteseiden*. *NRK Magn* 2074; *Td* 1734.

(102)   *Luråsgangar* (Hellosen in Dahle form). *NRK Magn* 1980 & 2074; *Td* 1732 & 1736; *RB* 17.

(103)   *Luråsen* III. *NRK Magn* 1984; *Td* 1728?

104a   *Luråsen* I. *NRK Arkiv* 53249; *RB* 2 & 4.

?   *Gangar* a. Myllarguten. *NRK Magn* 1984?

(106d)   *Den gamle Sevlien*. *NRK Magn* 952; *Td* 1727; *RB* 18.

(107)   *Duft*. *NRK* 952; *Td* 1739; *RB* 89.

108c   *Luråsen* II. *NRK Magn* 1985 & 1980? *Td* 1724.

(109)   = 172.

(110c)   *Gudbrandsdølen* (Gunnar Dahle). *NRK Magn* 951; *Td* 1733; *RB* 7.

111a   *Gjerki Haukeland* (G-d-a-e). *NRK Magn* 953; *Td* 1723; *RB* 56.

(112)   = 124.

(113)   *Filleva ren* (Soteruden) (G-d-a-e). *NRK Magn* 953; *Td* 1723; *RB* 77.

114d   *Skuldalsbruri* (Knut Dahle). *NRK Magn* 1983 & 2072; *Td* 1731; *RB* I, Halvorsen.
         = VII (II) 120a; ditto a. Hans Fykerud. *NRK Magn* 2072; *Td* 1738; *RB* 58.

115b   *Tussebrureferdi* (G-d-a-e) (Knut Dahle). *NRK Magn* 953; *Td* 1723; *RB* 5, Halvorsen.

117g   *Guro Heddeli*. *NRK Magn* 1983; *Td* 1726; *RB* 21.

118a-g   *Fjellmanngjenta*. *NRK Magn* 1978; *Td* 1730; *RB* 3.
         1. *Han dryfta godt spel, Knut* (Lurås form). = VII (II) 119d. *Luråsgangar* in Hellos form. *NRK Magn* 954; *Td* 1732 & 1736; *RB* 14 & 16.

120   See #114.

124b   *Gangar* a. Eivind *spelemann*, also called Eivind Tave; 2 versions? *NRK Magn* 951; *Arkiv* 52985; *Td* 1737.

169   *Gangar* a. Knut Sønnstaul. *NRK Magn* 2072; *Td* 1736; *RB* 99. Compare #117.

170   *Gangar*, learned from Lars Osa. *NRK Arkiv* 52985.

171   *Gangar* a. Tov Holte. *NRK Magn* 2808.

172	Hellosgangar, also called Luråsgangar. 2 versions? NRK Magn 1878, 2 recs.; Arkiv 52985, 2 recs.; Td 1736; RB 81. Compare #109.
173	Slik spela Pål (Tinn form). Same version after Håvard Gibøen; same version after Hans Fykerud (= 32). Only one form is printed. NRK Magn 1983 and Td 1725, 3 forms. NRK Arkiv 52985, 1 form.
Without number:	Gangar a. Håvard Gibøen (A-e-a-c#), not published. NRK Magn 954, 2 recs.; Td 1738; RB 88. Similar to Kivlemøygangaren. St. Tomasklokkelåtten (A-e-a-c#). NRK Magn 954, 2 recs. Eivind Groven's trans. # 1748.

Gangarar: 2/4

[*Gurvin II and III; Blom VII (III)*]

(65)	Gangar a. Håvard Gibøen. RB 36. See 201.
68	Grønskeimogen. NRK Magn 2073; Td 1727.
96	Trollhalling (Knut Dahle) (A-d-f#-e). NRK Magn 1985 and 2814, 2 recs.; Td 1737; RB 76.
(112a)	Luråsgangar = Kjeringi på Tinn. NRK Magn 2074; Td 1730 and 1732.
(115a)	Luråsgangar. NRK Magn 2073; Td 1726.
(118)	Triløytingen (Tinn form) (G-d-a-e). Same form after Håvard Gibøen: NRK Magn 953; Td 1723 & 1724.
(119a)	Langedraggangar. NRK Magn 1978; Td 1733; RB 12.
(123)	Ligangar, learned from Torkjell Haugerud. NRK Magn 2811.
(124)	Luråsgangar. NRK Magn 1978; Td 1731; RB 9.
(128)	Langåkeren. NRK Magn 1981, 2 recs.; Td 1753; RB 23.
(130)	Elgskyttaren. NRK Magn 1981, 2808; Arkiv 52985; Td 1734.
(132)	= 203.
133a	Lappen (Knut Dahle). NRK Magn 952; Td 1730. Compare springar 299.
(134)	Rekveen. Lacking in NRK; Td 1733; RB 14, Halvorsen.
139c	Torstein Brunsdalen (Knut Dahle). NRK Magn 1980; Td 1733; RB 31.
(140)	Gvannesen. NRK Magn 1979; Td 1730; RB 45.
(143)	= Margit Hjukse (without number).
(145)	Gangar, learned from Rikard Gøytil. NRK Arkiv 53831. Compare 200.

147c	*Gudvangen* (Knut Dahle). *NRK Magn* 2073; *Td* 1733; *RB* 32.
148a	*Kvamshallingen* (Knut Dahle). *NRK Magn* 2073; *Td* 1733; *RB* 34.
(150)	*Haugelåtten. NRK Magn* 2073; *Td* 1733; *RB* 21, Halvorsen.
(151)	= 201.
152a	*Fossegrimen* a. Håvard Gibøen. *NRK Magn* 952, 2 recs., 2074, 2807; *Td* 1735; *RB* 8.
(152f)	Ditto a. Myllarguten. *NRK Magn* 951, 952, 1986, 2 recs., 1981; *Td* 1740, learned from Eivind Groven.
(152g,h)	*Gangar* a. Håvard Gibøen. *NRK Magn* 1981.
(153)	*Hellosgangar. NRK Magn* 2072; *Td* 1736.
154d	*Rotnheims-Knut* (*Hallvorsen* a. Knut Dahle). *NRK Magn* 951; *Td* 1729; *RB* 7.
156l	*Floketjønn. NRK Magn 1982; Td* 1729; *RB* 11 (there called *Jon Vestafe*).
157 (e,f)	*Knut Bekkjin. NRK* 1980; *Td* 1730; *RB* 20.
(157i)	*Leirlien. NRK Magn* 1982; *Arkiv* 52985; *Td* 1725; *RB* 80.
(157k)	*Ringjaren. NRK* 1980; *Td* 1733; *RB* 80.
158b	*Bordkøyraren. NRK Magn* 951; *Td* 1728; *RB* 10.
	Gangar. Lacking in *NRK*; *Td* 1734; *RB* 28. This version has been derived both from *Bordkøyraren* and *Langåkeren* 128.
(159)	*Ha du kje hoppa. NRK Magn* 2072; *Td* 1732.
160j	*Talishaugen* = *Heit du fai min. NRK* 951; *Td* 1728; *RB* 50.
(160n)	*Valdresvelen. NRK* 20/4; *Td* 1737. Compare *Toloen.*
(160l)	*Fenta* after Knut Vågen. *NRK Magn* 1978; *Td* 1739.
161a & 162b	*Førnesbrunen* (A-d-a-c #). *NRK Magn* 954; *RB* 88.
(162d,e)	*Førnesbrunen* a. Håvard Gibøen. *NRK Magn* 1984, 2 recs.; *Td* 1724; *RB* 33. Ditto after Hans Fykerud. *NRK Magn* 1984; *Td* 1738.
(162l)	*Gangar* a. Hans Fykerud = *Eldhusgangar,* Anne Geituss. *NRK Magn* 2072; *Td* 1734; *RB* 40.
(199)	*Ola Bakken,* learned from Hølje Landsberk. *NRK Arkiv* 54001.
(200)	*Gangar* a. Knut Lurås. *NRK Magn* 2073; *Td* 1726. Compare # 145.
(201)	*Gangar,* form of Håvard Gibøen. The same form after Håkanes Førlid, not published. Compare # 65. *NRK Magn* 1979; *Td* 1732. Compare # 151.
202	*Gangar* a. Håvard Gibøen (G-d-a-e-). *NRK Magn* 953; *Td* 1723.

(203)   *Hoppe hægre. NRK Magn* 2072; *Td* 1730. Compare # 132.
Without   *Gjenta på Lauvøva, gangar* from Tuddal. *NRK Arkiv* 54001.
number:
           Margjit Hjukse (G-c-a-e), learned from Torkjell Haugerud.
           These lydarslåtts, which are composed by Lars Fykerud and
           Torkjell Haugerud, are built on an older *gangar* 143, known
           in Setesdal as *Systerslått*, forms b-d. In Lårdal, they call the
           slått Halling etter Langedragen or *Sæbyggjegangaren*, form e.

Springarar

[Gurvin IV, V; Blom VI, VII]

182   *Gibøspringar. NRK Magn* 1981; *RB* 82?
(203)   *Bakkhus-slåtten. NRK Magn* 1982; *RB* 63.
(238)   *Prillaren. NRK Magn* 1979; *Td* 1735; *RB* 70.
(239)   *Veumen* (Knut Dahle) = *Knut Dahles trollstemde springar*
           (A-d-f#-e). *NRK Magn* 2814; *Td* 1735; *RB* 83. Groven's
           trans. # 1318.
(242)   *Springar* a. Hans Fykerud = *Knut Eilevsen. NRK* 2072; *Arkiv*
           52987; *Td* 1738; Groven's trans. # 1314.
243   *Våen NRK Magn* 951; *Td* 1730.
244   *Dahlespringar* (Jon Skeie?). *NRK Magn* 942.
(249)   = # 626.
(258)   *Siklebekken,* learned from Rikard Gøytil. *NRK Arkiv* 53831.
260   *Myllarspringar* (Gunnar Dahle). *NRK Magn* 1980? *Td* 1725;
           RB 90.
(276)   *Tov Bøle. NRK Magn* 951; *Td* 1725; *RB* 84; Groven's trans.
           # 1256.
281   *Håvard's minne. NRK Magn* 1978; *Td* 1734.
293   *Springar* a. Knut Vandringen. *NRK Magn* 2073; *Td* 1726.
294   *Systerslått* = *Kivlemøyane* III (F-c-a-e). *NRK Magn* 1986; *Td*
           1738; *RB* 98.
295   *Håvard's sorg* (G-c-a-e). *NRK Magn* 953, 2 recs.; *RB* 77.
296   *Ruske-Sara. NRK Magn* 954; *Td* 1740; *RB* 87.
299   *Lappen. NRK Magn* 1982; *Td* 1730; *RB* 54.
301   *Frå morgon til kveld. NRK Magn* 951, 2 recs.; *Td* 1728.
337   *Springar* a. Brynjulv Roe. *NRK Magn* 2808.
338   *Springar* a. Tor Rønningen. *NRK Magn* 2808; *Td* 1740.
339   *Dakotaprærien. NRK Magn* 1983; *Td* 1725.

340	Springar a. Knut Dahle (A-e-a-c). NRK Magn 954; Td 1738. Reminiscent of Kivlemøyspringaren.
341	Springar a. Ole H. Bernos. NRK Magn 2073; Td 1737.
342	Den Torjei spela når han ikkje ville spela. NRK Magn 2073; Td 1728.
(368b)	Veneflamma. NRK Magn 1985; Td 1727; RB 68; Groven's trans. #1306.
369b	Springar a. Hans Fykerud (G-d-a-e-). NRK Magn 953; Td 1723-24?
370a	Springar a. Håvard Gibøen (G-d-a-e). NRK Magn 953, 2 recs.; Td 1723; RB 102. This slått is the foundation for a movement in the composition, Faldaføykir by Eivind Groven.
373a	Signe Ulladalen. NRK Magn 1981.
374a	Saltevju. NRK Magn 1983; Td 1735.
(375)	Sagafossen. NRK Magn 1982; Td 1728; RB 59. Groven's trans. # 1338.
376a	Rjukanfossen. NRK Magn 951, 1979 and 1985; Td 1724; RB 15. Trans. is really after 1979.
377a	Madson. NRK Magn 1981, 2807; Arkiv 52986; RB 60.
384a	Håvardstubben. NRK Magn 951, 2 recs.; Td 1730; RB 27.
(385)	Bægjuven (G-d-a-e). NRK Arkiv 52986, 2 recs.
387a	Fjellbekken. NRK Magn 2073, 2807; Arkiv 52985, 2 recs.; Td 1733; RB 64.
422a	Helge treisk. NRK Magn 1982; Td 1733; RB 69.
424b	Veggligjenta. NRK Magn 1978; Td 1727; RB 30.
(425)	Traskjen. NRK Arkiv 53831.
426c	Høytjuven. NRK Magn 2073; Td 1736.
(427)	Lars målar. NRK Arkiv 52985.
428a	Haslebuskane. NRK Magn 951, 2073; Td 1739.
430a	Grimeliden = Håkanes Førli. NRK Magn 2073; Td 1736; RB 73.
430b	Springar a. Tor Rønningen. NRK Magn 2808.
431a	Smågutspringaren. NRK Magn 2807; Td 1734; RB 79.
433b	Knut Dahles siste slått (G-d-a-e). NRK Magn 2074; Td 1723.
433c	Springar a. Tor Bøle. NRK Arkiv 52986.
437c	Springar a. Tor Rønningen. NRK Magn 2802.
440c	Den gode låtten. NRK Magn 951; Td 1733; RB 51.
447a	Luråsspringar. NRK Magn 1980; Arkiv 52985, 2 recs.; Td 1725; RB 76.
(455)	Gauken. NRK Arkiv 52986, 2 recs.

456a	*Signe* (Gunnar Dahle *NRK Magn* 3036). *NRK Magn* 954; *Td* 1739.
457a	*Fossekallen. NRK Magn* 2072; *Td* 1730; *RB* 66.
458a	*Gjestebodsgubben. NRK Magn* 1982; *Td* 1725; *RB* 42.
459a	*Gamle Gullbrand* = Håkanesgrisen (Knut Dahle *RB* 4). *NRK Arkiv* 53249; *Td* 1724.
(462c)	*Springar,* learned from Torkjell Haugerud. *NRK Magn* 2807. Groven's trans. # 1237.
464c	*Høyversdagen* (Gunnar Dahle *Td* 1071). *NRK Magn* 951; *Td* 1729; *RB* 53, there called *Margit Hjukse.*
465a	*Draum. NRK Magn* 2072.
467d	*Belarguten* in the form of J. Dahle. *NRK Magn* 2808.
468a	*Dusteruden. NRK Magn* 2073; *Td* 1737; *RB* 85.
469a	*Bøkårrennar.* (G-d-a-e). *NRK Magn* 953; *Td* 1734; *RB* 94.
470a	*Falkeriset. NRK Magn* 954; *Td* 1734; *RB* 101.
471d	*Svadden. NRK Magn* 2074, 2807, 2808; *Td* 1732.
475b	*Sønnstaulen. NRK Magn* 1984; *Td* 1729; *RB* 22.
476a	*Springar* a. Hans Fykerud (G-d-a-e). *NRK Magn* 953; *Td* 1723.
476d	*Springar* (G-d-a-e). *NRK Magn* 953, 2073; *Td* 1723.
477e	*Torgeir Miland. NRK Magn* 1981; *Td* 1726.
479b	*Sandsdalen. NRK Magn* 1979; *Td* 1735.
480d	*Systerslått* = Kivlemøyslått II (F-c-a-e). *NRK Magn* 1986; *Td* 1738; *RB* 97.
482e	*Brynjulv Roe. NRK Magn* 2072.
485c	*Tinnesand. NRK Magn* 954; *Td* 1739; *RB* 87.
486c	*Bokkoen. NRK Magn* 1982; *Td* 1732.
487a	*Morten sålebindar. NRK Magn* 951; *Td* 1730; *RB* 27.
489d	*Kari Midtigard. NRK Magn* 2073; *Td* 1736.
497c	*Springar* a. Ola H. Bernos. *NRK Magn* 2073; *Td* 1737. *Blinde-Torgeir. NRK Magn* 54001. (Not transcribed?)
498d	*Sauaren. NRK Magn* 951 and 2807. *Td* 1730; *RB* 26 & 67. *Springar* a. Knut Vågen. *NRK Magn* 1978. Groven's trans. # 1290; unpublished, = *Fivilboen.*
499c-g	*Siklebekken. NRK Arkiv* 52986. Groven's trans. # 1334.
500a	*Bokkoen. NRK Magn* 2073; *Td* 1734.
500b	*Tjugedalaren. NRK Magn* 52986.
502c	*Åttekrossen* = *Springar* a. Halvor Bøle. *NRK Magn* 2808.
505e	*Gaute Navarsgard. NRK Magn* 1978; *Tb* 1731; *RB* 100.
506a	*Gibøspringar* = Syrgjefuen. *NRK Magn* 1980; *Td* 1734; *RB* 34, 93.

507c	*Springar* a. Knut Vandringen. *NRK Magn* 2073; *Td* 1726; *RB* 92.
508e	*Ragnhild Hægard. NRK Magn* 1983; *Td* 1733; *RB* 3.
(509)	*Springar* a. Hans Fykerud. Lacking in *NRK*. *Td* 1739. Resembles *Gurosonen = Kålidalen. Steinsruden. NRK Arkiv* 54001.
510b	*Håvard's draum. NRK Magn* 1984; *Td* 1732; *RB* 52.
511e	*Springar* a. Hans Fykerud. *NRK Magn* 2072; *Td* 1738.
512a	*Kvenneslåtten. NRK Magn* 1984; *Td* 1726; *RB* 65.
513a	*Jon Vestafe. NRK Magn* 951; *Td* 1729; *RB* 11, Halvorsen.
(e,f)	*Bøheringen. NRK Arkiv* 52986.
514c	*Springar* a. Aslak Kleivane. *NRK Arkiv* 52985.
514d	*Springar* a. Tov Holte. *NRK Magn* 2808. The name, *Åttekrossen*, is wrong here. See 502c.
516a	*Grimeliden* (Knut Dahle). *RB* 61. Johannes Dahle played it in 2 forms: *Grimeliden* after Hans Fykerud (*NRK Magn* 2072) and after Håvard Gibøen (*NRK Magn* 2073). Eivind Groven's trans. 1328 & 1332.
516c	*Springar* a. Hans Fykerud. *NRK Magn* 1982; *Td* 1738.
517f	*Nordfjorden. NRK Magn* 2072; *Td* 1726; *RB* 91.
518f	*Springar* from Hovin. *NRK Magn* 2809.
519h	*Springar* a. Tor Rønningen. *NRK Magn* 2808; *Td* 1740.
520e	*Den blårandute. NRK Arkiv* 52985.
521h	*Springar* a. Ola Håkanes. *NRK Magn* 2073. There are 2 forms, Groven's transcriptions # 1321 & 1322, but only one is published. *Td* 1737.
521i	*Luråsspringar. NRK Magn* 2073; *RB* 44.
522d	*Vestafeen. NRK Magn* 1979; *RB* 26 & 62.
522e	*Igletveiten. NRK Magn* 1981; *Td* 1737; *RB* 43.
(523h)	*Flesbergingen. NRK* 1980; *Td* 1727, which has 2 forms, the last is shorter. Groven has transcribed both, but only one is published. *RB* 71, one form.
(523g)	*Bernåsen. NRK* 2808.
(523j)	*Nisien. NRK Arkiv* 52985.
524l	*Moguten. NRK Magn* 1979, 2 recs.; *Td* 1728; *RB* 74.
525g	*Springar* a. Hans Fykerud (G-d-a-e). *NRK Magn* 853; *Td* 1724.
525h	*Sigurd Jondalen* (G-c-a-e). *NRK Magn* 1986, 2 recs; *Td* 1737; *RB* 94.
526m	*Skjelleruden. NRK Magn* 2073; *Td* 1739.
526n	*Jarand Skinnarland. NRK Magn* 1980 & 1983; *Td* 1731; *RB* 19.

527q	*Kåte-Reiar. NRK Magn* 1978; *Td* 1740.
625	*Dåruden. NRK Magn* 2809.
626	*Springar* (A-e-a-e) *NRK Magn* 954; *Td* 1731. Compare # 249.
Without number:	*Bakkhusen. NRK Magn* 1982; *Td* lacking; *RB* 63. Groven's trans. # 1272 not published.

Håkanesen II *RB* 62.
Springar a. Ola Håkanes. *NRK Magn* 953, 2 recs.; *Td* 73, similar to # 476.
Steinsruden. NRK Arkiv 54001.

Fyryspel

Fyryspel a. Knut Sønnstaul. *NRK Magn* 2072; *Td* 1735.
Ditto a. Håvard Gibøen. *NRK Magn* 2073; *Td* 1731; *RB* 1.
Ditto a. Hans Fykerud. *NRK Magn* 2072; *Td* 1738; *RB* 10.
Ditto *Brynjulv Roe. NRK Magn* 2808; *Td* 1739.
Ditto a. Knut Dahle G-d-a-e. *NRK Magn* 953; *Tb* 1723.

Bruremarsjar

Myllargutens Bruremarsj (A-e-a-e). *NRK Magn* 954, 2 recs.; *Td* 1731; *RB* 55 og 72. Halvorsen.
Håvard Gibøens bruremarsj. NRK Magn 954; *Td* 1731; *RB* 13. Halvorsen.
Telemarkens bruremarsj (2 forms). *NRK Magn* 2074; *Td* 1729, *RB* 46, 47 og 78. Halvorsen, Groven's trans. 1867.
Visetone a. Knut Dahl, *NRK.*

Runddansslåttar

Clarinet *slått* a. Tomas Lurås (G-d-a-e). *NRK Magn* 953; *RB* 92. The slått goes in waltz time
Reinlender Td 1740.
Galopp. Td 1740.
Vals. Td 1739.
Masurka. Td 1740.

*F*ootnotes: Part I

Ethnography: an Aural Bibliography

1. Finn Vabø: transcription from tape. Bergen, Norway.
2. Director of Icelandic Broadcasting Company: field notes. Reykjavik, Iceland.
3. Finn Vabø: transcription from tape. Bergen.
4. Finn Vabø: transcription from tape. Bergen. The Norwegian spelling of *milieu* is *miljø*.
5. The *lur* is the Norwegian version of the Alpine horn: a long, slender, conical tube well over a yard long, fashioned from two hollowed-out sections of wood, bound together from birch bark. It is associated with the sæter women. The *munnharp* is a mouth harp (= jaw's harp). The *seljefløte* is a willow flute, about two feet in length.
6. The audible rhythmic tapping by fiddler and audience is in fact an integral part of the music, and this sound should not be dubbed out of commercial recordings—as was first pointed out to me by Morten Levy (Danish ethnomusicologist). Recent recordings of *hardingfele* music show an acceptance of this point of view.
7. Finn Vabø: transcription from tape. Bergen.
8. Finn Vabø: transcription from tape. Bergen.
9. Finn Vabø: transcription from tape. Bergen.
10. Johannes Dahle: translation from field notes. Tinn, Telemark.
11. Johannes Dahle: translation from field notes. Tinn.
12. Johannes Dahle: trans. from recorded interview. Tinn.
13. The *hardinfele* is essentially a solo instrument, playing its own mel-

ody and bass. Thus, when two or more players perform together (including the members of a *lag*), they usually play identical parts. Thus, ensemble playing is done for social, not musical, reasons.

14. John Helland: translation from field notes. Seljord, Telemark.
15. Eivind Groven: translation from field notes. Oslo.
16. Dagne Groven Myhren: quotation from field notes. Oslo.
17. Eivind Øygarden: quotation from field notes. Rauland, Telemark.
18. Sigrid Lid: quotation from field notes. Rauland.
19. As quoted to me in English translation by Eva Kostveit of Rauland school child.
20. Halvor Kostveit: quotation from field notes. Rauland.
21. Johannes Dahle: English trans. from field notes. Tinn.
22. Johannes Dahle: English trans. from field notes. Tinn.
23. Johannes Dahle: English trans. from field notes. Tinn.
24. Johannes Dahle: translation from field notes. Tinn.
25. Ola Øyaland: translation from field notes. Tinn.
26. Gunnar Dahle: translation from field notes. Tinn.
27. Dagne Groven Myhren: field notes. Oslo.
28. Einar Steen-Nøkleberg: field notes. Oslo.
29. Agnes Buen Garnås: field notes. Bø, Telemark.
30. Eva Kostveit: field notes. Rauland.
31. Ola Øyaland: translation from field notes. Rauland.
32. Finn Vabø: field notes. Bergen.
33. Finn Vabø: field notes. Bergen.
34. Finn Vabø: field notes. Bergen.
35. Finn Vabø: field notes. Bergen.

Footnotes: Part II

Chapter 1.   The Meaning of the Instrument

1. Jon Helland: translation from field notes. Seljord; 1967.
2. According to a physicist who has worked in this area: "We still believe that there are a very few people, who have spent most of their lives with violins, who can recognize an old one by its sound only, as we might know the voice of an old friend. However, so far we have found no one to tell us how they do this. We have shown by our analyses that the tone color as we have defined it is not adequate to explain any such miracle. . . ." (Saunders 1966: n.p.)
3. The fact that there was a title change in Playford's method for this instrument is interesting. In 1652, Playford called his book, *Musick's Recreation on the Lyra Viol;* but in a later edition (1661), he gave it the more explicit title, *Musick's Recreation on the Viol, Lyra-Way.*
4. *Also called Geigen Lyra.*
5. *A slightly larger version of the same instrument (lirone da braccio) was also held in this position.*
6. Also called *lirone da gamba, accordo, arciviolata, lira, lira grande, lirone perfetto,* and *lyra perfecta*—all names that bear additional testimony to the essential importance of the harmonic functions.
7. See Bessaraboff 1940 for a critical outline of this search and the term, *basse de viole d'amour* (fn. 690). Also see Sachs 1914.
8. Field notes from interview with Olav Fosslid.

Chapter 2.   Aural Structuring

1. Vabø later told me that the *slått, Sagafossen,* was named after the *spelemann,* Halvor Sagafossen, from Heddal, Telemark.
2. For *slått* variants, see O. Gurvin et al, *Norsk Folkemusikk* 1 (1958), 146-9 and V (1967), If. For the legend, see I. Aasen and J. Lindberg, *Norske Minnestykker* (1923), 75; R. Berge, *Norsk Bondelif i Segn og Sogu* (1910), 44f and 61; A. Faye, *Norske Folkesagn* (1844), 252; Gurvin et al, *Norske Folkemusikk* (1958), 308; V (1967), 265f; *Tidenskraft for Folkeminne* (Numedal; 1915-16), 96; and K. Tvedten, *Sagn fra Telemarken,* 94ff.
3. *Nordfjorden* is one of the most widespread of all the *hardingfele* slåtts. According to Bjørndal, its melodic material is derived from two western stevs. It was a required selection for all participants at Norway's first Hardanger fiddle competition in Grivi, Bø, which took place on July 8, 1888. (Bjørndal 1952). According to a personal communication from Johann Vaa, a *nystev* has attached itself to the *slått;* the text typically earthy, and we shall leave the missing words to the imagination of the reader:
   Kjeringi sat og mokka til graut
   Fekk ho sja ein . . . pa vatnet der flaut
   Kjeringi kasta byttar og spann
   For å få kara . . . i land.

   The old hag sat milking for porridge,
   When she spied a . . . floating on the lake.
   The hag cast away her buckets
   To bring the . . . ashore.

   For transcribed variants of this *slått,* see Blom et al VII, 516a-i; also see "Nordfjordspringar i Sogn og Fjordane Ringen" in *Spelemannsbladet* #4 (1977), 15.
4. Another example close at hand is *St. Thomasklokkene* (Ex. 9) Note tuning of strings given in Ex. 9b.
5. It is likely that the *gangar* and *springar* were once danced in succession as "coupled dances." Social dances were customarily performed in pairs during the 16th century in most European countries. The first dance, generally in a moderate duple time, was called the "stepped dance," and it was followed by the "leapt" or "jumping" dance in triple meter and a quicker tempo. The old *Pavane-Galliard* and the

Passamezzo-Salterello pairs were favorite coupled dances. The *Allemande*, which appeared about 1550, was followed by the tripla or proportz, and later, in the 17th century, by another "jumping dance" in triple meter, the *Courante (Corrente)*. In each pair, the second dance was a rhythmic variation of the first. (Bukofzer 1947: 44). Of course, the idea of grouping several dances together came long before their identification as a cyclic form.

Chapter 3. *Aural Thinking*

1. Whether notation actually performs this function is a matter of dispute (see Hopkins 1966).
2. In a review of two books on the subject of the relevance *to* arts education of research in cognition, Carol Robertson has emphasized: "The unjust pressure on the survival of the arts in general education may well derive from the myth that music and other figural activities are "inborn" talents, while mathematics (a body of information communicated in the most abstract of symbol systems) can be "taught" and "learned." (Robertson 1981: 530)
3. The *hardingfele spelemenn*, Kjetil Løndal and Knut Jorde (assisted by Øystein Odden, Ola Øyaland, and Johannes Dahle), have kindly sent me re-tapes of the commercially recorded examples, so that I could have an authoritative version with audible footbeating; it is upon these recordings that the measurement aspect of the project has been based. Ola Kai Ledang, Trondheim University, has also sent me a tape recorded by him in Telemark from the playing of Johannes Dahle in Tinn.
4. Robert Apfel, Yale University, has generously allowed me access to the machinery at the Mason Laboratory and has given me advice on how to use it. Burton Rosener and William Labov, University of Pennsylvania, have also given me advice in this area.
5. A first draft of this chapter was read at the national meeting of the Society for Ethnomusicology in 1975 (Wesleyan University). I am indebted to Thomas Burns, University of Pennsylvania, for valuable advice during the progress of research. The present version is a revision of a contribution to R. Falck and T. Rice, eds., *Cross-Cultural Approaches to Music . . . (Hopkins 1982), which in turn was a revision of the fourth chapter of my Ph.D. dissertation (Hopkins 1978).*

Chapter 4.   Musical Codes

1. This type of *stev*, called a *nystev*, bears no relationship to the old, four-line poem: the *gamlestev*. Nystevs are found mostly in Telemark and Setesdal. See Chapter 2, footnote 3 for another typical example.
2. *Stevjast*: to engage in an improvisatory dialogue, a contest in the improvisation of nystevs.
3. *Gnike*: squealing (as a result of a piece of machinery): 2nd def. in Haugen, Norwegian-English Dictionary. My translation does not attempt to convey rhyme or rhythm.

Chapter 5.   Emergence of the Classical

1. Interesting, in view of these findings, is the wry point of view implicit in the following riddle from Nordhordland, the area north of Bergen (as collected by Brynjulf Alver):

   > *8 proud guys*
   > *4 round magpies*
   > *All these things had the fiddle*
   > *Nobody could play*
   >
   > (Alver 1958: 309; my trans.)

2. Øyvind Anker originally published the Dahle/Grieg/Halvorsen correspondence (Anker 1943), and it is to him that I am indebted for my knowledge of it. Knut Buen's reprinting of the material makes it readily accessible today; thus my succeeding references are to the Buen sources.

*B*ibliography

Abraham, G. (ed.)   *Grieg: A Symposium*. London: Lindsay Drummond
1948   Ltd.

Anderson, O.   *The Bowed-Harp: A Study in the History of Early*
1930   *Musical Instruments*. London: Oxford University
  Press. Eng. trans. of *Stråkharpen*, Helsinki, 1923.

Anker, Ø.   "Knut Dale-Edv. Grieg-Johan Halvorsen" in *Årbok*
1943   *for Norsk Musikkgransking* 1943, 71.

Arbman, H.   *The Vikings*. New York: Frederick A. Praeger.
1961

Arneberg, H.   *Norsk Folkekunst: Kvinnearbeid*. Oslo: *Universi-*
1949   *tetsforlaget*.

Arnheim, R.   *Toward a Psychology oı Art*. Berkeley: University of
1966   California Press.

Arnheim, R.   *Visual Thinking*. Berkeley: University of California
1969   Press. Ref. here to 1972 paperbk. ed.

Babitz, S.   "Differences Between 18th Century and Modern Vi-
1957   olin Bowing" in *The Score* (March, 1957), 1.

Baines, A.   *Musical Instruments Through the Ages*. New York:
1975   Walker and Co. Ref. here to revision of 1961 ed.

Bakka, E.   *Norske dansetradisjonar*. Oslo: *Det Norske sam-*
1978   *laget*.

Bakka, E.   *Springar, gangar, rull, og pols*. Trondheim: *Rådet for*
1982   *Folkmusikk og Folkedans*.

Barzun, J.   "The Meaning of Meaning in Music" in *The Musical*
1980   *Quarterly* LXVI, #1, 1.

Beal, D.
1984

"Two Springar Dance Traditions From Western Norway" in *Ethnomusicology xxviii*, #2, 237.

Ben-Amos, D.
1974

"The Concept of Genre" in Ben-Amos, D. and K. Goldstein (eds). *Folklore: Performance and Communication*. Mouton: The Hague.

Berge, R.
1972

and O. Fjalestad. *Myllarguten/Gibøen*. Oslo: Noregs boklag.

Berliner, P.
1978

The Soul of the Mbira. Berkeley: University of California Press.

Bessaraboff, N.
1940

Ancient European Musical Instruments. Cambridge: Harvard University Press.

Bjørndal, A.
1952

"Hardingfela 300 År" in *Nordisk Musikkulture* Nr. 1,8.

Bjørndal, A.
1966

with B. Alver, —og fela ho let. Oslo: *Universitetsforlaget*.

Blacking, J.
1970

"Tonal Organization in the Music of Two Venda Initiation Schools," in *Ethnomusicology* XIV, #1.

Blacking, J.
1973

How Musical Is Man? Seattle: University of Washington Press.

Blom, J.
1961

"Diffusjonsproblematikken og Studiet av Danseformen" in *Kulture og Diffusion*. A. Klausen (ed.), Oslo, 101.

Blom, J.
1972

and J. Gumperz. "Social Meaning in Linguistic Structures: Code-Switching in Norway" in J. Gumperz and D. Hymes (eds.), *Directions in Sociolinguistics*. New York: Holt, Rinehart and Winston.

Blom, J.
1979-81

with S. Nyhus and R. Sevåg, *Norsk Folkemusikk* Oslo. *Universitetsforlaget*.

Blom, J.
1981

"Dansen i Hardingfelemusikken" in *Norsk Folkemusikk* VII (Oslo), 298.

Bloomfield
1933

Language. New York: Henry Holt.

Blume, F.
1970

Classic and Romantic Music. Eng. trans. New York: Norton.

Boyden, D.
1980

"Violin" in *Groves Dictionary of Music and Musicians*, sixth ed., XIX, 819.

Bright, W.
1963

"Language and Music: Areas for Cooperation" in *Ethnomusicology* VII, #1, 26.

Buen, H.
1978
with A. Garnås and D. Myhren. *Ei Vise Vil Eg Kveda*. Oslo: Tiden Norsk Forlag.

Buen, K.
1983
Som gofa spølå. Tuddal: Repesekken forlag.

Bukofzer, M.
1947
Music in the Baroque Era. New York: Norton.

Burrows, D.
1972
"Music and the Biology of Time" in *Perspectives of New Music* XI, 1.

Buvarp, H.
1952
"Studiet av folkemusikken" in *Norveg* 2,230.

Campbell, P.
1972
Rhetoric: A Study of the Communicative and Aesthetic Dimensions of Language. Belmont, Cal.: Dickenson Publishing Co.

Chase, G.
1960
America's Music. 2nd revised ed. New York: Macmillan.

Chase, G.
1972
"Pirogue to the Moon: The Mythologiques of Claude Lévi-Strauss" in *Yearbook of the I.F.M.C.*, 152.

Chase, G.
1973
Two Lectures in the Form of a Pair: Music, Culture, and History and Structuralism and Music. Brooklyn: I.S.A.M.

Chomsky, N.
1957
Syntactic Structures. The Hague: Mouton.

Claudius, C.
1931
Samlung of gamle musikinstrumenter. Copenhagen: Levin and Munsgaards Forlag.

Clemencic, R.
1968
Musical Instruments. New York: Putnam. Eng. trans. of original (Frankfurt) ed.

Closson, E.
1892
Edvard Grieg et la musique scandinave. Paris: Librairie fischbacker.

Cohen, A.
1973
with N. Cohen. "Tune Evolution as an Indicator of Traditional Musical Norms" in *Journal of American Folklore* 36, 44.

Conklin, H.
1969
"Lexicographical Treatment of Folk Taxonomies" in S. Tyler (ed.) *Cognitive Anthropology*. New York: Holt, Rinehart and Winston.

Cooke, P.
1978
"The Fiddle in Shetland Society" in *Scottish Studies* 22, 69.

Cooke, P. 1979	"The Pibroch Repertory: Some Research Problems" in Proc. R.M.A., 93.
Cooper, G. 1960	and L. Meyer. *The Rhythmic Structure of Music*. Chicago: The University of Chicago Press.
Dale, H. 1981	"Knut Dahle" in *Spelemannsbladet* Nr3,24.
Danks, H. 1976	*The Viola d'Amore*. Bois de Boulogne: Halesowen.
David, H. 1923	with A. Mendel, *The Back Reader: A Life of Johann Sebastian Bach in Documents and Letters*. New York: Norton.
Davies, J. 1978	*The Psychology of Music*. Stanford, Cal: Stanford University Press.
Deloria, V. 1969	*Custer Died For Your Sins*. New York: Macmillan.
Deloria, V. 1969	*We Talk, You Listen; New Tribes, New Turf*. New York: Macmillan.
Deutsch, D. 1982	*The Psychology of Music:* New York: Academic Press.
Diamond, S. 1974	"The Myth of Structuralism" in I. Rossi (ed.), *The Unconscious in Culture: The Structuralism of Claude Lévi-Strauss in Perspective*. New York: Dutton, 292.
Dolmetsch, A. 1916	*The Interpretation of the Music of the XVII-XVIII Centuries*. London: Oxford University Press. References here are to the 1946 revised edition of the original by A. Dolmetsch.
Dundes, A. 1964	"Texture, Text and Context" in *Southern Folklore Quarterly*, 25.
Dundes, A. 1969	"The Devolutionary Premise in Folklore Theory" in *Journal of the Folklore Institute* 6,5.
Dundes, A. 1957	and C. Pagter. *Urban Folklore from the Paperwork Empire*. Austin: University of Texas Press.
Einarsson, S. 1957	*History of Icelandic Literature*. Baltimore: Johns Hopkins Press.
Einstein, A. 1947	*Music in the Romantic Era*. New York: Norton.
Einung, H. 1942	*Tinn Soga*, 2 vols. Rjukan: Private pub.

Elsworthy, F. 1895	*The Evil Eye.* London: Western.
Evans, E. 1957	*Irish Folk Ways.* London: Routledge & Kegan Paul.
Evans, E. 1958	"The Atlantic Ends of Europe" in *The Advancement of Science*, 1.
Felber, E. 1911	*Die Musik in den Marchen und Mythen der verschiedenen Volker.* Report of the 4th Congress of the I.M.S., London.
Feld, S. 1974	"Linguistics and Ethnomusicology" in *Ethnomusicology* XVIII, No. 2, 197.
Feld, S. 1982	*Sound and Sentiment.* Philadelphia: University of Pennsylvania Press.
Feldman, B. 1972	and R. Richardson, eds. *The Rise of Modern Mythology 1680-1860.* Bloomington: Indiana University Press.
Fishman, J. 1972	*Language in Sociocultural Usage.* Stanford, California: Stanford University Press.
Fry, D. 1970	"Phonology" in I. Lyons (ed.), *New Horizons in Linguistics.* (Harmondsworth, Middlesex, England: Penguin), 26.
Fudge, E. 1970	"Phonology and Phonetics" in T. Sebeok (ed.), *Current Trends in Linguistics*, ix.
Galpin, F. 1910	*Old English Instruments of Music.* London: Methoen & Co.
Garnås, A. 1980	"Kvedarskogen hav runne på ny: 70-Åra" in *Årbok for Telemark* 1980, 115.
Giglioli, P. 1972	(ed.) *Language and Social Context.* Harmondsworth, Middlesex, England: Penguin.
Goldstein, K.	"The Ballad Scholar and the Long-Playing Record" in B. Jackson (ed.), *Folklore and Society*. Hatboro, Pa.: Folklore Associates.
Gombrich, E. 1960	*Art and Illusion.* Princeton: Princeton University Press.
Gourlay, K. 1978	"Towards a Reassessment of the Ethnomusicologist's Role in Research" in *Ethnomusicology* XXII, No. 1, 1.
Grame, T. 1973	"Sounding Statues: The Symbolism of Musical Instruments" in *Expedition*, 30.

Gregory, R. 1974	Concepts and Mechanisms of Perception. London: Oxford University Press.
Greni, L. 1960	"Bånsuller i Setesdal" in Norveg VII, 13.
Griffin, P. 1972	"Interview with Morton Feldman" in The Musical Times, August, 1972, 258.
Grinde, N. 1974	and Kåre Grøttum. Norsk Musikk. Oslo: Universitetsforlaget.
Grout, D. 1960	A History of Western Music. New York: Norton.
Groven, E. 1969	Equal Temperament and Pure Tuning. Oslo.
Groven, E. 1971	"Musikkstudiar—Ikkje Utgjevne før" in O. Fjalestad (ed.), Eivind Groven: Heiderskrift til 70 Årsdagen, Oslo: Universitetsforlaget.
Groven, E. 1972	"Myllar-Spel og Håvard-Spel" in Berge and Fjalestad, Myllarguten/Gibøen (Oslo: Universitetsforlaget), 233.
Gulik, R. van 1940	The Lore of the Chinese Lute. Tokyo: Sophia University.
Gumperz, J. 1972	and D. Hymes. Directions in Sociolinguistics. New York: Holt, Rinehart and Winston, Inc.
Gurvin, O. 1940	"Norske Serdrag i Musikken" in Norsk Musikkgranskning Årbok 50.
Gurvin, O. 1953	"Photography As An Aid in Folk Music Research" in Norveg 3, 181.
Gurvin, O. 1958	with A. Bjørndal, E. Groven, and T. Ørpen (eds.) Norsk Folkemusikk, Vols. 1 through V. Oslo. Universitetsforlaget.
Hajdecki, A. 1892	Die italienische Lira da Braccio. Amsterdam: Mostar. Reprint: Amsterdam: Antiqua, 1965.
Hallowell, A. 1955	Culture and Expression, Philadelphia: University of Pennsylvania Press.
Hamit, S. 1981	Contemporary Norwegian Music. Oslo: Universitetsforslaget.
Handler, R. 1984	with J. Linnekin. "Tradition, Genuine or Spurious" in Journal of American Folklore 97, #385, 273.

Harwood, D.
1976
"Universals in Music: A Perspective Derived from Cognitive Psychology" in *Ethnomusicology* XX, 521.

Haugen, E.
1965
The Norwegian Language in America. Bloomington, Indiana: Indiana University Press.

Heidegger, M.
Being and Time. New York: Harper and Row.

Helgason, H.
1972
"Organal Singing in Iceland" in *Beitredge fur Musikwissenschaft* XIV #3, 221.

Helmholtz, H.
1954
On the Sensations of Tone. Re-ed. of Ellis trans. New York: Dover.

Herndon, M.
1974
"Analysis: Herding of Sacred Cows?" in *Ethnomusicology* XVIII, #2, 219.

Herndon, M.
1976
"Reply to Kolinsky: Tarus Omicida" in *Ethnomusicology* XX, 21.

Herndon, M.
1980
Native American Music. Norwood, Pennsylvania: Norwood Editions.

Herskovits, M.
1948
Acculturation: The Study of Culture Contact. New York: Knopf.

Herskovits, M.
1948
Man and His Works. New York: Knopf.

Herskovits, M.
1972
Cultural Relativism: Perspectives in Cultural Pluralism. New York: Random House.

Hindemith, P.
Traditional Harmony. London: Schott.

Hollander, L.
1968
The Skalds: A Selection of Their Poems. Ann Arbor: University of Michigan Press. References here are to paperback ed. of orig. 1945 ed.

Holmboe, M.
1857
Norwegian Architecture: Past and Present. Oslo: Universitetsforlaget.

Hood, M.
1960
"The Challenge of 'Bi-Musicality'" in *Ethnomusicology* IV #2, 55.

Hood, M.
1963
"Music: the Unknown" in *Musicology*, Eds.: C. Palisca, F. Harrison, and M. Hood. Englewood Cliffs, NJ: Prentice-Hall

Hopkins, P.
1966
"The Purposes of Transcription" in *Ethnomusicology* X #3, 310.

Hopkins, P.
1967
"The Hardanger Fiddle and European Tradition", unpublished paper read at New England chapter meeting of Society for Ethnomusicology.

Hopkins, P.
1976

"Individual Choice and the Control of Musical Change" in *Journal of American Folklore Society* 89, No. 354, 449.

Hopkins, P.
1977

"The Homology of Music and Myth: Views of Lévi-Strauss on Musical Structure" in *Ethnomusicology* XXI No. 2, 247.

Hopkins, P.
1978

Aural Thinking in Norway: *The Lore of the Harding-fele*. Unpublished Ph.D. dissert. University of Pennsylvania.

Hopkins, P.
1982

"Aural Thinking" in *Cross-Cultural Approaches to Music: Essays in Honor of Mieczvslaw Kolinsky*. Toronto: University of Toronto Press.

Hughes, H.
1964

History as Art and as Science. New York: Harper and Row.

Huldt-
Nystrøm, H.
1966

Det Nasjonale Tonefall. Oslo: *Universitetsforlaget*.

Hymes, D.
1969

Reinventing Anthropology. New York: Random House. Reference here to 1972 paperback ed.

Hymes, D.
1974

Foundations in Sociolinguistics: An Ethnographic Approach. Philadelphia: University of Pennsylvania Press.

Hymes, D.
1974

"Breakthrough into Performance" in *Folklore: Performance and Communication* (eds., Ben-Amos & Goldstein), Mouton: The Hague.

Jakobson, R.
1971

Selected Writings of II. The Hague: Mouton.

Jóhannsdóttir, H.
1972

"The Fidla of Iceland" in Müller, (ed.): *From Bone Pipe and Cattle Horn to Fiddle and Psaltery*. Copenhagen: Musikhistorisk museum, 25.

Kauli, B.
1958

Norwegian Architecture. Oslo: *Dreyersforlaget*.

Klausen, A.
1977

Kunstsosiologi. Oslo; *Norbok*.

Klausen, A.
1979

"Norway's New Culture Policy and the Arts: Values in Conflict." Unpublished paper read at 1979 meeting of American Anthropology Association.

Korsten, B.
1969

Tonality and Form in Norwegian Springleiks. Bergen: *Kortsen*.

Koskoff, E.
1982

"The Music Network" in *Ethnomusicology* XX, # 3, 353.

Kubler, G.
1962

The Shape of Time. New Haven: Yale University Press.

Kuhn, T.
1962

The Structure of Scientific Revolutions. Chicago: University of Pennsylvania Press.

Kvifte, T.
1978

Om Variabilitet i fremføring av Hardingfeleslåtter. Unpublished Ph.D. dissertation: Oslo University.

Kvifte, T.
1981

"On Variety, Ambiguity and Formal Structure in the Harding Fiddle Music" in *Studia instrumentorium musicae popularis* VII, 102.

Kydland, A.
1983

Eivind Grovens 1. Symfoni. Unpublished doctoral dissertation. Oslo University.

Labov, W.
1972

Language in the Inner City. Philadelphia: University of Pennsylvania Press.

Laing, S.
1854

Journal of a Residence in Norway During Years 1834, 1835, and 1936. London: Longman Press.

Lange, K.
1958

with A. Östvedt. *Norwegian Music: A Brief Survey.* London: Dennis Dobson.

Langer, S.
1953

Philosophy in a New Key. Cambridge: Harvard University Press.

Langer, S.
1953

Feeling and Form: A Theory of Art. New York: Scribner.

Langer, S.
1967

An Essay on Human Feeling. 2 vols. Baltimore: Johns Hopkins Press. Reference here to 1970 paperbk. ed.

Larsen, K.
1948

A History of Norway. Princeton, NJ: Princeton University Press.

Leach, E.
1973

"Structuralism in Social Anthropology" In D. Robey (ed.) *Structuralism: An Introduction.* London: Oxford University Press.

Ledang, O.
1967

Song, Syngemåte, og Stemnekarakter. Oslo: *Universitetsforlaget.*

Ledang, O.
1971

"Seljefloyta—eit 'naturtoneinstrument'?" in *Spelemannsbladet* 30:8.

Ledang, O.
1974a

"Instrument-Player-Music on the Norwegian Langleik" in *Studia Instrumentorum Musicae Popularis* III, Stockholm (= *Festschrift for Ernst Emsheimer) 107.*

Ledang, O. 1974b	"Folkemusikk i smeltedigelen. Frå Hardanger til Trøndelag" in M. Mortensin (ed.), *I Forskningens lys*, 311.
Ledang, O. 1975	"Folkemusikkforsking—Intellektueit Spel Eller Målretta Kulturarbeid?" in *Tradisjon* 5, 1.
Ledang, O. 1975	"Frå Kunstmusikken til Folkekulturens Musikk" in *Forsknings* Nytt XXI, #1, 2.
Leipp, É. 1965	*Le Violon*. Paris: Hermann.
Lévi-Strauss, C. 1962	*La Pensée sauvage*. Paris: *Plon*.
Lévi-Strauss, C. 1964-71	*Mythologiques*, 4 vols. Paris: *Plon*.
Lévi-Strauss, C. 1966	*Le Cru et le Cuit* (= *Mythologiques* I) Paris: *Plon*.
Lévi-Strauss, C. 1971	*The Savage Mind*. Eng. trans. of *La Pensée sauvage*. London: Weidenfeld and Nicholson.
Lévi-Strauss, C. 1972	*l'Homme Nu* (= *Mythologiques* IV) Paris: *Plon* Plon-Julliard.
Levy, M. 1974	*Den Staerke Slått*. Hojbjerg: Wormianum.
Levy, M. n.d.	"Norwegian Fiddle Music" in *D.F.S. Information* (Copenhagen: *Dansk Folkemindesamling*).
Lid, O. 1981	"Vi må *bruke* nynorsken" in O. Rue (ed.), *Nynorsken i 80-åra*. Oslo: *Det Norske Samlaget*.
Liestol, M. 1973	"Det norske folkevise-omradet i begynnelsen av 1800-tallet" in *Norveg* 16, 85.
Lindblom, B. 1970	"Toward a Generative Theory of Melody" in *Swedish Journal of Musicology* 52, 71.
Lindeman, L. 1953-67	*Ældre og nyere norske fjeldmelodier*. Christiania: C. Warmuths Musikforlag.
Ling, J. 1967	*Nyckelharpen*. Stockholm: K.W. Potratz.
Lomax, A. 1968	*Folk Song Style and Culture*. Washington, D.C. American Association for the Advancement of Science, Pub. No. 88.
Lyons, J. 1970	*Noam Chomsky*. New York: The Viking Press.

Mace, T. 1676	*Musick's Monument*. Fac. of 2nd. ed. Paris: *Editions du centre national de la rechersche scientifique.*
Malthus, T. 1966	The Travel Diaries of Thomas Robert Malthus (ed.) P. James. Cambridge: Cambridge Univ. Press.
Marcuse, S. 1975	*Musical Instruments.* New York: Norton Ref. here to paperback ed. of 1964 ed.
Mason, D. 1903	*Masters in Music* I. London: Bates and Guild Co.
McAllester, D. 1971	"Some Thoughts on 'Universals' in World Music" in *Ethnomusicology* XV, #3, 379.
McAllester, D. 1979	"The Astonished Ethno-Muse" in *Ethnomusicology* XXIII, #2, 179.
McLuhan, M. 1971	The Gutenberg Galaxy: *The Making of Typographical Man.* Toronto: University of Toronto Press.
McNeill, M. 1973	*The Scots Cellar.* London: Reprographia.
Merriam, A. 1955	"The Use of Music in the Study of a Problem of Acculturation" in *American Anthropologist* 57, 28.
Merriam, A. 1964	*The Anthropology of Music.* Evanston: Northwestern University Press.
Merriam, A. 1977	"Music Change in a Basongve Village (Zaire)" in *Anthropos* 72, #5/6, 806.
Mersenne, M. 1635	*Harmonie Universelle.* Paris. Ref. here to Chapman trans. 1957. The Hague: M. Nijhoff.
Metcalfe, F. 1858	*The Oxonian in Thelemarken*, 2 vols. London: Hurst & Blackett.
Meyer, L. 1956	*Emotion and Meaning in Music.* Chicago: University of Chicago Press.
Meyer, L. 1967	*Music, The Arts and Ideas.* Chicago and London: University of Chicago Press.
Michaelsen, P. n.d.	"The Hardingfiddle: An Investigation of its Sympathetic Strings." Unpub. paper: Oslo University, Institute of Physics.
Mockler- Ferryman, A. 1896	*In the Northman's Land.* London: S. Low Marston & Co.
Mozart, L. 1951	*Grundliche Violinschule.* Ref. here to 2nd ed. of Eng. trans. by E. Knocker: *A Treatise on the Funda-*

mental Principles of Violin Playing. London: Oxford University Press.

Munch, P.
1956
A Study in Cultural Change: Rural-Urban Conflicts in Norway. (= *Studia Norvegica* No. 9) Oslo: H. Aschebourg & Co. (W. Nygaard).

Myklebust, R.
1982
Femti år med folkemusikk. Oslo: Det norske samlaget.

Nattiez, J.
1971
"Situation de la semiologie musicale" in *Musique eu jeu* 5, 3.

Neal, M.
1978
"Flatfele and Hardingfele Parties in Oslo" Unpublished paper.

Nettl, B.
1983
The Study of Ethnomusicology: Twenty-Nine Issues and Concepts. Urbana: University of Illinois Press.

Nketia, J.H.K.
1962
"The Problem of Meaning in African Music" in *Ethnomusicology* VI, #1, 1.

Nyhus, S.
1973
Pols i Røsostraktom. Oslo: *Universitetsforlaget.*

Nyhus, S.
1969-81
with J. Blom & R. Sevåg. *Norske Folkemusikk,* VI & VII. Oslo: Universitetsforlaget.

Osa, S.
1952
Hardingfela. Oslo: Musikk-huset.

Oxenstierna, E.
1965
The Norsemen. English trans. by Hutter. New York: New York Graphic Society.

Pálsson, H.
1971
Hrafnkel's Saga. Harmondsworth, Middlesex, Eng.: Penguin.

Panum, H.
1920
Langeleiken. Hamar.

Panum, H.
1920
Middelalderens Strengeinstrumenter. . . . *Ref.* here: Eng. trans. by G. Pulver, *String Instruments of the Middle Ages.* London: W. Reeves.

Parks, G.
1979
"Expressive Dimensions of Politics in Helgeland". Unpub. paper read at symposium: *Expressive Culture in Scandinavia.* AAA annual meeting, Cincinnati.

Pekkilä, E.
1983
"'Musikki' and 'Kappalevalikaima' Aspects of the Ethno-theory of a Finnish Folk Musician" in *Suomen Antropologi* 4, 209.

Pincherle, M.
1956
Corelli: His Life, His Music. N.Y.: Norton. Trans. by H. Russell of *Corelli et sons temps.*

Plato 1885	B. Jowett, trans. *Phaedrus in Dialogues* 25. London: Oxford University Press.
Playford, J. 1682	*Musick's Recreation on the Viol, Lyra-Way*. Ref. here to fac. ed. with intro. by N. Dolmetsch. London: Hinrichsen, 1960.
Porter, J. 1977	"European Folk Music" in *Ethnomusicology* XXI, No. 3, 435.
Powers, H. 1980	"Language Models and Musical Analysis" in *Ethnomusicology* XXIV, #1, 1.
Praetorius, M. 1619	*Syntagma musicum* III, Wolffenbüttel. Ref. here to facsimile ed. by W. Gurlitt, Kassel: Bärenreiter: 1950.
Propp, V. 1968	*Morphology of the Folktale*. Rev. ed. of Eng. trans. Bloomington, Ind: Research Cent. in the Language Sciences.
Radcliffe- Brown, A. 1952	*Structure and Function in Primitive Society*. N.Y.: MacMillan. Ref. here to 1965 paperback.
Ramsøy, N. ed. 1974	*Norwegian Society*. N.Y.: Humanities Press. Eng. trans. of *Det Norske Samfunn*. Oslo: *Universitetsforlaget*.
Read, H. 1956	*The Art of Sculpture*. New York: Pantheon.
Reese, G. 1940	*Music in the Middle Ages*. N.Y.: Norton.
Rice, T. 1980	"Aspects of Bulgarian Musical Thought" in *Yearbook of the International Folk Music Council* 12, 43.
Robey, D. 1973	*Structuralism*. London: Oxford University.
Rue, O. (ed.) 1981	*Nynorsken i 80-åra*. Oslo: *Det Norske samlaget*.
Sachs, C. 1914	"Die Viola bastarda" in *Zeitschrift der Internationalen Musikgesellschaft* 15, Heft. 5.
Sachs, C. 1920	*Handlbuch der Musikinstrumentenkunde*. Leipsig: *Breitkopf & Härtel*.

Sachs, C.
1961

The Wellsprings of Music. The Hague: Martinus Nijhoff. Paperbk. reprint by McGraw-Hill (N.Y. 1965).

Sahlins, M.
1983

"Other Times, Other Customs: The Anthropology of History" in American Anthropologist 85, #3, 517.

Salus, P.
1968

with Taylor and Auden, eds. Völuspá: The Song of the Sybil. Iowa city: The Windover Press, University of Iowa.

Sandclef, A.
1958

"The Combination of Seafaring and Farming" in Ulster Folklife IV, 15.

Sandvik, S.
1983

Vi Byggji Hardingfele. Oslo: Tiden Norsk Forlag.

Sandys, W.
1864

The History of the Violin. London: W. Reeves.

Sapir, E.
1921

Language. New York: Harcourt, Brace and World.

Sapir, E.
1958

Writings on Language in D. Mandelbaum (ed.), Selected Essays. Berkeley: University of California Press.

Saunders, F.
1966

"Violins Old and New: An Experimental Study" in American String Teacher, Summer and Fall issue.

Schlesinger, K.
1914

The Precursors of the Violin Family. London: W. Reeves.

Schmitz, H.
1962

Die Kunst der Verzierung im 18. Jahrhundert. Kassel und Basel: Bärenreiter-Verlag.

Seashore, C.
1938

Psychology of Music. References here are to Dover paperback edition, 1968.

Seeger, C.
1960

"On the Moods of a Music-Logic", in Journal of the American Musicological Society 13, 224.

Seeger, C.
1961

"Semantic, Logical and Political Considerations-Bearing Upon Research in Ethnomusicology" in Ethnomusicology V #1, 77.

Seeger, C.
1971

"Reflections Upon a Given Topic: Music in Universal Perspective" in Ethnomusicology XV, #3, 385.

Seeger, C.
1977

"The Musicological Juncture: 1976" in Ethnomusicology XXI, No. 2, 179.

Seeger, C.
1980

"United States of America: Folk Music" in The New Grove 19, 436.

Sevåg, R.
1972

"The Harding Fiddle" in *From Bone Pipe and Cattle Horn to Fiddle and Psaltery. M. Muller* (ed.) (Copenhagen), 18.

Sevåg, R.
1973

Det gjaller og det laet, Oslo: *Det Norsk Samlaget*.

Sevåg, R.
1974

"Neutral Tones and the Problems of Mode in Norwegian Folk Music" in *Festschrift to Ernst Emsheimer* (Stockholm), 207.

Sevåg, R.
1975

"Geige und Geigenmusik in Norwegen" in W. Deutsch & G. Haid eds., *Die Geige in der europäischen Volksmusik*. Vienna: A. Schendl.

Sevåg, R.
1979

"Die Hardingfele: Instrument-Spieltechnik-Musik" in *Studia instrumentarum musicae popularis* VI, 71.

Sevåg, R.
1980

"Norway II: Folk Music: in *The New Grove Dictionary of Music and Musicians* XIII, 322.

Sevåg, R.
1979-81

with J. Blom and S. Nyhus, *Norske Folkemusikk* VI & VIII. Oslo: *Universitetsforlaget*.

Sharp, C.
1932

and M. Karpeles, *English Folk Songs of the Southern Appalachians* I. London: Oxford University Press.

Sibley, F. (ed.)
1971

Perceptions: A Philosophical Symposium. London: Methuen & Co. Ltd.

Simson, C.
1659

Division-Violist. London. Ref. here to 1972 facsimile ed.; N.Y.: Schirmer.

Smith, J.
1977

"The Singer or the Song? A Reassessment of Lord's Oral Theory" in *Man* 12 (N.S.).

Smith, L.
1962

Modern Norwegian Historiography. Trondhjem: *Universitetsforlaget*.

Solheim, S.
1952

Norsk Saetertradisjon. Oslo: H. Aschehoug & Co. (W. Nygaard).

Solheim, S.
1956

Horse-Fight and Horse-Race in Norsk Tradition Oslo: H. Aschehoug & Co. (= Studia norvegica III) No. 8.

Springar, G.
1956

"Language and Music: Parallels and Divergencies in M. Halle (ed.), *For Roman Jakobson* (The Hague: Mouton), 504.

Stewart, J.
1953

The Folk Arts of Norway. Madison: University of Wisconsin Press. Ref. here to 2nd enlarged ed. N.Y.: Dover, 1972.

Stocking, G.
1968
Race, Culture and Evolution: Essays on the History of Anthropology. New York: The Free Press.

Stone, R.
1982
Let the Inside Be Sweet. Bloomington: Indiana University Press.

Straeten,
E. van der
1933
The History of the Violin I. London: Cassel & Co. Ltd.

Strunk, O.
1950
Source Readings in Music History: N.Y.: Norton.

Sturluson, S.
1964
Heimskringla, 2 vols. Ref. here to rev. ed. London: Dent.

Tax, S.(ed.)
1949
Acculturation in the Americas: Proceedings of the 29th International Congress of Americanists. Chicago: University of Chicago Press.

Thorsteinsson, B.
1909
Islenzk Thjødlög. Copenhagen: Kostnad Carlsbergs Jodsins.

Tirro, F.
1967
"The Silent Theme Tradition of Jazz" in The Musical Quarterly 53, 313.

Tomassen, F.
1975
Review: Norwegian Society by N. Ramsøy (ed.). (Eng. revised ed., 1974) in Current Sociology IV, 539.

Vaa, J.
1981
"Folkemusikk-Debatt" in Spelemannsbladet March-April, 15.

Virdung, S.
1511
Musica getutscht. Fac. ed. Bärenreiter: Kassel, 1970.

Waschsmann, K.
1971
"Universal Perspectives in Music" in Ethnomusicology XV, 385.

Waschsmann, K.
1980
"Folk Music" in The New Grove Dictionary of Music and Musicians VI, 693.

Westermarck, E.
1926
Ritual and Belief in Morocco, 2 vols. London: Macmillan.

Whitney, C.
1974
A Study in Small Worlds. Unpub. doctoral dissertation. Wesleyan University, Middletown, Connecticut.

Wilson, D.
1966
with O. Klindt-Jensen, Viking Art. Ithaca: Cornell University Press.

Wittgenstein, C.   *Tractatus   Logico-Philosophicus*. London: Kegan
    1922   Paul.
Yoell, J.   *The Nordic Sound*. Boston: Crescendo.
    1974

Index